Afternoon Tea with Mary and Marcus Braybrooke

Helen Hobin

Afternoon Tea with Mary and Marcus Braybrooke

Copyright© 2019 Helen Hobin+

The rights of Helen Hobin as author of this work have been asserted
in accordance with the Copyright, designs and patents act 1988

Cover design: Copyright© 2019 Helen Hobin
The cover design is inspired by the window in Marsh Baldon Church
by the artist Nicola Kantorowicz

Braybrooke Press, Abingdon OX14 3EN
www.lulu.com

ISBN 978-0-244-96888-5

Afternoon Tea with Mary and Marcus

Contents

1. Travelling with Mary and Marcus — 5.
2. The Parliament of the World's Religions — 6.
3. Mary's Childhood in Cambridge — 10.
4. Marcus' Childhood in Cranleigh — 18.
5. How did Mary and Marcus meet? — 27.
6. Courtship and Marriage — 34.
7. Highgate - 17 Bisham Gardens — 40.
8. Frindsbury, Strood and the Medway Towns — 47.
9. Swainswick, Langridge and Woolley — 52.
10. To Wells Again — 65.
11. Box and CCJ — 76.
12. Christ Church, Bath — 86.
13. Interfaith Pioneers — 93.
14. The Baldons and Nuneham Courtenay — 107.
15. An International Interfaith Centre — 115.
16. Farewell to the Baldons — 127.
17. Clifton Hampden — 130.
18. Books, Gardening and Much More — 140.
19. A Rather Large Afternoon Tea — 154.

Afternoon Tea with Mary and Marcus

O love of God, how strong and true!
Eternal, and yet ever new;
Uncomprehended and unbought,
Beyond all knowledge and all thought

O love of God, how deep and great,
Far deeper than man's deepest hate,
Self-fed, self-kindled like the light,
Changeless, eternal, infinite.

O heav'nly love, how precious still,
In days of weariness and ill,
In nights of pain and helplessness,
To heal, to comfort and to bless!

O wide-embracing, wondrous love!
We read you in the sky above,
We read you in the earth below,
In seas that swell and streams that flow.

We read Thee best in Him who came
To bear for us the cross of shame;
Sent by the Father from on high,
Our life to live, our death to die.

We read thy power to bless and save
E'en in the darkness of the grave;
Still more in resurrection light
We read the fullness of thy might

O love of God, our shield and stay,
Through all the perils of our way,
Eternal love, in Thee we rest
Forever safe, forever blest

This hymn was written by Horatius Bonar (1808-89). The tune was written by J.J Maunder (1858-1920), who was a relation of Mary's mother. The hymn was sung at the wedding of Mary and Marcus and also at the funeral of Ronald Reagan. The prayer below was written by Mary and Marcus.

May the spirit of compassion help us to feel the suffering of the peoples and all the creatures of the world;

May the spirit of love melt the cold hearts that trample on human rights;

May the spirit of beauty help us to preserve the unique splendours of each country;

May the spirit of wisdom help us to treasure the mystical insights of all religions;

May the spirit of patience and endurance strengthen those who are oppressed and exiled from their homes;

May the spirit of courage strengthen those who speak for those who have no voice;

May the spirit of non-violence bring healing peace and justice to all the peoples of the world;

May the spirit of unity help us to recognise people of every nation as brothers and sisters and our unity with all creation.

1. Travelling with Mary and Marcus

Never travel with your grandparents! Round and round the airport carpark we went—the bright lights and noises of Heathrow blaring, my grandmother and grandfather pointing in opposite directions, and our sense of déjà vu increasing with each lap.

Sitting in the back seat of the car, and occasionally attempting to suggest a third option, I couldn't help but wonder what I'd gotten myself into. I'd been to interfaith events before, on occasion, but the quinquennial Parliament of the World's Religions—held in 2015 in Salt Lake City— was on a rather larger scale than most. This time, a quick day commute to London was replaced by a 10 hour flight, a transfer, and a five day conference in the USA. And I'd be there with the two people who, to me, have long represented the spiritual movement to bring about peace between religions. They have also represented Ferrero Rocher chocolates left on pillows, hot summer days of cycling and the most adventurous of childhood bath-times but that, for now, is beside the point.

More than anything, I have heard them described as opposites; as chalk and cheese, yin and yang, and perhaps it is this essential differentness which makes Mary and Marcus Braybrooke such an impressive team.

Our fourth lap of the Heathrow airport had begun. We were, rather ironically, looking for the valet car parking area. In the end we pulled over and a very kind staff member assured us that the valets would come to meet us.

Wherever we went, my grandparents would run into friends—people they'd met from all over the world throughout the years. Some they'd spent an evening with, others had perhaps hosted them for weeks abroad, or been looked after by them for years in the UK. Although Mary and Marcus were always delighted to reunite with old friends and acquaintances, occasionally I was nudged forward to introduce myself first, so that the newcomer would be prompted to say her or his own name, and thus jog my grandparents' memories!

Even in the airport at Dallas, Grandma and Grandpa suddenly found themselves being embraced by a lovely young woman who they'd entertained and helped with her project on interfaith history. We were later to bump into each other again at the Parliament.

The Chapel of Thanksgiving at Thanksgiving Square in Dallas

2. The Parliament of the World's Religions and Childhood Memories

The Parliament itself was a colourful, buzzing event— the opening evening began with a beautiful parade involving people of all faiths processing together. One sweeping glance through the crowd would pick out the wings of those decoratively dressed as angels, along with turbans, bells, drums and indigenous dress. There were a number of excellent opening talks, including some beautiful singing, though Mary found it rather ironic that despite female equality being one of the headline themes, the stage was usually dominated by men.

We went to dinner with Bishop Bill Swing and his wife Mary, to a sushi restaurant. Bill and I both wished to order an old Japanese whisky to drink, but as I did not have I.D. and looked under 35 (!) I was refused any. When Bill placed his tumbler subtly at my elbow I took the hint, and was pleased to try it. The evening was filled with laughter, not least when Mary began a sentence with the rather bizarre statement 'Marcus *loves* the toilet'—she was referring to the twinning of their Clifton Hampden toilet with one in Burundi, but was cut off by mine and Bill's uproarious laughter.

Everywhere one wandered there were fascinating people to talk to and things to look at; peaceful scrolls giving instruction for a harmonious life, candles, posters of the Dalai Lama, Buddhist carvings, numerous books of scripture, Interfaith jewellery featuring symbols from many faiths and all sorts of cuisine. Brahma Kumaris friends kindly shared with us a delicious homemade vegetarian meal. There was a group of friendly Sikhs providing turbans and wrapping them for anyone who wished to experience the process. Seeing people of all different nationalities and faiths wearing turbans throughout the conference was thoroughly refreshing. The amount of vendors and stalls were so many that I spent a solid hour looking for a necklace my Grandmother would like. There were also wonderful art exhibits. A South African artist was creating a huge wall of portraits of anyone who asked. It was a fascinating collective 'self-portrait'.

We attended one of the keynote talks, unfortunately only arriving in time to catch the end of the preceding film, 'The Man who Saved the World'. Among the panel were Bishop Bill Swing, the excellent female Rabbi Lyn Gottlieb and Jane Goodall. Mary was particularly struck when the latter mentioned that primates were violent to each other over their territory.

The children's choir at the Parliament of the World's Religions 2015

On our last evening we went to the Mormon Gospel Choir Tabernacle to attend an Interfaith evening of song and dance from all faiths. A particular highlight to an amazing evening was the children's opening song, which was a colourful blend of traditional costumes and seemed almost a youthful coming to life of Norman Rockwell's famous Golden Rule painting.

At the beginning of devotional time, which my grandparents led, we were reminded of what Lao-Tzu said 2,500 years ago: 'If there is to be peace in the world, there must be peace in the heart.' Through the centuries, spiritual writers of many faiths have repeated this message, but most of us still have yet to learn it. It is one contribution each of us can make to a more peaceful world. The session began with some readings from several different faith traditions, accompanied by pictures, as we tried to still the body and the mind. Then in silence, we opened our heart to the compassion of the Holy One as we reclaimed our true humanity. Then in our imagination, like ripples in a pond, we radiated that compassion to our family and friends, to all at the Parliament, to leaders who shape our destiny, to refugees and victims of violence, and to animals and the world of nature. The programme included music and visual images. As my grandfather said softly, "The practice we shall learn is a treasure we can take in our hearts as we return home, and it will help us spread the peace we long for".

My Childhood Memories

My own childhood memories of my grandparents are a patchwork of images at the Rectory in Marsh Baldon. Digging in the garden for the little potatoes my grandfather grew, realising years later that he'd already found and retrieved them, only to cover them with earth again so my sisters and I would have the pleasure of succeeding. The clip-clop of hooves as we rode our piebald cob Kelly up the long Rectory drive, to find my grandmother waiting to feed our dear horse with —of all things— a waffle.

Sarah and I in the Rectory garden with Grandpa.

In the church at Marsh Baldon, my grandpa laying out a picnic blanket scattered with toys so that should the younger members of the congregation lose interest in the sermon, we'd have something else to occupy us. I can only hope that the tractor noises I inevitably made didn't obscure too much of the chosen reading.

One of the stories that my grandparents recall most, of my many adventures with them, is the occasion on which we played hide-and-seek in the large woodland arboretum nearby. I was three at the time, and, to put it succinctly, I won. I remember standing under a pine tree, with only my feet poking out, for some time. Eventually I emerged, and a kindly woman spotted me and helped me to reunite with a rather frantic Mary and Marcus. Utterly oblivious to quite how panicked they were, I was rather pleased to have won the game.

Of course, the memories that I have involve a wide range of emotions; on one occasion whilst staying overnight (a lovely tradition that allowed my sisters and I to spend some individual time with our grandparents) I had my first taste of 'Appletiser' and kept coming downstairs to sample more. Grandma had a few friends round, sitting together at the kitchen table, and eventually she quipped, to a general round of laughter, "You'll be weeing all night!" Mortified, I returned to my room. The embarrassments and reactions one experiences as a child are certainly interesting with hindsight.

I recall sitting on the lawn outside the Rectory, having a family picnic. On confessing to my dear Auntie Amanda that my favourite type of dog was a Golden Labrador (spontaneously mentioning our 'favourite' things seemed like an important aspect of conversation back then), she returned that they were rather smelly. I was utterly indignant, incensed on behalf of all Labradors, and retorted using a line that I'd heard from *Sabrina the Teenage Witch*. However, saying "What's the matter? Cat's got your tongue?" immediately after she had just spoken somewhat nullified my argument. I stormed off, with all the bravado and bluster a child could manage. (If you're reading this now Amanda, I apologise for the outburst!). At an even younger age, I hosted a circus on the lawn for my grandmother. Under a selection of bed-sheets, held up by chairs, I placed a range of cuddly toys, and coerced them into various stunts. Watching back the footage now, I can recognise the increasing weariness in grandma's voice as she says, "That's lovely, Helen. Shall we go back inside now?" You can guess my answer. At one point, whipping a skipping rope at the floor (thankfully I have much more developed opinions on the treatment of animals and even the use of circuses now), I spent a good few minutes with my head inside the mouth of a cuddly toy lion, before bowing and saying "Thank you! Thank you!" Given that the lion was approximately the size of a football, and that his mouth only opened roughly one centimetre wide, the reception to my act was quite generous.

Many adventures indeed took place on that garden lawn— which was immaculate except for the molehills that perpetually frustrated my gentle grandfather. We filmed a series called 'Toffee to the Rescue' there, in which our adored apricot Toy Poodle, Toffee, played the starring role, gallantly saving us from all sorts of unfortunate situations. As a puppy, he had loved to chew on a little half-size blue and silver brush, previously used for sweeping the floor. And, as resourceful film-makers, we took advantage of this. There is a particular scene, carefully stored on VHS tape and now DVD, in which I, as the villain who has just stolen jewellery from the house, am tackled by Toffee. Lying on the grass, I waved the brush from my left side to the right and back again, resulting in some lovely footage of our four-footed hero not only guarding my fallen figure, but leaping tirelessly back and forth to prevent me from sitting up. A method that police dogs should perhaps consider!

My grandparent's poodle features in so many special parts of my childhood; from waiting in the primary school playground with my mother when he was staying with us, to teaching me how to bark (I loved to try animal impressions as a child, and the doorbell ringing provided a great chance to impersonate him barking), to winning a blue rosette at the Harwell Village Feast with me, in the obedience competition. I must confess though, that particular challenge was entitled 'Won't eat a sausage', and our success came less from Toffee deferring to my handling skills, and rather more from him being a terribly fussy eater. My grandfather being the incredibly compassionate man that he is, he would always get down on his hands and knees whenever Toffee turned his nose up at a plate of fresh chicken (or another similar meal) and try to coax him with gentle words. Indeed, I recall noticing the quirky poodle once enjoying a bowl of cornflakes and ice-cream. He passed away recently, and whilst his loss is heart-breaking in so many ways he lives on in our memories, and couldn't have had more devoted parents than Mary and Marcus Braybrooke during his long and happy lifetime. There is a carefully tended grave in the garden at 17 Courtiers Green.

Toffee was a wonderful friend growing up, though there were also occasions in which he was, metaphorically, in the dog house. My grandparents had a generous habit of leaving little gifts on the pillow when we came to stay—whether a chocolate or a tiny notebook, it was always a very exciting moment to rush upstairs and 'put away our bag'. One day, I found a beautiful hanging mobile waiting on the bed, with intricately painted lions and unicorns dangling from the wire. I went downstairs to say thank you, but on returning after supper, found that the entire thing had been chewed beyond recognition by a certain curly-haired companion. On another, unrelated, occasion I received a plastic replica of the famous 'Heart of the Ocean' necklace, from the film *Titanic*. Being a child, I earnestly believed that it was the actual necklace itself, and carefully hid it away in my box of precious items, so that it wouldn't become lost or stolen. Had I realised, I perhaps would have worn it instead.

My sister Kathryn mentioned a few years ago that one of her favourite smells from childhood came from the splashing of water on the hot tarmac of the Rectory drive, as we four attempted to 'wash' all of the cars present, in between bouts of playing 'bicycles and policemen'. The aforementioned game consisted of riding around in circles, with one of us occasionally stepping forward to hold up a hand, redirecting the traffic.

There are so many little portions of the large Rectory which hold particular memories; the bathroom which featured a portrait of a nude woman on a giant seashell surrounded by angelic figures was a source of constant fascination; I was later to learn that her name was Venus. The little guest bedroom in which my grandparents would slice up pieces of apple and read us stories came alive with images of mice dancing and disobedient puppies running across hilltops. My grandfather has always been an extremely perceptive man, and it was thanks to him that a health issue I experienced in childhood was solved. I adored apple juice from a young age, and used to drink it all the time from a little beaker. At eighteen months old, I was drinking so much of it that I didn't feel hungry enough to eat properly, and became very poorly at my grandmother's 60th birthday party. He put two and two together and to my personal disappointment my access to the drink was severely restricted. I became well again. Perhaps such an addiction contributed to my later love of Appletiser — and, even later, the cider of my university days!

I am very fortunate to be close to my grandparents, and to not only have so many wonderful childhood memories, but to be constantly making new ones with them. I suggested this biography some years ago, whilst I was still studying at university. Between studies and full time work, I can only apologise for how long it has taken to make this book a reality. My grandparents are people who, given how much they have done, how widely they have travelled and how many people they have impacted, should be better known. They are not famous, nor do they desire to be. But they are important: to me and to many people. I wanted to write this biography for a few simple reasons. To make a record of the lives they have led, the work they have done, and of how they have viewed the world as it changed over the last eight decades - a patchwork quilt of memories, stories and experiences. One of the main aspects of their lives which fascinates me is their involvement with the Interfaith movement. I honestly believe that, in a world full of complex problems, efforts to understand, accept and work alongside people of all different backgrounds, religions and nations are crucially important. I will arrive in detail at the subject of their interfaith work, but first, I had better start at the beginning.

3. Mary's Childhood in Cambridge

Mary was born in Cambridge on January 25th 1935. She was a small baby – six and a quarter pounds. Her mother Phyllis (née Rowsell) breast fed her with rich milk so she became 'rather a plump child' (her words) and later at school she was called Tubby.

Mary's earliest memory was of the outbreak of World War II. She was in Exmouth at the Withycombe Methodist Chapel, where in 1935 she had been baptized. As she heard the Declaration of War she cried because everyone looked serious. She was soon taught how to wear a gas mask at the little private school, called St. Collettes, which she attended. She also sometimes, with her brother Paul, who was nearly four years older, slept in the Morrison shelter in the study of their Cambridge home. Mary and Paul, however, spent some of the war in Exeter with Auntie Joan and Uncle Don, although Exeter had far more bombs than Cambridge.

Mary in her sandpit.

Hers was a happy childhood and she remembers spending a lot of time on her swing and playing ball and with her little dolls who lived on a punt. Mary from an early age adored dogs, but her father refused to let her have one, because as an Australian he thought dogs should live outdoors. So Mary used to take other friends' dogs for walks instead. They had two cats, Peter and Tim, to whom she was devoted.

Soon after the start of war Mary began to suffer from asthma, which has been a problem right through her life. Her parents smoked: her mother up to 60 cigarettes a day and her father a pipe. As well as cats they had feather pillows and eiderdowns, so it was not surprising she developed asthma, though she thought it was psychosomatic because she missed her father, who, during the war, was in Harrogate working with the Ministry of Aircraft Production. 'I lived on ephedrine tablets' she says, 'and had tests which showed I was allergic to dust.' (An excuse for letting other people do the dusting!)

Mary's father, Dr George Walker, was a graduate of Sydney University. He came to Cambridge to do a PhD in pure mathematics. He met Mary's mother when he stayed with the family during a vacation at their home in Exmouth. He only went back once to Australia, where he received a great welcome, but he always regretted that he never said a personal farewell to his mother before she died in 1939.

Afternoon Tea with Mary and Marcus

Mary says, 'I loved my mother, but she was a complex character. She was mostly taught at home by a governess and was always very outspoken'. She was a Land Girl during World War I. During World War II, she provided accommodation for evacuees and then for some RAF officers. Mary says 'She loved my father but was shattered when she discovered, after they had married, that he was an eminent Free Mason. Their marriage worked on the whole but they rowed quite a lot – especially about whether cats were allowed upstairs!' Mary met her Australian grandpa once. Her only memory is of him letting her precious tortoise Humpty (pictured here) get lost by leaving the tennis gate open.

Mary's maternal grandpa Philip Foale Rowsell, son of Benjamin Joseph Rowsell of Yeovil in Somerset, was a rather grand person with a loud voice. In 1895 he married Florence Elizabeth Turner. A pharmacist by profession, he was a Justice of the Peace; Mayor of Exeter from 1921-4 and a member of the Central Advisory Committee that set up the National Health Insurance. He was Liberal candidate for Bridgwater in 1914, but the election was postponed because of the outbreak of war. In 1929, he stood as Liberal candidate for Totnes, but was beaten by a narrow margin. In 1938, he was awarded a CBE. Mary was not allowed to attend his funeral as she was only 11. Mary did not know her grandmother, but saw something of Philip Rowsell's second wife, 'Popsy' (F.I.M. Norton), whose grandson Paul Thomas was an usher at Mary's wedding.

Mary and Paul spent their holidays in Devon, either staying at Ladybrook, which was a lovely bungalow on Dartmoor – now a Christian Centre for Young People - or at Dawlish Warren or Exmouth. Once with Aunt Joan and Uncle Don, Paul and Mary were cut off by the tide at Sandy Bay and had no way of communicating their anxieties and fears. Fortunately, someone in a rowing boat finally came and rescued them. A traumatic experience for young children! Marcus also remembers nearly being cut off there when the family were staying with his mother's cousin Violet, who also took the children for what seemed to them very long walks.

In Cambridge, Mary had local friends of her own age. Meriel, who lived next door but one, was her best friend. They used to drop notes to each other frequently. Mary had piano lessons nearby from Mrs Brown but now wishes she had practised more. When she was eight, Mary went to the Cambridgeshire High School for Girls - a grammar school, known as 'the County.' She joined a small preparatory class of 'very privileged little girls' – to quote from the vivid reminiscences of Nin Twyman (née Andrews). Nin recalls that 'We had a charmed existence, (apart from maths) of drawing, plays, and music. We had a fierce regime of learning Marion Richardson hand-writing' – a distinctive style that Nin still uses, but to which Mary's writing has little resemblance.

Afternoon Tea with Mary and Marcus

Mary's school friends in later life

My grandmother always enjoyed singing in choirs, and was fortunate that the now famous Colin Davies was for a time conductor of the County Girls school choir. Mary and her class-mates all passed the eleven plus. Mary had a choice of going to the Perse School (Paul was at the boys school), but she opted to go to the County which had a real mixture of girls and was not snobbish! It helped that the chosen school was only down the road.

When they started at the County, she and her class-mates were separated, but were reunited when they were thirteen, as they all got into the A-stream. 'Mary,' Nin says, 'was always much respected and very sensible in a class of very bright but rather naughty young girls – but she too had her moments. We are all ashamed of our behaviour in history. Mary was always in the top five in exams and invariably voted in as class prefect, and, as we knew she would, became Head Girl.'

Nin recalls that when, newly married to Michael, they returned to Cambridge, Mary's parents were very kind to them. She also remembers playing tennis at Kersell and 'the ferocity of George's service. Mary's service wasn't bad either.' Mary was delighted, on moving to the Baldons, to renew her friendship with Nin Twyman, who was living quite near-by. Years later, Nin painted a gorgeous picture of my sisters and me jumping through waves in the sea.

Mary has also kept in touch with other school friends who have spread across the world. Cecilia settled in Jerusalem and, on several occasions, was the guide on the pilgrimages that Mary and Marcus led to the Holy Land. Shirley, who was particularly good at sport, moved to South Africa, but returned recently for a school reunion. Sheila, however, Mary met again when they discovered they were both working in the Kidney Unit at the Churchill Hospital in Oxford. Gabriele Reifenberg (Buschi), who has spent a lot of time helping in the Buddhist kingdom of Bhutan, said, 'My memory of schooldays are very sketchy but I find it amazing that Mary kept on with her work until age 75. We do meet up most years, with several other schoolmates, so I suppose one of our abiding traits is loyalty to friends.'

In her primary years, Mary was off school a lot with asthma. 'Every time,' she says, 'my mother bought me a new Enid Blyton book, which I read avidly.' For treats the family went to the Regal Cinema and had baked beans on toast at the café there. On weekends they went punting in Hemingford Grey or visited friends who always seemed to live on farms in the country. They attended West Country socials where Mary, then eleven, learnt to dance with her first boyfriend David (aged 13), who was a brilliant dancer. Sometimes the carpet at home was taken up so family and friends could do old time dancing which Mary loved. When the family had parties, Mary's father organized lots of lovely games, including charades and Murder. In 1945, Mary and her brother Paul joined with friends to form a 'Celebration Society' to mark the ending of the war. The society's eight or so members met in a shed at the end of the garden, discussed hopes for the future and had picnics. Mary and friends also played tennis a lot and table-tennis, at which she became quite good.

I asked her brother Paul, for his perspective on this time in their lives.

He wrote to me, 'When the Second World War began in September 1939 I was just 8 and Mary 4½. We have some shared memories but in many ways our wars were very different. We both remember Chamberlain's short speech announcing that we were at war with Germany – announced by the radio in the Withycombe Methodist church.

Because of the perception that Cambridge was likely to be bombed because of the large number of RAF aerodromes in the surrounding area it was thought that Mary and I should be 'unofficially' evacuated. We had spent regular summer holidays at 'Red-a-ven' in Countess Wear – a couple of miles on the Exmouth side of Exeter. It was owned by our Uncle Don and his wife Joan, shared with their dogs Jack and Kit (loved by Mary). Mary and I moved to Red-a-Ven during the first few months.

As it turned out, Exeter had serious bombing raids, and leaving our Anderson shelter in the garden we experienced the sky lit up by red glows due to fires in Exeter and on different occasions, some 50 miles away, Plymouth as well. As it turned out, Cambridge – protected by its university status, only had minor incendiary bomb damage. This was much later in the war – and maybe the bombs were abandoned before pilots returned to Europe.

The decision was made that we should return to Kersell in Cambridge. Mary went first, and I stayed to complete a year at the village school in Countess Wear. Our memories are a little uncertain regarding the journey home – we wonder whether this was the occasion when we both clearly remember watching an aerial dog-fight above the train a short while after we left.

Later in the war we both remember sharing a Morrison indoor shelter (erected in the study at Kersell). We have shared our thoughts when we heard the engines of a V1 'doodlebug' (pilotless flying bomb) stop, although I don't recall the explosion which one expect to follow a little later. The later V2 rocket bombs of course gave no warning before they exploded.

At the end of the war, when Mary was 10, we took over the shed at the bottom of the garden as headquarters of the Celebrations Society. We made some wooden 'C S' letters to go on the door, but otherwise how we celebrated and the membership (other than her friend Meriel) is a mystery. No doubt food came into it – supported by our mother. Tennis was a favourite occupation.'

Mary remembers adolescence as an exciting time, when she was full of romantic ideas, idealism and a desire to make the world happier! School she found interesting – thanks to excellent teachers.

Mary and Paul resting after playing tennis. Who won?

Mary adored the theatre and cinema and collected the autographs of Ivor Novello, Michael Wilding Robert Donat and others. Recently she rediscovered her old autograph book in a shed – thankfully the mice had not found it. I remember once discussing with my grandmother an essay that I was writing during my literature degree, and upon bringing up the subject of 'hero-worship' I was surprised to hear Mary refer to back to her days of waiting at stage doors for celebrities. I recently looked through the autograph book myself, and in between the stylized signatures of actors and cricketers, I particularly took note of two pages. They were divided up into neat, hand drawn rectangles, which formed a self-titled 'Wall of Friendship'. Friends and family had followed Mary's instruction to 'please add a brick', and it was covered in little notes and names. One Australian cousin had also folded back the corner of a later page with a firm note: "Private. Don't look." As I inevitably peeled it back, curiosity triumphing over politeness, I had the surreal experience of being put in my adolescent grandmother's place. "I knew you would."

At school, Mary did lots of acting and also joined the Debating Society. She remembers playing cricket against the 'County' boys, who gave the girls 50 runs, played left handed, but still won! Mary, who had been to a local Church of England Sunday School when she was young, later attended the Cambridge Unitarian church with Meriel and her family. The Unitarians had interfaith services and so when she later met Marcus his interest in this was nothing new to her. Mary always enjoyed academic discussions and went to university functions at Emmanuel College where her father had been a Fellow, although by this time he was Principal of the Correspondence College in Burlington Place. He also took Mary to some Masonic events, as her Mum would not go. Mary became a St John Ambulance cadet and passed various courses in First Aid and Fire Fighting. When she was only 15, she helped in local hospitals and remembers being embarrassed at giving men bed baths. For help with social care she visited an old Jewish lady, Miss Steinberg, a refugee from Germany every week for several years. These visits began when Mary was around thirteen and continued until she was twenty, and she stuck to them religiously, even though Miss Steinberg was not easy to please. One day she threw some eggs at Mary because they were not the right sort! She wanted to teach her German but Mary was more interested in French and Spanish. Mary's first trip abroad – aged 15 - was with Meriel to Besancon, France.

Mary was very interested in languages and when she was 17 stayed with the Denis' family in Nancy. It was there she first met Odile, who with her husband Roger, have been life-long friends and have visited my grandparents on several occasion – and later with children and grandchildren making exchange visits. Josephine and I have been the most recent generation to interchange. It is interesting that when Mary exchanged it was with Odile's brothers Jean and Pierre and not with her, because Odile's parents did not consider her education so important. Odile and her husband Roger, who sadly died recently, became good friends – Odile visited Mary recently. Mary also did school exchange trips to Spain to stay with Margarita and her family in Valladolid.

Mary avec Monsieur et Madame Denis et Odile

At 17 Mary's life changed and she fell madly in love with Nigel, a second year language student at Emmanuel College, who was four years older than her. 'I first saw him acting the main part in Ibsen's *The Wild Duck*. Nigel wrote poetry, had a beautiful singing voice, was full of ideals and was very romantic.' During her last year at school she was seeing Nigel regularly although, she says, 'I did go out with other boys a bit too.' She and Nigel had an intense relationship for 4 years.

Nigel was distant from his father and step mother and lost his mother when he was 4. Mary's mother, who was fond of men, became rather over-attached to him too, which, at times, was problematic. They bonded over music; Nigel would sing while Phyllis played. Nigel and Mary were unofficially engaged and he gave Mary his Mother's engagement ring, but Mary wore it on her right hand, feeling too young to be engaged.

When Mary was in Nancy in France, she had a letter from Miss Battensby, her headmistress, informing her that she had been elected Head Girl. 'I was very surprised and frightened! I had always lacked confidence and this gave me a bit more belief in my ability to cope with everything. I had always appeared strong in my ideals and beliefs and very sad at the state of the world!' Her outer self-assurance must have been discernible, as eight hundred children voted for her to become Head Girl. Indeed, Mary recalls that several of the younger girls seemed to have crushes on her, and would go out of their way to walk with her, which she found embarrassing and difficult to cope with.

Given Mary's determination to change the injustices of life, she was much influenced by a conference of the Junior Council for Education in World Citizenship (CEWC) in Berlin on Group Tensions. She also remembers going to the Resi Nightclub, which, on each table, had private telephones to arrange a partner for a dance.

At school, Mary says, 'I loved History, Spanish and French in the sixth form, but could not see a career in languages. At school there were some girls from dysfunctional or poor families – especially one who was incredibly bright. This was the beginning of my interest in becoming a social worker. I, therefore, applied to Bedford College London to read Sociology and was given a place.' Mary's brother Paul recalls, 'We agree that we had mainly happy childhoods, within the limits imposed by the war, and sometimes fractious adults. Strangely we were aware of strong disagreements, both between our parents and Auntie Joan and Uncle Don. We remember late evening arguments between parents – probably after the war as Dad was away for much of the war – and we were both upset by them. I don't know whether Mary had similar thoughts but it always worried me how much I was responsible for the arguments.'

'We attended,' Paul said, 'West Country Socials in a Cambridge Hall, where the activity was mainly Old Time Dancing. Mary tells me that she loved these evenings – and that she regularly danced with David Mann, a school friend of mine. When Mary talked about these events I was surprised to be reminded of the name of her dancing partner, and of his prowess. We also had parties and old time dancing at Kersell during the late 1940s, and 'murder' was also on the menu! After the war we had some very happy excursions within about a 30 odd mile radius of Cambridge. A regular destination – which Mary and I both much enjoyed – was Hemingford Grey, where we picked up a punt with Dad as punter. We usually set off in the Huntingdon direction for a picnic. Our chosen spot was near a little used railway line which crossed the River Great Ouse on an old timber bridge. We clambered on this bridge – trains were very rare! Disappointingly Mother often opted out of these trips. She got up very late in the day (and went to bed similarly late!). Visits to Devon continued, both to Red-a-Ven and to the bungalow on Dartmoor, which was also theirs. Mary and I grew to love the moor around Belstone – a difficult haven to beat even now. Throughout her childhood Mary had asthma badly. I remember how upsetting it was to see her struggling for breath. At the time much less was known about the disease than now. I had the same concerns for our Patrick many years later.'

Afternoon Tea with Mary and Marcus

'Mary and I were several times invited to Stratford-upon-Avon for a couple of days by Florrie Kenyon (who was a friend of our mother), where we attended a number of Shakespeare plays. We both thoroughly enjoyed these excursions – when Diana Wynyard and Anthony Quayle were at their height at the Memorial Theatre. This reminds me that Mary had her film star and actor favourites at this time – including Michael Wilding, Robert Donat and Ivor Novello. I agree about the last two! She met Michael's brother, who came to Kersell. And films she enjoyed included two wartime ones – Mrs Miniver and The Way to the Stars. In 1949 Mary and I went together to see Ivor Novello's penultimate show – King's Rhapsody – in which he starred. A lovely evening out – a complete contrast to the grim years we experienced in the first half of the forties.'

Mary's Health

Before we continue the story, this seems the place to say a word about Mary's health. She has never had good health, although you would not notice it from her energy, activity and interest in everything going on in the world. And with her great sense of colour co-ordination, she always dresses well (from her well stocked wardrobe!) – with earrings to match. My sisters and I used to enjoy hunting through her jewellery to find the closest matching shade among her earrings. I remember once asking her if she minded my rather more eclectic tastes, only to find that my bright orange leggings and red t-shirt were readily welcomed with a hug. But whilst her impressive style may distract from her imperfect health, physical ailments have been a factor to cope with throughout her life. As a child, as we have seen, she had asthma from the age of four. She also had knock knees, for which she had to do exercises. She enjoyed outdoor games but, she says, 'Running made me breathless, so I was never very daring.'

Her most serious illness, when she was 28 years old, was viral encephalitis which, even more so then, was life-threatening. Mary says, 'I nearly died and was admitted to an isolation hospital - Brookfield in Cambridge. I was off work for three months. A Baptist minister who visited chose to read the passage "in my Father's house are many mansions", which is usually read at funerals.' Marcus remembers his anxious journey to see her while she was in hospital, even if Mary was not well enough to recall it. Even so, Mary says, 'Being very ill seemed to help me to decide to marry Marcus.'

In adulthood she suffered for several years with a slipped disc (after lifting Jeremy at 14 months). In those days rest was prescribed – one doctor even told Marcus to put some bricks into bags to tie to her ankles and help stretch her back. She had her appendix out at 40 and has had a lot of chest infections. Nonetheless she always went to work.

In later life following the menopause, Mary developed painful arthritis in both knees. After putting up with this for many years, she had two total knee replacements, which have made her more mobile. After the second one she had a lot of sickness. The surgeon was Indian and came to visit her so often, that one of the nurses said 'Are you a private patient?'

Mary has worn glasses for much of her life. She has had a cataract and other operations and now has age-related macular degeneration in both eyes which may lead to partial blindness at some stage. She also suffers from Sjogrens syndrome which leads to a lot of discomfort because it causes very dry eyes and a dry mouth.

She has had a number of falls. A little while before they moved to the Baldons, Mary and Marcus were going to the opening of the Global Retreat Centre in Nuneham Courtenay. In Oxford, Mary tripped over a bicycle that was lying across the pavement. Fearing A&E would take all day, the chemist suggested a doctor who might help. His methods were old-fashioned and he stitched the leg with a large black needle, while the dog wandered around and eventually licked the wound!

With various ups and downs with their health - often on holiday - Mary and Marcus have experienced health care in several countries and are grateful for the help they have received.

Mary learning to drive – outside Kersell.
She passed first time

Mary with her Mother

It is time now to introduce Marcus.

4. Marcus' Childhood in Cranleigh.

Marcus was born in Rose Hill Nursing Home in Dorking, Surrey, on 16th November 1938. His sisters Bryony and Susan were taken to the maternity home where there were a number of new-born babies. 'The Matron,' Marcus' elder sister Bryony says, 'suggested we might like to select our brother. Marcus was our third choice, not because we did not fancy him – but because we did not expect red hair.'

At about the age of two – war having started – the family moved to Cranleigh. They spent several months with their maternal grandparents before they moved to Box Cottage ('Box' because of box bushes not the shape of the house) in Mount Road – a house that his parents originally rented for six months and continued to rent until his father died nearly fifty years later.

Marcus as a child

'Cranleigh was in the path of bomber raids,' Bryony says. 'I know that Mother often left Marcus in his pram in the garden during air-raids, much to the consternation of the neighbours. Mother felt he was safer there than indoors and she was probably right.' One of Marcus' first memories was of VJ Day. 'I can picture walking through the village of Cranleigh to the common, where a great bonfire was burning. Everyone was happy. At last World War II was over. How much did I know about the war? I can almost smell and feel the green linoleum in the play-room where, with my mother and sisters, we would hide under a table listening to the whine of a doodlebug – hoping it would not go silent, a sign that it was about to drop.'

The family was away when a bomb fell in the village in Surrey where they lived. They got back the day afterwards, to find some windows had been blown in and to be told the Rector had been hit on the head by a falling stone and that the Church's stained glass had been blown out.

Originally Box Cottage was two-up, two-down with a small box room which was Marcus' bedroom. It had a window looking out onto the road. 'I remember,' Marcus says, 'peeping out and seeing Bryony kiss her current boy-friend when he brought her home. She was not pleased with me.' He still has in his bedroom a picture of a shepherd driving his sheep home in the evening, which he had in his childhood bedroom. They now also have a beautiful woven tapestry of Jesus the Good Shepherd, which they bought in Cyprus.

The kitchen was minute. After the war, two rooms were added on. Marcus and his sisters went to Scotland on holiday whilst much of the work was done. 'The house was amazing when we got back – both its size and the new furniture.' Quite soon, however, Marcus' grandmother Hilda came to live with the family so the downstairs playroom became his father's bedroom. 'We had to play in the sitting room, which meant at bedtime knocking down the model village I had just built.' The great attraction of Box Cottage was the garden, used as a cricket pitch and clock golf course, which even with hens and rabbits, Marcus' mother kept beautifully. There were two large apple trees, which were ideal for climbing.

Another of Marcus' earliest memories is of walking over a wooden bridge at the nearby home of his grandparents. His maternal grandfather, Alfred Leach, held his hand. Alfred Leach was a retired clergyman, who had also been a great cricketer. Before he was married he served as chaplain on several liners to South Africa. Marcus remembers going to his bedroom to say goodbye, shortly before his death. Both Marcus' paternal grandparents died before he was born. His grandfather William Braybrooke was also a clergyman. Marcus recalls going to Oakhill in Surrey and to Surbiton to see churches in which he had served. The Braybrooke name goes back a long time. One of King John's 'evil counsellors' was Richard Braybrooke.

Marcus' father, Arthur Rossi (always called Rossi) was away a lot in the war. Marcus remembers him coming home once, with a sword and a dagger – booty from Germany – and also a damaged soft stone cross, which Marcus still has. This had been given to his father by a Polish soldier who was dying -– some Poles had got to England at the start of the war and served with the allies. Marcus' Dad was for a time with the army's public relations team (or that's what we would call it now) handling the press, and had stories about Monty (Montgomery), King George VI and Ike (Eisenhower). Once when he stayed at Wells, Mary gave him a tape-recorder to recount these tales. He was disappointed that the BBC did not want the tape.

Marcia in her beautiful garden

Marcus' mother, Marcia Nona (née Leach) was a wonderful mother - very loving, good fun, with a great sense of humour and who enjoyed her children's company.

She also had a great knowledge of nature and, as she was a talented painter in water colours, did pictures of many wild flowers so that her children might learn their names. (Books were scarce in wartime).

His Mother worked very hard to look after the family. Marcus remembers her on her knees washing the sheets and hoping it would not rain. There were few mechanical aids in the home and less money. Despite a tiny budget and rationing, she cooked delicious meals. She also had an allotment, which supplied a lot of fresh vegetables for the family.

Afternoon Tea with Mary and Marcus

Marcus' Mother had a deep faith, as shown in this hymn that she wrote:

As we kneel before thy altar,
Heavenly Father, may we know,
The wonder of thy living presence,
On our hearts thy peace bestow.

Give thy courage and compassion
To thy priests, who day by day,
Strive to serve Thee to Thy glory
Strive to lead us in Thy way.

Grant that all who share Thy blessing
May with all Thy blessing share
Give us fellowship in living,
Who seek fellowship in prayer.

Thus each humble life may mirror
Some reflection of Our Lord,
And by faithful service witness
To Thy Light's Incarnate Word.

Here, with thankful hearts, we pray for
Those who've passed beyond our sight,
That their love may still enfold us,
Their bright faith still shed its light.

Down the years, as generations
Come within this Hallowed place
Draw all hearts, in love, to enter
The great kingdom of Thy grace.

War-time meant that everyone had to make do, so the family's genteel poverty and the wearing of handed-down clothes that did not fit, was not unusual. Probably the years after the war were even tougher, especially the great freeze of 1947. Food was rationed until the early fifties.

When Marcus was about three or four his sisters put him on a horse called Cornish for a little ride – but Cornish was a bit wild, bolted and threw Marcus off. He was unconscious for a while. 'When I came to, I kept asking for Cornish to come and see me in bed.'

Bryony says that because she was six years older and Susan was three years older, 'Marcus became a very independent and self-contained child. He spent hours playing with his model village, built out of Lotts bricks (a popular toy then), where he invented an imaginary life for its inhabitants. There were three plaster figures and one lead soldier who became real in his imagination and became part of our family.' Marcus adds that one of his best Christmases was when his mother made lots of food out of modelling clay for the shops in his village. He also produced miniature newspapers for the villagers, based on what he read in the *Daily Sketch* – with the scores of the imaginary football matches he played with his toy footballers.

Afternoon Tea with Mary and Marcus

'Later,' Bryony says, 'he invented his own game of cricket played against a brick-wall – with teams and their scores recorded.' Marcus admits that he sometimes wished has friends had not come round to play and spoil an exciting match! Marcus first school, Hesketh, was in the next road – Bridge Road. He had a lovely young infant teacher, Pam Baxter, whom he met up with again, just before she died at a local care home near Oxford. She remembered that he was devastated when he lost a toy metal soldier called 'Gungadin.'

Marcus moved to his next school, Cranleigh Prep school, when he was nearly eight. He cycled every day to the school which was about one and a half miles from the house. At thirteen he went on to Cranleigh Senior School – quite a good public school – where he was one of the few day boys. He has generally quite happy memories of his school days. He is still in touch with two fellow Cranleighans –Christopher Morgan and Bob Matthews.

Some of the many tiny newspapers Marcus created, some smaller than a matchbox.

He was not too bad at sport and got into first or second teams for cricket, because, with a weird action, he bowled leg-breaks. He also played hockey, rugger, as a scrum half, and fives. The school had an unheated indoor swimming pool, which, thankfully, was seldom used. It was surrounded by hot baths, which Victorian pupils would have had before plunging into the icy water – the stuff of Empire, which by the time Marcus went to school was fast disappearing.

Marcus was bright, but some boys at the junior school were very bright, and as Marcus says, 'It's best not to appear to be clever'. At the senior school his A-level subjects were History and English. On one of his reports, Bryony says, 'the Scripture teacher said, "Marcus shows a keen sense of humour in this subject" – which is still apparent in his sermons.' On another report the Headmaster wrote at the bottom, 'Wholly laudable.' A friend who was staying told his Dad, 'That's worth ten bob of anyone's money!' His Dad paid up. Bryony also says that when Marcus was eight, someone asked him, 'What do you want to be when you grow up?' and Marcus replied, 'A Bishop.' Now, he's thankful he wasn't.

When the time came to consider university, his headmaster suggested Magdalene College, Cambridge, where the Master was Lord Braybrooke. His headmaster had been there himself and told Marcus, 'With a name like that, you are bound to be accepted.' – He did, in fact, get a scholarship to Magdalene. Marcus was shy but had some good friends and does not remember being bullied.

Marcus and his sisters had a lot of fun together, but with typical ups and downs. Card games were very competitive and often ended in tears. Marcus also knew it was best to keep away when a new dress was being made for one of his sisters – it never seemed to be quite right! The family all played tennis and a kind neighbour, Mrs Chappell, would sometimes ask them to tea and to play croquet.

Marcus loved cycling – and would ride around the local streets pretending the bike was a bus and ringing the bell. He would also cycle long distances and had some cycling and youth hostelling holidays in England, and, when he was 14, in Holland and two years later in France. On the real local bus there was a kind conductor called William who let him shout out the names of the stops.

Marcus says, 'We had a lot of freedom as children and learned from my mother to appreciate the beauty of the countryside. We had rabbits and hens and cats and a dog. Susan and Bryony with friends bought a large retired hunter – Kim. I remember the excitement of waiting for the horse-box, hooked on to the steam train, to arrive at the station. Holidays were staying with relations – best of all on Uncle Dick's (Richard Leach) farm in Scotland, where we earned some money picking berries - but also with Cousin Muriel in a little cottage near Wotton-under-Edge, where we had to get the water pumped up from a well.'

For about five years after the war, as already mentioned, his Dad worked raising money for the Conservative Party (Labour was in power). He presumably received reasonable pay and was provided with a car. After falling out with the Tories, he stood twice as a Liberal candidate for Parliament and then founded his own 'Patriotic Party.' He was a colourful candidate and *The Guardian* described him as a 'political chameleon.' He had various jobs for a while – but there was quite a long time when he was on the dole. That was a difficult time and his mother got a job charring as well as her tiring work at a nursery garden. Later on she was a helper at the cottage hospital—my own mother remembers at the age of ten, going along with her on a Sunday evening, volunteering after the staff had all gone home. She distinctly recalls the huge kitchen with massive gas grills, and making lots of toasted cheese for all the patients, "Granny always got it just right". Marcus was about 16 when Dad was out of work and he wishes now that he had been more sympathetic. The County Council took on paying his fees and when a new headmaster introduced school uniform he was allowed to go on wearing his old sports jacket as the family could not afford the uniform.

Life at home was not always easy. His Dad's moods were as changeable as spring weather. He could be great fun and very funny but also very angry. His Mum had to hide money for the rent round the house to stop his Dad going off with it. As Marcus now realises, this was probably for his Father's other family. It was presumably also why he was away, most weeks, for a couple of nights as a Special Constable with the Thames River Police.

Marcus' parents were both children of clergy – both his grandfathers also wore the cloth. (Once, as Marcus was walking back from church, a man called out 'I'm also a man of the cloth – I'm a window cleaner'). His father, before Marcus was born, had for a time been a clergyman, but went back to soldiering when the War started. He did not stop believing in God – but was often angry with the Almighty. For several years when his grandmother lived in Box Cottage, his Dad moved out of his bedroom to make room for her. Even so, Grandmother, who always wore a long black dress, avoided speaking to Marcus' Dad because she so disapproved of how he had treated her daughter years before. With the children, Grandmother Nora Leach could be great fun - if they behaved.

Marcus umpiring at Cranleigh Tennis Tournament.

As children, the family (except his father) went most weeks to Matins, although after Marcus was confirmed he usually went to the eight a.m. Holy Communion service. Certainly by his early teens he thought he would like to be a vicar. 'I was about twelve,' he says, 'when I went to stay with an elderly cousin. In the afternoon I went swimming at a nearby pool and ventured out of my depth (I could swim but not too well). Some older boys splashed me and I swallowed water and began to sink. I came up once but went under again but then struggled to the side. I had been told that if you went under three times you would drown. Anyhow as I was cycling home, I kept thinking of words from the General Thanksgiving– "Show forth thy praise not only with our lips but by giving up our lives to thy service." Certainly by the time I went to the Senior School some of the teachers knew that what I wanted to be was a clergyman.'

'I don't know if I was insufferably religious – but I did try to be good. But, of course, sex and religion have always had an uneasy relationship. We knew far less about sex than teenagers do today (there was no sex education) and there was a culture that suggested it was 'dirty.' So trying to be good made me shy and inhibited – and I was not well informed - but had the usual urges. One of the few things I remember from confirmation classes was the headmaster saying that masturbation was quite natural, and certainly among the boarders there was a fair bit of homosexuality. I realise now that a bachelor, who was a friend of a family we knew, was 'grooming me' and eventually invited me to stay in his cottage and got me into his bed - although didn't persist when in the morning I said I wanted to go home. (I feel my father should have warned me). As teenagers there were dances and my sister's friends were often in the house, but even when I danced I kept my partner at a distance. I think I did once briefly kiss a girl called Jane when I said goodnight, but Mary has been the one and only "woman in my life."

National Service

In those days all young men had to do two years' National Service. It was thought best for Marcus to do this before going to university, although this meant getting special permission to enlist when he was seventeen and so younger than most of the other conscripts. Because his Father had been an officer in the King's Shropshire Light Infantry, he wanted Marcus to do his National Service with his old regiment.

Afternoon Tea with Mary and Marcus

Marcus was not a natural soldier and, with no sense of rhythm, he could not march in step. Eventually the sergeant major ran out of abuse, stopped shouting and tried to help him. The first weeks were in Shrewsbury. Marcus remembers the first night and deciding if he did not kneel down in the large dormitory in which there was no privacy on that first night to say his prayers, it would be even more difficult on the next night He admits it was hard to concentrate. Basic training involved endless marching or standing to attention, cleaning, learning to use a rifle, ceaselessly polishing his kit – later on, brasso in the bloodstream caused blood poisoning: but the medical orderly had such a broad Yorkshire accent that he and Marcus never understood each other. Marcus was also given a 'housewife' so he could sew on buttons. There were a lot of buttons on the great coat which Marcus wore on his first leave. In the underground one by one the buttons came off and rolled around the train – to be sown on properly by his mother when he got home.

Marcus was initially with the group picked out to be officers– recruits that had been at public schools! – and was transferred to Strensall in Yorkshire. It soon became clear that, as the O.C. put it in his letter to his Father, 'Marcus was still rather too young' – anyhow if you cannot march in step you are not much use to the infantry. After being sent back to Shrewsbury for a while – where he spent days on the Wrekin, stopping the public wandering onto the range and getting shot – he was transferred to the Intelligence Corps to Maresfield near Hayward's Heath. (You had to have an IQ of at least a fourteen year old – or so it was said – to join the Intelligence Corps). Marcus remembers a happy day of freedom wandering around the beautiful city of York. Whilst he was at Strensall, Prime Minister Anthony Eden embarked on the disastrous and dishonest invasion of the Suez Canal on November 5, 1954. Those who might have to fight there were told nothing of what was going on and the *News Chronicle*, which opposed the action, was banned from military premises.

Maresfield was very different from the army barracks of Marcus' basic training. The camp consisted of old huts divided into two wings with six or eight soldiers in each half. Rumour had it that the camp had been condemned after the First World War. When there was heavy rain, water bubbled up from under the floor. The huts were heated – if one can use that term - by coke burning stoves. In Marcus' hut, one recruit was a qualified solicitor and another a senior manager at a large business – they were older, but at least the conversation was stimulating. Life was more relaxed – there were classes on the organisation of the army and a little about interviewing techniques and much else that was quickly forgotten. Once the training was over, many people had a long wait before they were deployed, which was bad for morale. They were expected to do 'fatigues' – cleaning the loos or spud-bashing: but the solicitor advised Marcus always to carry a bucket so people would think he had a job to do.

One of the officers at Maresfield was a keen Christian. He held a Bible study evening in his home once a week, which Marcus went to and where he met other recruits who were Christian. Marcus says that the verse which kept him going was St Paul's words, 'I have learned in whatsoever state I am, therewith to be content.' He and some others also went regularly to the local church. Some weekends Marcus would get leave and happily cycle some twenty five miles home to Cranleigh: but not so cheerfully back to Maresfield. He recalls that one evening he was quite depressed at the thought of going back and had gone to bed early on the Saturday evening. He was just going to sleep when his mother came in to say there was a telephone call for him. It was from someone who was even more of a misfit in the army, who had become a friend. When he went back to his bedroom, Marcus says 'it was filled with light - as if my friend was an angel reassuring me of God's love.'

Marcus was quite quickly deployed to Libya. Because of the tensions with Egypt after Suez, he was told to wear civilian clothes. The aircraft was a cargo plane – but it was the first time Marcus had flown. The plane was headed for Benghazi, but at almost the same time a plane heading for Tripoli crashed – killing some of the soldiers aboard. The BBC was only allowed to report it was going to North Africa – so his parents were

Afternoon Tea with Mary and Marcus

very distressed. Eventually, Marcus' uncle, Andrew Geddes, a retired RAF Group Captain, managed to find out that the plane Marcus was on had arrived safely.

Benghazi was the main centre for the British military in Eastern Libya. The Intelligence Corps had a house in the city. Marcus, however, was initially sent to the sub-office in Derna – much further to the East - to work with the staff-sergeant who was based there. There was a lot of routine work, but also some attempt to discover about political developments – it was not long before the Sennuysi king was deposed. Marcus slept in a room adjoining the office – rather isolated at night – and ate with the firemen whose base was quite nearby. Almost every meal was a fry-up and there was not much concern for hygiene. Not surprisingly Marcus developed dysentery. 'It was,' he says, 'one of the worst nights of my life. I kept drinking grapefruit squash and have never again wanted to drink grapefruit squash!' In the morning Marcus was put in a military ambulance to be taken to hospital in Benghazi. The driver and orderly had been told that there was a dance that evening – and as life in Derna was so dull – they raced as fast as they could for more than two hundred miles on a very bumpy road.

Marcus spent quite a lot of the summer of 1957 in hospital– and for some years had recurring digestive trouble. When he was better Marcus joined the Intelligence Corps office in Benghazi. The work was clerical – vetting the locals who applied for jobs with the army to see if they had a record for theft or dishonesty. The tedium of the work was compensated for by the fact that the working day was from 7.30 a.m. to 1.30 p.m. which meant there was plenty of time to spend the afternoon on the wonderful sandy beaches and swimming in the warm water.

There were three other privates and all four became good friends. Two were quite a lot older: one was to become a professor of Greek. He and Marcus eventually got a week's leave to visit the ancient Greek and Roman remains at Cyrene. They also made friends with a couple who were lecturers at the infant Benghazi University. Marcus also went regularly to the garrison church and often baby-sat for the Padre's son. He also had his first lessons in driving, including crashing into a gate. On the cook's day off, Marcus took his turn in doing the cooking and also quite often was the barman in the sergeants' mess, to which Libyan police officers often withdrew to refresh themselves, especially during Ramadan, and to swap information.

There was some question as to whether Marcus should apply to become an officer, but he felt that time abroad was more interesting than a return to the parade ground. Late in 1957, it was decided that the British army should leave Libya – so then it was time to burn endless Top Secret files, whilst the Libyans helped themselves to land-rovers, typewriters and other equipment.

Marcus was then posted to Cyprus to the Port Security Unit at Limassol. Eoka guerrillas were determined to drive out the British and gain independence for Cyprus. Whilst he was there Hugh Foot was appointed Governor and made it clear that the British would agree to independence, provided they could keep military bases. The thought of independence, however, reignited the hostility of Greeks and Turks for each other. It was a volatile situation and soldiers were not allowed out of camp except on duty and then they had to be armed. Marcus says he is thankful he never had to use his pistol. Usually two soldiers were deployed together, but on one occasion Marcus was sent by himself to an isolated landing stage. 'It was one of the few times I have really felt afraid. I was a sitting target.'

On the whole relations between the soldiers and Greek and Turkish dock officials were quite good. The soldiers' role was to check that no weapons or subversive literature were being smuggled into the country. Anyliterature in Greek had to be impounded until an officer had come down from Nicosia to look at it. There was a student returning from Athens who had books in Ancient Greek. Marcus, who knew some Greek, says 'The student was stopped and I was told to guard him. I suppose Thucydides could be considered subversive. Guarding someone was a strange feeling. Do you talk to him? But he would not want to talk to you.' Marcus persuaded the officer that returning pilgrims should not have their Bibles taken from them. There was often time to swim in the port – the water was probably none too clean. One sergeant was a very good swimmer and Marcus learned a lot from him. Marcus was billeted in a large tented camp on the hill above Limassol. There was a constant shortage of water. 'Just as I had soaped myself, the shower would run out of water.' Again, there was some Christian fellowship, but also some opposition. One of the other soldiers in the tent much disliked the fact that Marcus was a Christian, which on one occasion he showed by urinating on Marcus' bed. Thankfully my grandfather was not in the bed at the time and, with some explaining, was able to get fresh bedding. The soldier had, as usual, had too much to drink, but the two went for a beer soon afterwards.

Marcus' regret was that there was no chance to see anything of Cyprus – other than a week at the Army Chaplaincy's Centre in the beautiful and historic port of Kyrenia, in the north, which he and Mary visited for a holiday in 2010 and again, briefly, in 2017. Marcus did, however, with a friend, have a week's leave in Israel in 1958 – before Israel had occupied the West Bank. Israel at the time was seen as the underdog. Marcus and his friend Barry stayed in Tel Aviv but had a chance to visit West Jerusalem, the Dead Sea and Galilee in all its beauty. The visit was enough to give Marcus a feel for the human Jesus who lived in this land – a land Marcus has returned to on many occasions. One day crowds rushed past the hotel where Barry and Marcus were staying and they thought a riot was starting - in fact, the first super-market in Tel Aviv was being opened.

The final days in the army were frustrating. The due date for Marcus' demob had passed, but Marcus was still in the sweltering heat of the transit camp at Nicosea – over 40 degrees. When eventually they did get back to Maresfield, it was too late to go home that day, because there were forms to be filled in. Marcus says, 'I find it hard to remember the couple of weeks back at home before setting off for Cambridge: but it was wonderful to see Mum and Dad again and the rest of the family: but it's strange how little time there is to share experiences and hard to go back from being in charge of one's life to being a child again - which was all the more difficult when I went home from Cambridge in the vacations.'

How did this dynamic pair begin their life together?

5 How did Mary and Marcus meet?

Before we answer that question, let's find out about life at university. Mary, although she lived in Cambridge chose to go to Bedford College, which was part of London University, because Cambridge did not offer a degree in Sociology and, anyhow, Mary wanted a change of scene.

Mary in London: Bedford College

Mary started at Bedford College in the autumn of 1953. The college, now amalgamated with Royal Holloway, was then in the centre of Regent's Park. Mary lived at Nutford House Hall of Residence near Edgware Rd, which had female students from all the University colleges. It was a pleasant walk from Nutford House to Bedford College. A fellow student living at Nutford House was Susan Braybrooke – but more of that anon.

'These were three very happy years,' Mary says. She loved Sociology, but found time for a lot of other activities. 'At university in my first term I helped to start a pipe smokers club. It didn't last long!' Mary also captained the college table-tennis team and chaired the UNSA (United Nations Student Association) society and was also on the committee of the Student Christian Movement (SCM). 'We spent a lot of time in coffee shops, which were then very popular, and talked endlessly about politics and religion. I twice attended Billy Graham meetings. When I was nineteen, I had a Christian conversion and deep spiritual experience when I felt "Christ in me" - a feeling of coming to the end of myself and being in Christ. This is a commitment which has always been with me. I shared this with Nigel and we believed we would start a Christian community of believers who would live a peaceful nonviolent life and would try to change the world!'

Mary became great friends with her room-mate Barbara, who was reading Social Science at LSE. They both helped, each week, at a club for 'un-clubbables' in Shoreditch - it was burnt down several months after they left. Mary also taught cooking at another club in Bermondsey.

'As chair of UNSA,' Mary says, 'I invited speakers to meetings. I had one nasty experience and was probably naive. The Nigerian High Commissioner invited me to dinner at the Strand Palace Hotel and I went up to his room, where he nearly raped me. A Nigerian reporter friend was in the next room and rescued me. The High Commissioner wrote to me after that and implied I was not free - quoting "Stonewalls do not a prison make."' Later, as a child care officer in Cambridge, several men tried to forcibly kiss her and she had various offers from male clients too but she managed to maintain her professionalism. 'Such actions today would not be allowed,' Mary says, 'but I just thought it was the way men are!' She also had a number of boy-friends –quite a few of whom sent her Christmas cards for several years. Marcus was never jealous and says 'I am not surprised, she was, and is, so attractive.'

Mary passed her Economics exam in her second year and in the following year she gained a second class degree in Sociology, with which she was quite satisfied. 'Looking back,' Mary says, 'University was a time of great awakening. They were three very happy years.' One summer she worked in a Schweppes factory but mostly she travelled. On one occasion, she spent ten hours or so in a Spanish security cell, having been arrested for travelling from Valladolid to Madrid without a passport. She told the officials that she knew a nun in Madrid, but they said they could not believe a nun. The men on the train gave her their business cards and offered to help. There was a great fear of the Government and she made matters worse by telling the police what she thought of the dreaded General Franco, at that time the Spanish dictator. She was finally freed after her passport arrived and she then spent a few hours with a delightful Spanish student seeing the sites of Madrid.

Mary's First Job.

In 1956, Mary started her first job, at the age of 21. Marcus, at the same time, was starting his national service. She worked for two years as Assistant Organiser of Children's Care work with London County Council, based in Hammersmith. Mary had hoped to do a post-graduate child care professional course, but was told to get some experience first. (She eventually got the professional qualification at Bath University in 1976). 'My job,' she says, 'was very interesting and involved dealing with various school care committees as well as arranging and attending child health clinics with specialist doctors in Fulham, Notting Hill Gate and Ladbroke Grove (in one street most of the dads were in prison). 'I followed up,' she says, 'the most deprived children who did not attend, and interviewed parents. One clinic was for enuresis and children were told to hold on as long as possible to develop bladder capacity and given bells which started ringing as soon as they weed and woke them up.'

'Soon after I started work,' Mary says, 'Nigel finished with me. I was devastated for a long time, but know now that the relationship would not have worked, because of his sexual orientation, of which at the time we were both unaware.'

She shared a basement flat in Kilburn with her brother Paul, who recalls 'that it was fungus ridden and that Mary had to pass through my bedroom to reach our other room' 'The arrangement did not work very well, ' Mary says. 'I drove him to marriage! Having just got unengaged I wanted to be out, but he had just got engaged and wanted to save money. He also expected me to do the cooking!' Every weekend they got an early train at about 5 am – it only cost five shillings - to spend weekends with their parents in Cambridge, where they were sure to get plenty to eat. The damp in the flat was also a reason for Mary leaving after nine months, but she was a happy bridesmaid at his wedding – her third time as a bridesmaid.

After leaving Paul, Mary moved into the top room of a large house in Earls Court, which belonged to the parents of her friend Pat Sterne, who also read Sociology. Pat was living with her boyfriend, Michael. Mary, at the top of the house, shared with four other girls. They got on well, although one girl always left her washing up. There were no such things as dishwashers in those days (1957/8)! No television either except in very few homes.

Leisure time was spent going out with friends in London. Mary says, 'I was introduced to the Christian Community in Hampstead, by Denis Wight a friend of Dr and Mrs Hay, our next door neighbours in Cambridge. Denis shared many of my ideals and we were both members of the Fellowship of Reconciliation (FOR). At the Christian Community, I became very friendly with lovely people from all over the world, especially many Germans from Stuttgart, where Anthroposophy was started by Rudolph Steiner.' Mary did not join the community, ultimately because she was asked to do so by Dr Heidenreich, the top person, who had promised not to put pressure on her. 'Besides this,' Mary says, 'although everyone was delightful, it was elitist. Almost all the members were intelligent and artistic and I wanted somewhere where all could feel at home.'

Mary Back in Cambridge

When she went back to Cambridge, in 1958, Mary eventually joined Wesley Methodist church, going back to her parental roots. 'It was,' she says, 'a time of real hope and idealism.' She ran a youth club, was on the Leaders' meeting, helped in the Sunday school and made many friends. David Frost, who became a very well-known broadcaster, also attended the church. Whilst there, she taught John Morris, the minister's son, to drive. She recalls him being naughty and smoking all the time, although when he passed his driving test she felt very pleased with herself. Later, John and his wife Cheryl came on several of the tours my grandparents led and they were sad that John died quite young. He and Mary competed to take the best videos of their tours. My grandmother's informal travel films, when I have watched them, have always been excellently narrated, although I do recall during one family screening myself and my sisters couldn't stop laughing. This was due to a period of about five minutes during which she recorded footage of some small rocks and could be heard to repeatedly ask my grandfather 'Marcus, where are the birds? Where?'

A Child Care Officer

Mary's new job was to be a Child Care Officer in Cambridge. She found these years doing child care very fulfilling. They involved work in fostering, adoption, court-work, preventing children from coming into care, chasing runaways from approved schools and Borstals (Young People's Detention Centres), doing lots of home visits to families with problems. She was provided with a car and worked all hours including Saturday mornings with no extra pay - even for being on call at weekends - but never even thought about it! She had excellent support and supervision and was a member of a very happy little team and knew well all her colleagues, such as court officials and probation officers. She worked there for six years and had a wonderful time. After she left, her predecessor, Jane Fletcher - also a relation - came back to her old job. This meant that these children only had two social workers to relate to during their whole childhood – a continuity unheard of today.

Mary recalls two unusual incidents 'Once I had to take a rather active boy of 9 with autism on a commuter train toa special school in Surrey. The compartment was full of city men, all reading newspapers. They clearly thought I was an incompetent mother and disapproved. Suddenly the boy banged all their newspapers and they were forced to put them away. I explained the situation and fortunately they all laughed and began to talk to us both. Phew!' On another occasion she was travelling with her (male) boss to a case conference by train when a slightly dishevelled man came to sit by her. He said, Mary recalls, "I know you are a Social Worker because you are reading the *Guardian* and wearing a pendant. I have escaped from a mental hospital in Kent." Mary managed to ring the hospital and they were there to meet him at the next station. 'Needless to say my boss ignored the whole scenario and when I asked him why he did not support me he said I could manage perfectly well. Was he anxious about not coping with a client!?'

One client, who we'll call Belinda, was 13 and lived in a local children's home. She had a very disturbed background of living in 5 different foster homes, all of which had broken down. She was diagnosed as mentally ill as she had jumped out of a window, though Mary never really agreed with the diagnosis. Belinda spent several years in the local mental hospital. After Mary left the job, she kept in touch with her and visited when she could. Belinda came to stay several times at their home in Frindsbury, and, as we shall see, she was eventually married in the church there.

Life in Cambridge

Mary went back to living with her parents. 'I wanted to be fiercely independent so I had 2 rooms upstairs, a little bedroom and my old red room as a sitting room. I remember some beautiful flowers painted by my maternal grandmother on the walls. I was upset when my father painted over them.'

Mary became secretary of the local World Refugee Year and also of the Cambridge branch of the Fellowship of Reconciliation, a Christian pacifist group, of which she is still a member. Marcus later came along to it too because, he said, it was the only way to see anything of Mary!

'Cambridge,' Mary says, 'was a very exciting place to live and there were lots of great social events. A number of undergraduates came to have tea and play tennis including Marcus. I went to several May Balls – only the last one was with Marcus, and then we were chaperoned by my brother and sister- in-law, Paul and

Pepita, and by Marcus' sister Bryony and her husband Paddy. I also had time to do quite a lot of foreign travel and I had the chance to practise my French and Spanish'. Paul recalls, 'It is difficult to comment dispassionately on the subject of boy and girl friends! When I met Mary recently it was intriguing that she could remember more of the names of boys at my school than I could! Unsurprisingly we both met boys / girls through friends of the other.

'Mary had a long lasting friendship with Nigel – although technically she met him through a college friend. In the end we both met our wives/husbands independently – Mary meeting Marcus through his sister Susan who was at Nutford House – a hostel for London University. This reminds me that I met Margarita through Mary – a delightful Spanish girl – my first, but thankfully not my last, connection with Spain! Thinking about Pepita reminds me of the great respect we both have for Marcus – his gentle approach, his deep concern for everyone and (particularly for me) his care that one should not be misled or put in the wrong position.'

Paul reminisced upon the other memories of his sister which stood out to him; 'A visit to Mary at London University with an army friend; a great week on the Broads when I scored no points with my sister – but achieved a sore bottom when stepping back from the deck I had been mopping and fell on to the rowlock of a dinghy; the May Ball we attended with Mary and Marcus - when Marcus and Pepita punted us out to Grantchester at first light – a great night'. And he added that the memories are ongoing, with 'continued regular meetings when we share everything good and bad that went before and discuss the trivia and the deep.'

Pepita's perspective gives wonderful context to these memories, especially to the trip on the Broads; 'I think I first met Mary at her 21st birthday party at Bedford College and then I gradually got to know her on visits to Cambridge. She was my bridesmaid when I married Paul and I her matron of honour at her wedding to Marcus at Wesley Methodist church in Cambridge. No doubt many people have commented on Mary's and Marcus's abilities and pastoral care – so I'll leave that to them – save getting myself into trouble!

Paul and Pepita after their engagement.

Afternoon Tea with Mary and Marcus

'However I will relate a few stories, mainly about Mary. In, I think, 1956 George and Phyllis organised a holiday on the Norfolk Broads. There were six of us: - George, Phyllis, Paul, Mary, a friend called Colin Cope and me. It sounds ridiculous but we had four boats: a cruiser with a sailing dingy and a sailing boat with a rowing one.'

'One afternoon we moored up so we could go sailing. We had been joined for the day by Vaughn Lewis and family. Mary was to have 'lessons' in the sailing dingy with Vaughn. I was in charge of the sailing boat and Paul was rowing around in the other dingy. All was going well until a sudden gust of wind hit Mary's dingy which started to keel over. 'Let go!' shouted Vaughn. Mary, obedient to the last, let go of everything – sheet and tiller. The result was that the boat turned turtle leaving its passengers in the drink. Paul grabbed his camera. His sister was not impressed that he didn't rush to rescue her, although she did eventually manage to scramble into the dingy. I don't know if she has ever forgiven her brother!'

Pepita remembers that 'One Christmas Mary and Marcus bought theatre tickets for us all to go to Stratford on Avon. I think the group was Mary and Marcus, Marcus's sister Susan and her husband David; Bryony, his other sister and Paddy and Paul and me. It was agreed that we meet in the cafeteria for lunch prior to the show. Much to our embarrassment and the amusement of other clients, Mary had brought Christmas crackers with her, which she insisted we pulled and wore the paper hats. No choice! – We put them on as told!'

'My first memory of Marcus,' Pepita says, 'was when we went to the Magdalene May Ball. There were six of us, Mary and Marcus, Marcus's friend Max, later to be his best man, and his girlfriend, Paul and me. I don't recall much about the actual Ball but I do remember punting at about four o'clock in the morning. We set off with Marcus, (I would say at the helm but I don't think one can say that with a punt – may be it is at the pole!), gliding us along the Backs. It was mild and gentle, a perfect summer's daybreak. I had never punted before but someone persuaded me to take over. Fortunately, under Marcus's tuition, we all survived! Mary is forthright, kind, loyal and when you don't know her a bit scary. When I first met her she made me feel inadequate – maybe it was because I was worried she would not think me good enough for her brother. Marcus is a holy man in the true sense of the phrase. He too is gentle and kind, willing to listen and offer sound advice. In some ways you might feel Mary and Marcus are not compatible but when you meet them together you know they are a perfect match.'

Marcus at Cambridge

Looking back to his Cambridge days, Marcus says, 'Mum and Dad, to give me a good start, loaded the rather aged car with my possessions and drove me there. We then went to Ely for lunch with the Jefferson Smiths. Peter, who, had been a good school friend, kindly wrote regularly to me while I was in the army.

'When I think back to Cambridge,' Marcus recalls, 'my first memory is of the beautiful banks in May, full of flowers and blossom. The best thing about the years at Cambridge was falling in love with Mary. I have happy memories also of the kindness of her parents and the tennis and delicious meals at Kersell. I also enjoyed my studies and all the new horizons they opened up. I made a few lasting friendships and my faith was broadened and deepened.'

'I was probably too full of self-questioning and uneasy about the elitist life-style to be really happy,' he continues. 'I felt then, much as I do if I am asked to a London club, appreciative, but not somewhere that I belong. If I had not met Mary, I think I could have given into the depression that I sometimes felt. Indeed working hard was a way of escaping from myself. I think too although I valued the Pastorate, I was never quite at ease with its rather evangelical ethos and did not feel I really belonged there either.'

Money was always rather a problem. Although a good part of his expenses were covered by his scholarship and county grants, Marcus' father was expected to make a contribution which he was not in a position to do – so it meant for Marcus eating frugally, not being able to afford social drinking and doing a holiday job, usually at a nursery garden. At least, he is thankful, that he did not accumulate big debts, as students do today. During two summer vacations, he helped at a children's holiday camp near Deal in Kent.

Magdalene is one of the smaller colleges. There was a family connection to the college, which was founded by Thomas Audley - an ancestor of Lord Braybrooke, who was visitor of the College and to whom Marcus' family was distantly related. A Lord Braybrooke edited the first edition of Pepys' diaries and Pepys library is housed at the college.

'For my first year,' Marcus says, 'I had had a room to myself in the older part of the college. For the next two years I shared with Max Hebditch, who later was my best man. Max and his wife Felicity have continued to be great friends. I made a few other lasting friendships, most of who were from grammar schools rather than public schools. I was never part of the rugby/rowing/drinking set. For the fourth year I was in digs. Very sadly, my delightful landlady died and I moved to a very cramped room – of which the only advantage was that it was much nearer the college.'

For his first two years Marcus read History – mainly Medieval and Ancient History. His tutor for Ancient history was Robert Runcie – later to be Archbishop of Canterbury. He then changed to Theology. He says that he enjoyed the intellectual side of university life - reading and studying and listening to some brilliant and original lecturers.

He was regular at chapel services, but also joined the Pastorate, which was linked to Holy Trinity Church and which arranged Sunday tea discussions for students. 'It was at Holy Trinity,' he recalls, 'that listening to a sermon by Cuthbert Bardsley – then Bishop of Coventry – that I had a never-forgotten awareness of Jesus' forgiving and all-accepting love. I realised that I no longer had to try to be a good Christian – all I needed to do was hold fast to the assurance that God loved me as I am.' There was a lot of interest at the time in Christianity. Mervyn Stockwood invited outstanding and controversial speakers to a late evening Sunday service at Great St Mary's.

Marcus joined the United Nations Association and the Liberal Club, partly because his father was at that time a Liberal candidate, and Marcus took an active interest in politics. He played some hockey and cricket and croquet and his punting was good enough not to fall in! In terms of his subsequent life, it was Marcus' links to the Society for the Propagation of the Gospel that was to have the most lasting effect. SPG was an Anglican missionary society and it had a special fellowship for those considering missionary work. The fellowship met every year in January at High Leigh Conference Centre. 'Quite a lot of the time,' Marcus says, 'was spent in the unheated and freezing chapel. One year the emphasis was on dialogue with other religions and the speakers included Bishop George Appleton and Kenneth Cragg, a renowned scholar of Islam – both of whom were to become my mentors – and Dr Basu, a Hindu lecturer at Durham University, who compared Teilhard de Chardin and Aurobindo'. Their talks and the preliminary reading stimulated his interest in the theological and spiritual encounter of the world religions.

At the university, there was also a small SPG group which he regularly attended. One of his friends, Edward Bailey, who was a year senior had successfully applied for a World Council of Churches' scholarship in India. So Marcus thought he would do the same and was given a scholarship to Madras Christian College. Before leaving, he went to see Dr Bouquet, who was one of the very few Anglicans at that time to have studied world religions. Marcus remembers his advice, 'If you eat dry biscuits and bananas, you will probably survive.' The academic year in Madras (now Chennai) started in late June – so, to be there on time, Marcus did not stay for the degree ceremony. It was to be the start of life-changing experiences and friendships with people of many different faiths – some of whom are pictured below. But, before we follow Marcus to India, we need to back-track to Mary and Marcus' first encounter playing table-tennis - ping-pong would be a misleading way to describe their dynamic relationship!

The Senior Sister of the Feng Shui Temple in London welcomes Vinod Kapashi, and Charanjit and Ajit Singh, who are leading members of the World Congress of Faiths (above).
Members of the Peace Council (below).

4. Courtship and Marriage

Following her early experiences, Mary was wary of commitment. She says, 'it took me five years to decide to marry Marcus, who waited patiently and was about to give up when I said yes! I had many male friends but Marcus was always there in the background and I knew he was a very special, unusual person whom I could always respect, and that he was highly intelligent and a great Christian. I had never imagined marrying an Anglican priest, but then Marcus has never really been a typical cleric and has become increasingly less so. He has an amazing sense of humour. He also played a good game of tennis and had managed to beat me at table tennis. I had always said I would marry the man who could beat me!' 'It was not until he returned after a year in India that decisions were made. I had come to know his parents well and initially it was his sister Susan, with whom I became friends at London University, who introduced us. Sadly by the time we were married she was in New York working for architects where she remained for 16 years. I regret that Rachel's second name was not Susan but we were not keen on the name at the time she was born.'

They saw a lot of her in later life when she returned to England. After she married David Goldhill, a Jewish atheist, they lived nearby for a time. Sadly Susan died in 2011 and eventually David went into residential care near Godalming, where Mary and Marcus visited him at least once a month. He died in 2017. At the funeral, there were readings from Isaiah and Trotsky – both about social justice. Their ashes are buried in the family grave in Cranleigh.

Jeremy, Amanda, Susan, David, Mary and Marcus.

To India

In June 1963, Marcus climbed up into an Air India 'Palace in the Skies' on his way to Madras – now Chennai. 'It was also the real start of my interfaith journey.' His interest in world religions, as we have seen, had been stimulated by membership of the Society for the Propagation of the Gospel – but now he was to live with members of some of those religions.

Marcus had been awarded a scholarship by the World Council of Churches (WCC) to study for a year at Madras Christian College. The college was founded in the middle of the nineteenth century – as part of educational work which Christians saw as a 'preparation for the Gospel' – in the sense that the Hindu world-view was so different that it made it hard for Hindus to understand the context of the Christian message.

Many of those who taught at these colleges had a deep appreciation of world religions and by their translations and writings helped to make them known in the West. They believed that God had never left himself without witnesses and that all that was good in other religions would be taken up and fulfilled in Christ. This was in contrast to others who saw 'pagan religions' as idolatrous and the realm of darkness.

The college was originally in the centre of the city but had moved out to Tambaram - to what was then 'countryside'- some years before the Second World War. Chennai has now spread beyond Tambaram. By the time Marcus went to Tambaram there was an always crowded electric train into the city. The college has a beautiful campus planted with a wide variety of trees. When Marcus arrived in 1963 everyone showed Marcus much kindness. Almost immediately Mrs Devanasssen took Marcus to buy 'a cot,' which turned out to be a hammock-like bed, as white Englishman 'could not be expected to sleep on the floor!'

Marcus had a room in Bishop Heber Hall, one of the students' halls of residence named after the first Anglican bishop in India. He shared the life of a student and adapted to student food, choosing to be mostly vegetarian. One difficulty was that the World Council of Churches assumed that scholars would live as locals – and were paid at that rate – but for health reasons this was not easy. Marcus had little money with him and was rescued by the Revd Duncan Forrester – later a professor at Edinburgh University – until after many hours at the local bank he could transfer money from England. Bishop Heber Hall had a beautiful chapel, which kept up some high church traditions that Anglicans had contributed to the Church of South India (CSI).

CSI came into being by a union of Anglican and Protestant churches in South India. It combined the South India United Church, which was itself a union of the Congregationalists and the Presbyterians, the Anglican Dioceses of South India and the South Indian District of the Methodist church. Some Lutheran and other churches have subsequently joined CSI. The CSI liturgy was very beautiful and among the first of the new liturgies which are now widespread. It was there that Marcus first met with 'the Peace' – a greeting which had deep meaning in a still caste-ridden society. As is customary in places of worship in India, shoes were removed before entering the chapel.

There was a communion service there on Sunday mornings. In the late afternoon there was another service in the main hall to which Christian members of staff and students were encouraged to come – usually it was a service of the word, but occasionally it was a communion service and Marcus remembers his hesitation the first time he received the sacrament from a lay person – something still then unknown in the Church of England. There was also each day in the halls of residence a morning assembly, which, although Christian, emphasised universal themes in the hope that students of other religions would come too. Few of the students who were not Christian took much interest in their own religion – they mostly reflected the pervasive agnostic secularism of Pandit Nehru. The more observant would have gone to other colleges.

Marcus says he made a few good friends among the students and rather more among the staff: but 'it was strange being the only 'white face' among several hundred students – travel to India from the UK and US had not yet become popular nor commonplace.

There was no formal course, but Marcus attended some seminars at the University and joined the philosophy classes at the College – there were no courses in theology or the study of religions. The head of the department Dr. C. T. K. Chari gave him special tuition and invited him to his home for the various Hindu festivals. CTK's brother Dr Venugopal had converted to Christianity, but Dr. Chari saw good in both Hinduism and Christianity, and was sympathetic to the teaching of Sri Ramakrishna, who, based on his own experiences, claimed that all religions lead to a mystical union with the Divine. The differences, it is said, are due to the different languages and images that holy people use to talk about an experience that is inherently ineffable.

Practical experience of helping at a Leprosy clinic with students of different faiths, where the doctor was a devout Hindu, also inspired Marcus with the vision of all people coming together to serve those in need. The smiles of the children, he says, soon rid him of inherited prejudices about the disease. Marcus also had time to travel, third class, to several holy sites and stayed with generous Indian families. He visited Jyotineketan, an ashram founded by Fr Murray Rogers, who became a lifetime mentor. Marcus remembers complaining about the mosquitoes, only to be told, 'this has been their home long before we came here.' He also remembers Murray saying, 'The exterior dialogue with other people must be matched by an inner dialogue with the Lord.' This is why Marcus has been more interested in learning from other religions, rather than just learning about them. He also vividly remembers a Christmas he spent in a remote village in Andhra Pradesh with his college-friend Samuel's family and seeing the joy that faith in Jesus had given to these former outcasts. There was some talk of Mary visiting India, but she felt she needed to stay with her mother, who was unwell. They corresponded regularly and Marcus remembers the thrill of seeing the blue airmails. However Mary recounts that his letters, which survive, were mainly factual and far from romantic!

Wells Theological College

For three months after Marcus got back from India, before starting at Wells Theological College, he had an internship at SPG in London. This meant a daily commute to Waterloo – there was then still a station in Cranleigh. He helped research material for leaflets about world religions that the Society planned to publish. The Mother's Union HQ, close to SPG's HQ in Westminster, had an excellent and cheap café on its top floor so for a short while Marcus was an honorary member of the MU.

Whilst living back at home he had time to spend with the family. I personally have often found the transition from a long period of travel back to 'normal life' quite peculiar, particularly the shift in independence. My grandfather says that 'It was lovely catching up with the family and friends, but as I heard them talk there were big gaps in my knowledge of what had been going on - for example, Susan had got engaged but I did not know about the difficulties they mentioned. I was still wondering whether Mary would say yes - and we had too little time together, but also there was the great worry about Mary's encephalitis.'

Marcus had been to see two theological colleges before he went to India. He visited Cuddesdon at the beginning of Holy Week, when everyone was in silence. He felt it was too austere and high church for him. Wells Theological College was much more relaxed. By the time Marcus went there Tom Baker, who had recently become the principal, had changed all that and was imposing greater spiritual discipline. Everyone was expected to be in chapel by 7am for meditation and Matins followed by Holy Communion (which was optional). On Saturday evenings silence after Compline was the rule. During one visit in November (the same weekend when John F. Kennedy was assassinated) Mary tempted Marcus to break this instruction. Earlier that day he had taken her for a walk in a muddy field, where they were chased by cows. A romantic weekend indeed!

Whilst Marcus was at Wells, the staff went to visit Pontigny, which was the training college in France for worker priests. When they came back, the staff stopped wearing cassocks and students started addressing them by their Christian names. The members of staff were theologically radical, which was not a problem for Marcus who was aware from Cambridge days of the theological debates, but it was disquieting to many members of the college. Marcus, to gain pastoral experience, regularly visited a very disturbed person at the Mendip Hospital. He recalls, 'At Wells Theological College, besides occasional practice preaching in village churches, we were expected to gain some pastoral experience and I chose the option of visiting someone at the Mendip Hospital which was one of the now outdated large Victorian buildings for the mentally ill. (Perhaps also because Mary's social work had made me much aware of the issues). Many of the patients -all together in large wards - were very disturbed. Sometimes I could have some conversation with the man I was asked to visit - sometimes after an hour, I wondered what had been the point. It started my interest in the healing ministry of the church, which at the time was very much neglected and in Highgate I trained as a Counsellor at the Counselling Centre at the Methodist Church, where Mary also helped, and was supervised by a Clinical Psycho-therapist. I think all this helped me to recognise that we all have a shadow side, which needs to be integrated, rather than suppressed, which has been the approach of much Christian moral teaching.'

His only memory of the class on pastoralia was of a Bishop telling the students always to wear a hat when walking in the parish so you could take it off when you saw a member of the congregation and keep it firmly on when you saw a Papist or Dissenter. He stopped short of telling them to spit at atheists!

As a student Marcus lived in one of the houses in Vicar's Close, which is said to be the longest continually inhabited road in England. The fact that students lived as small communities encouraged close fellowship and took away the usual institutional character of colleges. Marcus had a particular friend Tim with whom he often played tennis and always lost because Tim had been at Junior Wimbledon. For a term Marcus was 'head boy,' although there was some more ecclesiastical title which he has forgotten.

On Sundays, students had to attend the Cathedral service and then spent lunch dissecting the sermon. Sermon class was something everyone dreaded. A couple of victims had to preach a trial sermon which staff and students then commented on. The first time Marcus attended he breached the convention by saying what he actually thought about the sermon. Marcus, so recently involved in the United Church of South India and aware of India's poverty, found college life rather parochial and gossipy – a feeling often repeated at subsequent deanery chapters and other meetings of clergy. The sheer beauty of the Wells Cathedral, the city and the countryside around, did much to counteract this. Marcus has especially happy memories of a visit his mother made to Wells at this time and her delight in its beauty, which was at its best in the summer sunshine.

Together at Last: Engagement

Despite the muddy November walk, by the end of 1963 at last Mary yielded to Marcus' long pursuit. The next difficulty was for Marcus to get his would-be father-in-law's permission. Mary's father, George, however, chose to spend the Saturday afternoon after Christmas examining something underneath his car. Time was going by – and the hope of buying a ring before the shops shut was fading. So Marcus knelt down and joined George on the ground and got his blessing. History does not record whether Marcus knelt to Mary as well as to George! There was time to get a ring – and perhaps the only secret Marcus has kept from Mary was how much the ring cost. Mary and Marcus celebrated their engagement by going to a dance at the University Arms Hotel with George, Jenny Johnston who was a relation, the Hays from next door and Paul and Pepita, whilst Mary's mother, Phyllis, baby-sat for Mary's nephews.

Mary and Marcus were engaged for 6 months. It was a very happy time. Marcus continued at Wells Theological College and Mary was still working in the Children's Department in Cambridge. Mary wrote letters to various disappointed male friends to put them in the picture.

Mary and Marcus went to see the Rev Arthur Valle, the Methodist minister at Wesley Church, Cambridge, to arrange a date for the wedding. They wanted the same weekend as Mary's parent's wedding (21st June) and asked for 20th June 1964. Arthur with his tongue in his cheek said there was already a funeral that day! But he agreed to the date. Later on they had a very tiresome time with the Bishop of Ely. Marcus' future vicar Harry Edwards agreed to celebrate communion with Arthur Valle's agreement but when permission was

Afternoon Tea with Mary and Marcus

asked of the Bishop he refused because of the "delicate" position between the Anglicans and the Methodists, who were courting each other at the time. He wrote, that 'The regulations of Convocation of the Church of England are quite clear and I am bound by them" (8th May 1964). Mary was furious but several letters made no difference. It was very disappointing and both Mary and Marcus were upset. Fifty five years later The Churches' courtship has made little progress There has been a recent suggestion that Anglicans might 'gladly bare' with the 'temporary expedient' of accepting the ministry of Methodists minsters – even though no episcopal hands have touched them. In response, Mary wrote to the *Church Times*. The letter is reproduced below.

Anglican-Methodist ministerial interchangeability

From Mrs Mary Braybrooke
Sir, — I hope when the "Methodist question" (News, 21 June) is put, that members of the General Synod will consider the pastoral implications as well as the theological and historical ones.

I am still sad that the then Bishop of Ely refused permission for my husband Marcus's vicar to celebrate communion in the Methodist church where we were married — even though the minister kindly agreed to the use of wine.

I "gladly bore" with being confirmed as a "temporary anomaly". I should have remembered that in God's sight "a thousand years is like a single day" (Psalm 90.4).
MARY BRAYBROOKE
17 Courtiers Green
Clifton Hampden
Abingdon OX14 EN

From the Revd Geoffrey Squire
Sir, — In 1983, I was ordained in Exeter Cathedral, but the following year I had to return to that cathedral to be ordained again that I might preside at the eucharist and pronounce the absolution after confession. So, was my first ordination

The Wedding

Mary's mother was thrilled to assist with the preparations and George helped make many of the arrangements – including installing two new loos. He also instructed ladies not to wear stiletto heels that would damage the tennis court. Mary chose her nephews, Phillip and Tim, as page boys. Bob was an usher with Paul Thomas and Tony Vernon Harcourt, and of course Mary's brother Paul. The two little bridesmaids, Amanda Peters and Katherine Puckel, looked lovely in the green that Mary chose because it irritated her that green was supposed to be unlucky. Mary was radiant in her simple cream dress, which Marcus later had cleaned to be on show at their Golden Wedding. Marcus was still able to get into the second-hand morning dress at Sarah's wedding in 2017.

The marriage was in Wesley Church Cambridge and Mary's father arranged everything. The wedding service was lovely. The best man Max and his wife Felicity brought their baby daughter aged three months so there was some baby noise – recorded on the tape of the service - but it did not matter. Mary was thrilled that a number of her clients attended the service as well as six members of her Youth club. There were about one hundred and twenty guests. A small children's choir sang 'May the Grace of Christ Our Saviour.'

The very happy reception was in a marquee on the tennis court. There was a finger buffet and as well as fruit cake, which Mary would not eat, there was also a Madeira cake, which was unusual then. Mary's Uncle Don made a speech saying Mary was his favourite niece and then spoilt it by saying she was his only niece! There were lots of telegrams including one hoping for child care continuity. They did not realise how quickly Mary and Marcus would fulfil this! Mary had even made Marcus agree to adoption if they could not conceive as she had dealt both with adoption and childless couples in her work. One sadness was that by the time they were married Susan was in New York.

Newly-weds Mary and Marcus.

Honeymoon

After a night in London, the happy couple set out to Austria for their honeymoon. The flight over the Channel in a thunderstorm was frightening but all else went well. After a night at Cologne they stayed in near Innsbruck in the beautiful and picturesque little village of Inzing. Their room looked out onto the beautiful mountains. Marcus climbed some of them: Mary waited half way! They also spent time walking together by the river. A highlight was a Mozart concert in Innsbruck. They believe that Rachel was conceived in Freiburg, where the coach tour made an overnight stop. Mary soon realised that she had married a man who never wasted a moment. Rachel arrived 9 months to the day and date of the wedding and Jeremy came just under a year later! The family was complete and their wonderful children have given them so much joy.

7. Highgate - 17 Bisham Gardens

Mary and Marcus moved into their first proper home, 17 Bisham Gardens in Highgate Village just before the ordination. The vicar in effect moved in too – he was an expert at painting and decorating and set to work to make the house liveable, whilst Marcus stained the rough wood floors - fitted carpets were a thing of the future. The house was a late nineteenth century three storey terrace house. From the attic study there was a view over London as far at St Paul's Cathedral. There was a tiny garden – soon to have a sandpit. In those days telephone exchanges had a name – theirs was Fitzroy 0542.

Just below Bisham Gardens there is the lovely Waterlow Park, which was an ideal place, although hilly, to push a pram. At the end of the road the extremely steep Swains Lane led to the very overgrown Highgate Cemetery – best known for the grave of Karl Marx. Russian visitors liked to take pictures of the clergy - to show relatives at home what a medieval pre- Communist society was like.

The Family Grows

Both the children were born in the Queen Mary Maternity Hospital in Hampstead, during the time that Mary and Marcus were living in Highgate, and while Marcus was curate at St Michael's. The evening before Rachel was born, Marcus and Mary were running a Youth club, when Mary realised something was happening. She did not tell Marcus and said nothing when in the morning he was telephoned and asked to go and sit with a dying woman. 'I do not know to this day what he would have done if he had known I thought I was in labour!' Mary says. 'He was a very conscientious priest and it would have been a difficult decision for him. For many years the widower sent us a Christmas card'.

Later that day both went to the Maternity Hospital, but the nurse said it was unlikely Mary was in labour and sent Marcus home. Later that night she phoned to say Mary was definitely in labour, so Marcus cycled through the early morning from Highgate to Hampstead to be with Mary, but had to wait downstairs until the baby was born (Dads were kept out of the way in those days). He occupied the time by reading Trollope. Rachel was born on March 20th, 1965. She was face presentation, which was unusual as only 1 in 500 births are 'face presentation.' All the staff, therefore, came to watch. One day later Rachel thoughtfully sent her mother a Mothering Sunday card (with Marcus' help). When Jeremy was born he was face to pubis, ('looking upwards') which is also unusual – only 5 births in 100. Mary was told she must have a large pelvis! Because Mary was afraid of being again told she had come to the hospital too early, she waited until almost the last moment. Thankfully, their good friend Millicent was there to drive them to the hospital. Jeremy was born within the hour of Mary getting to the hospital - Marcus had to find the midwife when he thought he saw the baby's head. The date was March 9th, 1966.'

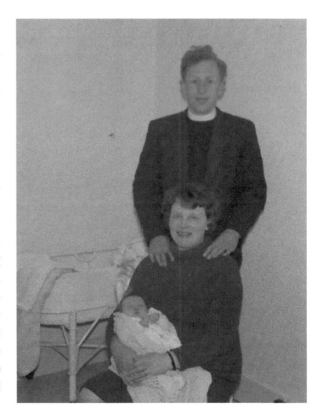

Happy parents

Millicent, who was godmother to my mother Rachel, remained a dear friend of all of our family. I remember visiting her a few years ago in her lovely nursing home in the Cotswolds, before she passed away. Her room was peppered with little carved wooden ducks, and we later exchanged several letters. When my mother was a child she would go to stay with her godmother, making fabric collages and artwork, and to this day we still have a huge collage of hers on the wall—her own daughter had tragically passed away at the age of two, and Rachel's visits meant a lot to both of them.

'The birth of a baby,' Mary says, 'is utterly miraculous and the joy immediately after the pain and hard work is indescribable. My only sadness is that I was unable to breast feed properly and was not given much encouragement. However it meant that Marcus could bond quickly by helping with the feeding.'

'At that time we stayed in hospital for 8 to 10 days in a two-bedded ward. When Jeremy was born, the other bed was occupied by a lady whose second baby, sadly, was born with Down's syndrome. Because I was a Social Worker it was thought that I could support her and cope: but I found this very hard. She was not told that there were problems and excitedly wrote to her friends that she had a beautiful baby girl. I knew from looking at her baby about the Down's syndrome. When she was told the day before she went home about the situation she left her baby behind and it was heart breaking. I never knew the outcome but hope she changed her mind because these children can bring so much joy.'

'I loved the babies and was thrilled to be a mother and it was a delight to have two so close together. I was frightened when I came home with Jeremy that Rachel would not recognise me as she had stayed in Cambridge with my dear mother for three weeks. At once, she gave me a lovely smile and all was well and, of course, she never remembered life without Jeremy. They were always great companions.'

Mary as a young mother

Members of St Michael's were thrilled to have two babies and were very supportive. They arranged a Baby Shower and provided a nappy laundering-service, so that Mary could join in parish events. Mary and Marcus never lacked baby sitters and bought a very simple second-hand black and white T.V. set for five pounds to entertain them – but also to watch a series of programmes by Wedgwood Benn's wife on how to bring up babies.

Parish Life

Although Marcus is better known for his interfaith work and his writings, he has always thought of himself as a parish priest. He and Mary have shared the life of a number of churches.

1964 was not only the year of Mary's and Marcus' marriage. It also the year in which Marcus was ordained a deacon at St Paul's Cathedral on Michaelmas day, September 29th. In fact, Marcus' Ordination was delayed so that he could be married first. London Diocese at the time had a rule that a clergyman could not be married in his first year as a curate – perhaps it would be too distracting? The Suffragan Bishop of Willesden asked the Bishop of London to make an exception – it had been a long courtship – but the Bishop of London refused. The Suffragan Bishop, therefore said, 'You had better get married first then.' As already mentioned, Rachel actually arrived nine months to the day and date of their wedding – did the Suffragan Bishop have the gift of prophecy?

The ordination to be a deacon was at St Paul's Cathedral. There were some 50 men being ordained as deacon or priest. The coach bringing them from the pre-ordination retreat was very late – it arrived about five minutes before the service and suddenly there was this group of men hurrying to the crypt – where there was, at the time, the only loo in the building. Ten minutes later they were all dressed in white surplices with their minds on higher things. Before his ordination to be a priest his vicar Harry Edwards said of Marcus: 'Everybody recognises he was born to be a priest; that he will do well by the Church; and that the Church of England is fortunate to have such excellent young men entering its ministry.'

Besides the family, Archbishop Desmond Tutu, whom Marcus' parents often had to tea when he stayed in Cranleigh during his holidays as a student in London, and Aatchen Thomas, who was chaplain at Madras Christian College, were among those who came to the service and back afterwards to Bisham Gardens for lunch.

Marcus had come to Highgate on a parish visit from Wells Theological College. The vicar Harry Edwards was left-wing in his views. Most of the parishioners were wealthy and seldom agreed with what he wrote in the parish magazine. Harry always wore a long black cassock – he said it was the only garment that did not identify him with a particular social class. Marcus did the same for six months. There was, each day, an early morning service and evening prayer. Harry was very good with children and on Sundays there was a crowded family service at 10am, followed by traditional Matins – as well as an early communion service and evensong.

All services were from the *Book of Common Prayer* (liturgical revision was for the future). Visiting was a priority and over a couple of years every house was visited – this was usually appreciated by both those who did and those who never came to church. It also meant that Harry and Marcus had usually met people before they came to enquire about a baptism or a wedding or a funeral. There were also regular services in local Care Homes and visits to hospitals.

Very soon after Marcus and Mary arrived Harry and Norah Edwards went for six months to Australia to see some of their family. A retired Australian vicar Sydney Ball and his wife Elsie took charge of the parish. Sadly there was an acrimonious dispute with Harry as to whether Sydney could use the parish car – and several of the parishioners sided with Sydney. There was also a Lent course entitled 'No small change' during which many suggestions for change were made – but not welcomed by Harry on his return.

Afternoon Tea with Mary and Marcus

Sydney and Elsie, like Harry and Norah, were very kind to Marcus and Mary. Mary and Marcus' first Christmas is one they have never forgotten. At Christmas, there were a lot of services – Midnight, 7am, 8am Holy Communions, 10am Children's Service; 11am a.m. Matins and then another communion at 12 noon. 'I think both Sydney and I were surprised to see Mary and Elsie sitting at the back during the 12 noon service,' Marcus says. 'Hadn't they been to enough services? When the verger came up with the collection he whispered to Sydney "Do you have keys for the vicarage. Your wife has forgotten hers." So Sydney fished in his pocket and put them in the collection plate for the verger's return journey. The Balls did not know how to work the night storage heaters – so the house was freezing and the turkey wasn't cooked till after 4pm'

Another, now amusing, incident, took place on Highgate Hill. Mary says, 'Marcus was a very enthusiastic, dutiful young priest and for the first few months, like his vicar, he wore a cassock. Once, walking with me when I was heavily pregnant, outside Holy Jo's (St Joseph's Roman Catholic church), my pants ('knickers' in those days) fell to the ground, the elastic having broken. Overcome with embarrassment Marcus walked quickly on ahead ignoring me. I was not amused! Marcus' excuse was that for a priest to be seen helping a lady with her knickers might be misconstrued.

Parishioners were very kind: offering places to stay for holidays, even lending them cars. Their first holiday, when Rachel was just a few months, was rather ambitiously in Douglas in the Isle of Man. Another year they stayed at a Holiday Centre for Clergy at Wells-on-Sea. Early on they had mackerel, which Marcus said he enjoyed – as a result they had it every other day for the rest of holiday. In their third year the lovely Cooper family, who were to become great friends, offered them the use of their tiny cottage called Toad Hall just behind the sea wall at Dymchurch. The sands were wonderful, but a major tragedy was when the wind took hold of the lovely big beach ball that Rachel was holding. Marcus chased after it for half a mile, but the wind was faster. The miniature railway was a great success. Their next door neighbours, the Millers, very generously lent them their car. In those days the clergy used to get an annual bonus. The Easter collection went to the vicar and the Whitsun collection to the curate. (Now clergy are one of the few groups not to get a bonus). They received £116. 4s 3d (the Vicar had received £265 at Easter) and spent some of the money on a portable radio.

Harry gave Marcus a lot of encouragement and freedom. He was allowed to work for a Master's degree at London University instead of the usual Post-Ordination training - nicknamed Potty training. He also, while he was at Highgate, became Hon. Secretary of the World Congress of Faiths, about which there will, later, be much to say. There were good relations with all the other churches. Marcus started a Christian Aid Committee – at the suggestion of Brian Frost with whom Mary and Marcus still keep in touch. It was an exciting time in the church's life and some people in Highgate were leading the changes. The radical weekly *New Christian's* offices were down the hill from Highgate and Marcus and Mary got to know the editor Trevor Beeson and both wrote several reviews. David Edwards, the editor of SCM Press, which published John Robinson's *Honest to God*, lived in Highgate and Marcus and Mary got to know him. David's successor at SCM, John Bowden and his wife Rachel became life-long friends. Mr Hawkins took them to hear Martin Luther King speak (Marcus later met his widow Coretta) and encouraged them to join the Movement for the Ordination of Women to the Historic Ministry of the Church of England (MOW), which like Anglican-Methodist union, they expected to happen within at most ten years.

Mary and Marcus kept up with Highgate friends for several years - sadly many of them have died. Rosemary Beattie still comes to visit them. She's always been very kind at keeping in touch with all of their grandchildren, including myself, remembering every birthday and encouraging our love of reading by sending us book tokens. She thoughtfully took my pony-mad mother to see the Olympia Horse Show, and gave her a special childhood toy—a Tiny Tears doll.

Afternoon Tea with Mary and Marcus

Phillippa Regnault (née Cooper) tells how they first met her family and their subsequent encounters: 'I met your grandparents in 1965. They were newlyweds! We lived in Highgate where Marcus was the curate at St. Michael's church and it was he who prepared me for confirmation. On a couple of occasions I went to their home to baby sit for Rachel, and later on for Jeremy. The highlight of our relationship was when Marcus celebrated my marriage in Dymchurch to my French husband Alain. Another memorable and emotional occasion was when he officiated at my stepfather's funeral in Broad Chalke.

Marcus and Mary have stayed with us a couple of times in France. I hope you know that your grandmother still speaks excellent French! The last time was in 2012, when I had been recently widowed but when they came, and some of my children were there too, it was just like old times. In fact Mary paid me the greatest compliment. She said that I had very easily slipped into Alain's role as the leader of the family. It was a lovely thing to say as I was battling with bereavement. But as you probably know both of your grandparents have the knack of saying just the right thing at just the right time. We talked a lot over the years about differences in faith (my husband was Catholic, one of my sons-in-law is Muslim), how certain experiments between Jews and Muslims living together in the Middle East do work out, social attitudes, single parents, and the like. There have been bits of advice given over the years, some taken, some not. When I was engaged to be married my then fiancé had come over to Dymchurch to do a summer job and Mary and I were staying with my family at our cottage down there.

One evening Alain was off duty and came over from the local hotel where he was working. We had some kind of lovers' tiff and Mary said to me. "Philippa, you weren't very kind to Alain". Well do you know, from that day till the day he died I tried to be "kind". I had been caught red-handed and I spent 40 odd years trying to put it right! Thank you Mary! I like to believe I succeeded.

Helen, you ask me what defines Marcus and Mary. It's pretty difficult to put in a nutshell! I would say a mixture of deep spirituality and great fun. These are totally compatible but all too rare in clergymen and their wives! Their greatest quality, I'd say is tolerance and open-mindedness. On the few occasions we've met over the years, every single time I've met them I have a real sense that they have so much empathy that they can understand where people are coming from and thus, accept them for what they are. I wish one could emulate! The older one gets the wiser, but I always felt they were pretty wise from the start!

One great memory for my half French/half English children was when we went to tea with Mary. It was when they were living in Wells or Bath. The children (all now between 30 and 40) still remember that tea. A proper English one! While they were playing Mary and Alain and I were chatting. She was a mine of information. It went from the differences between Catholics and Anglicans to why she thought it was important that children should have pets to look after! Rachel had a pony at the time. We stayed so long that Marcus came in quite late and found us there – an added treat.

One great memory was when we were taking them back to the Gare du Nord. Mary saw the grand wheel on the Place de la Concorde and literally overflowed with glee at the idea of people taking a ride. I immediately picked up on the unspoken enthusiasm and asked her if she wanted to go up. We decided we had time before their train left. And she did – go up.

Now what do I find most surprising about them? Maybe that Mary is overflowing with energy, fun, determination, despite the painful arthritis while walking round the gardens in Versailles with us. Marcus is peaceful, quiet, never gets rattled, - the epitome of kindness and gentleness. Two different temperaments: but total symbiosis as a couple. It radiates and it does people so much good. There was a political slogan years ago "La Force Tranquille". That's Marcus - an incredibly intelligent industrious mind and strong character in a soft and gentle envelope.

Afternoon Tea with Mary and Marcus

Marcus once told us about one of his visits to the Holy Land and I said I'd love to go. Mary said "I'm not sure that Alain is quite ready for it yet"! Although he (and I!) grew more tolerant as we grew older, it was not, shall we say, our main quality! But maybe we have learnt something from your grandparents though. I like to think so. And just for the *petite histoire* I'm going to Israel next Sunday!'

There are other Highgate friends with whom they are still in touch, including Peter and Alison Austin, who is Jeremy's godmother. At Peter and Alison's wedding, Rachel was a bridesmaid. Peter was taking rather a long time over his speech, and the guests were beginning to grow a little restless. From Marcus' arms young Rachel, who was four, called out loudly "Hurry up, Peter!" It was a joy for Mary and Marcus to attend Peter and Alison's 50th wedding anniversary in 2019 in Whitstable.

Mary's Social Work

Mary was seven weeks pregnant when they moved to Highgate. Having enjoyed driving around the Somerset countryside in a provided little car she was offered a job as senior child care officer in the London Borough of Hackney and had the use of a much larger old black car. She found the culture somewhat different. A very busy office with several workers to supervise where occasionally owing to pressures, arrangements to receive children into care (now called "looked after children") were made on the telephone and 'freedom from infection' certificates were done later!

World Congress of Faiths

It was while he was at St Michael's, that Marcus joined the World Congress of Faiths (WCF). He saw a small advertisement at the bottom of the front page of *The Times*, about the WCF Library at Younghusband House, which was quite near Paddington Station. As he wanted to keep up his interest in world religions, he enquired about this and went to a meeting at which Geoffrey Parrinder, a leading scholar in the field, was speaking. He joined the Congress and soon afterwards started as an external student working for a Master of Philosophy degree, supervised by Geoffrey Parrinder, who

Marcus making a presentation to Lord Combermere

became a good friend. The thesis formed the basis of his first book, *Together to the Truth*. His efforts to gain a doctorate were not so successful. The distinguished scholar Ursula King and Lord Combermere, later chair of WCF, were among his fellow students.

Marcus' first published article, 'A Christian looks at Hindusim' was published in the WCF journal *World Faiths* in 1965, and a year later he was invited to be one of the Honorary (or voluntary unpaid) secretaries. His responsibilities included helping to arrange the lecture programme and the annual conference, and this gave him the chance to meet many outstanding scholars and spiritual teachers including the Sufi leader Pir Vilayat Khan, Archbishop Anthony Bloom, head of the Russian Orthodox Church in Britain, Professor Alister Hardy, known for his pioneering work on religious experience, Otto Frank, and HH the Dalai Lama, as well as Christian pioneers of interfaith dialogue including Edward Carpenter, soon to be Dean of Westminster, and George Appleton, at the time Archbishop in Jerusalem.

Each year WCF arranged an 'All Faiths' service in which people of many religions joined together. At the time they were very controversial and many Christians saw this as a betrayal of Jesus Christ – the only son of God. Marcus' participation in such a service was reported, rather critically, on the front page of the *Church Times.* He wrote to the paper and explained that as a 'mere curate' he had only represented Christianity because Archbishop Bloom had been delayed. One of the members of St Michael's congregation told him not to put himself down. The most memorable services were when the Dalai Lama took part.

Time to Move On

After Mary and Marcus had been in Highgate two and a half years, the Bishop persuaded the vicar to have a second, rather way-out, curate. The parish did not want to pay for a second curate – so Mary and Marcus began to think about moving. Marcus approached Graham Leonard, the then Bishop of Willesden – not the one who helped about their marriage. When he went to see him, the Bishop was double-booked and gave Marcus five minutes and suggested a parish where he could do a second curacy. Marcus happened to know someone who had lived there and gave him a ring. His friend told him that the vicar was impossible and the two previous curates had both had nervous breakdowns – so much for episcopal oversight!

Harry Edwards, early on, had advised Marcus that 'the less you see of bishops, the happier you will be.' (Poor Bishop Bill Swing if he reads this!).

St Michael's, Highgate

8. Frindsbury, Strood and the Medway Towns

With his confidence in episcopal advice diminished, Marcus took the then desperate step of looking at clerical advertisements. At that time it was almost unheard of for clergy posts to be advertised – but just a few were in the radical *New Christian* magazine. That weekend there was one advertising a position in a Team Ministry for Strood, which, Marcus said, 'I discovered was in Kent – so I wrote in and to my surprise was asked to go and have a look – and to my even greater surprise was offered the job.'

The family moved to Frindsbury in December 1967. Frindsbury, with its old church, was a village on a hill above the river Medway. There was an amazing view of the Medway towns, with boats, trains and cars always on the move. The parish also included the large newish housing estate of Wainscot. Down the hill was Strood. The whole area was impoverished. There were three churches in Strood and they and Frindsbury had only recently been joined together in one of the first team ministries. Traditionally clergy worked by themselves as vicars or rectors of a parish – often they were quite lonely and suffered from stress and depression. Moreover parishes were isolated – maybe jealous – so that no overall strategy could be planned for an urban area.

The leader of the Team was John Waller, who had been hoping to work in South Africa but had been barred from doing so by the apartheid South African government, which must have known and feared such a dangerous and radical clergyman. John had enormous nervous energy and an exciting vision for a new pattern of church life.

Life at Frindsbury did not get off to a good start. The house was small, although an extension was eventually built on. There was a back-boiler which was meant to heat the house and the water but did neither efficiently. Marcus had gone ahead, so Mary and the family arrived the next day driven by Mary's Dad. As he turned in at the gate, his car went off the narrow raised drive. There was no damage – but not the best welcome. Mary's relationship with John also quickly went off track. The family had moved in just before Christmas – so one of the first services was the carol service. Mary and Marcus and the children sat at the back. John was keen to welcome families – but when Jeremy fell off the pew and started crying John said loudly: 'Please take the child that is crying out of the Church.' Mary was furious. Admittedly John's son was singing a solo at the time. Mary and Marcus took the family home – and after the service John came to see them. It was a long evening and Father Christmas did not get any help with filling the stockings of either household. By the morning all involved tried to act on the angels' message of 'goodwill to all people.' Mary started a crèche immediately.

In time Mary and Marcus and John and his wife Pam developed a deep friendship and trust. Marcus worked particularly closely with John as they both had primary responsibility for Frindsbury as well as their roles in the wider life of the Team. Marcus says he learned a lot from John about relationships and the dynamics of leadership and giving members of the congregation a real share in decision-making. Relationships among the team of clergy were sometimes tense. Those clergy whom John had inherited quite soon moved on. One of the new members who was already there, to whom both Mary and Marcus were especially attached, was Peter Absolon.

A lot of changes were introduced – some of which at the time were very daring, although now commonplace. The altar was moved forward – despite a furious protest by the Mayor – so that the clergy could face the congregation. This was to emphasise that clergy and laity together are the people of God and that Christ's presence at the Communion is in the thankful gathering of his people rather than just in the bread and wine. To emphasise that all life is holy, instead of wafers, an ordinary loaf of bread was brought to the altar and broken and shared. The trial modern language order for communion – to become known as

ASB when published in the subsequent Alternative Service Book – was introduced. As was the peace – when members shook hands and greeted each other with the words, 'the peace of the Lord be with you.'

Marcus, as we have seen, was used to this in the Church of South India, but such physical contact was alarming for some members of the congregation. As a child, the sharing of the peace was one of my favourite parts of the service – partially because it involved getting up and moving actively around, but also because it was a lovely way to meet and interact with all the varied members of the congregation. Elderly and lonesome parishioners would respond with such warmth to being blessed by a child.

Members of the laity too were asked to lead the prayers. So many of these changes are now taken for granted. Some people left – and St Mary's down the hill would not go along with the changes. But new people came, especially many of those who took part in Lent discussion groups and perhaps for the first time, were discovering the relevance of the Gospel message of God's love for them. Real efforts too were made to help people see the meaning of baptism – one colleague was against infant baptism which he thought was often a sham. Mary and Marcus had baptism groups at their home for parents and produced a simple service which talked about God's love – there was no mention of the devil. (In 2016, the Church of England's new alternative baptism service did the same).

While Mary and Marcus were at Frindsbury, there were high hopes that the Church of England and the Methodist Church would come together. It was arranged that on the Sunday after the vote the local Methodist minister would share in the communion service – at that time anyone who was not a confirmed member of the C of E had to seek special permission to receive communion. The proposal to unite was passed – but not by a sufficient majority for it be acted on. Marcus was very near to resigning – but John decided they would go ahead with the invitation to the Methodist minister. When he consulted the Bishop, he was told that the Bishop himself was going to the Methodist church on the Sunday morning. From then on, Marcus says, 'I have always invited all "who love the Lord Jesus" to receive communion.'

At that time someone who had been divorced was not allowed by church rules to marry in church – and if they had a blessing it had to be an austere affair – no hymns, no flowers and very few witnesses. But when Belinda, who, as we have seen, was one of Mary's clients in Cambridge, met someone in the hospital and fell in love, she asked Marcus to take the wedding. It was so wonderful that Belinda had at last found someone really to love her, that Marcus turned the blessing service into a quasi-wedding service. It was a day to celebrate. Rachel was a beautiful bridesmaid. They had a lovely baby. Mary kept in touch with family and was with Belinda shortly before she died, very bravely, of cancer. Hers, Mary says, was 'a very courageous, brief life.' Later, when the Church Synod rejected attempts to change the rules, Marcus told his Bishop that he would ignore church rules and - as allowed by Parliament (the so-called 'A P Herbert clause') - that in some cases he would marry a couple where one person had had a divorce. The Church has now relaxed the rules.

Besides a very busy parish life – with lots of baptisms and funerals – John did most of the weddings – and visiting the sick and newcomers: Marcus continued as Hon. Secretary of the World Congress of Faiths, coming back late at night to a deserted Strood station. One of his responsibilities was to arrange WCF's annual conference, with Mary's help. Marcus also started a local branch of WCF - there were about a dozen such branches in the country at that time. Meetings were usually held at the Chatham Unitarian Church.

Marcus took on encouraging ecumenical links in the Deanery. He was also was persuaded by John Bickersteth, who was later to be his Bishop when they moved to the West country, to become chair of the Medway Towns Christian Aid and Freedom from Hunger Committee. As a result every year towards the end of April an enormous lorry drew up outside their house with 72,000 envelopes and leaflets for Christian Aid

Week. These then had to be distributed to churches across the towns. Almost all churches took part. There was also a Freedom from Hunger shop in Strood – charity shops were then quite unusual. A group of dedicated women ran the shop, but Marcus had to get involved with persuading the local council not to charge rates etc. The Christian Aid Committee arranged each year a lecture on the need for aid in Rochester Guildhall – one of them was by the first person to be appointed Minister for Overseas Aid.

Much of the money was given to a project in Rajasthan, India, to drill wells in villages which had no clean water. 'On one of my trips to India for an interfaith conference,' Marcus says, 'I was able to visit one of these villages and to see how the well had improved peoples' lives. There was much less illness and women and children did not have to spend hours walking to collect dirty water and carry the heavy jars back home. One condition was that the well was to be used by all the villagers – thus helping to break down the caste barriers in the area. More controversial was the aid to Uganda. When Idi Amin seized power the whole front page of the local paper was devoted to attacking my decision to continue sending help for the poor to the churches in that country. My view was that the poor in Uganda needed help even more urgently and that because the money went through the churches it was reaching those for whom it was intended.'

Marcus' name was quite often in the local paper as he helped to found a local Action for World Development Group (AWD) – later to be known as the World Development Movement. It was clear that development aid was not enough to reduce poverty – a change to international trade rules and government policy was needed. A particular issue was the effect on West Indies' sugar production of Britain joining the Common Market. The AWD group presented the local MP, Mrs Fenner, with a heart made of sugar, to draw attention to the crisis. Mrs Fenner's predecessor was Anne Kerr – one of the most left wing Labour MPs. On one occasion John Bickersteth and Marcus went to see her to express their deep concern for people of Biafra – an area of Nigeria where civil war was waging. Anne Kerr agreed and got onto the telephone and was at once put through to the Prime Minister Harold Wilson.

Peter Absolon and Marcus also took the lead in forming a local Community Relations Council. 'We were particularly close to the local Bangladeshi community: raising money to help the victims of devastating floods in East Pakistan and then supporting the efforts of the people of Bangladesh people to achieve their independence. We also got to know the local Sikh community and discovered that they had to meet in the back room of a pub for their worship (mostly Sikhs are teetotalers). We arranged for them to use a church hall. Just at a time when there was a national debate about whether 'non-Christians' could be allowed into 'Christian' buildings. We wrote a letter to the *Times* and sent a copy to the Bishop of Rochester, who said it was the first time he had opened the post to find the letter he had just read was also in the newspaper!'

Marcus was also a member of a group set up by the British Council of Churches (BCC) to discuss both the use of church buildings by members of other faiths and also the sale of redundant churches to other faith communities to turn into mosques or gurdwaras. 'The arguments continue,' Marcus says. 'I soon discovered that people seldom bother to find out what has been said on a subject before pontificating on it. I was also part of a BCC group to discuss whether people of different faiths could on special occasions join together to pray – that debate also still goes on.'

As if this was not enough to do, Marcus also was a very part-time lecturer on world religions at Bristol University. This involved a long commute which with the teaching took up most of his day off – Mary's tolerance was amazing. Marcus was still not sure whether he wanted an academic career, but at that time very few universities offered courses in so-called 'comparative religion.' Marcus says he was glad to have had the experience of teaching there (and later at Westminster College in Oxford) and was rather sad when the full time post was offered to someone else, but looking back he is glad that it was. Marcus also acted as chaplain at Cobham Hall – a progressive private school for girls, where the Head Teacher encouraged girls to learn about world religions.

'It was a busy life,' Marcus says, 'and Mary had a very responsible job as a Social Work team leader. She was also suffering from back problems. I hope we gave the children enough time.'

Mary – Another Team Leader

Rachel was 3 and Jeremy 2 when the family moved to Frindsbury. Quite soon Mary was visited by a Social Worker called Kay, who pleaded with her to resume working. Mary agreed to 10 hours a week and two friends from the Wives Fellowship, Uta and Janice, kindly looked after the children. It helped also that Marcus worked from home. Mary first worked in Chatham and Gillingham but as time went on the hours became 15 and later, when she became acting team leader of about 20 people - including Child Care officers, Home Care organisers, and Occupational Therapists - she worked for 30 hours or more.

By this time both the children were at the local Roman Catholic school, English Martyrs, where they were the only non-Catholics. The school was the nearest one and had a lovely atmosphere and an outstanding reception teacher, whom Rachel adored. My mother used to have a game of pretend-schools, and would play her ukulele, pretending to be her teacher, who played a guitar. She even tried to cut her hair to a similar style, with a sweeping fringe, but each attempt bore worse results! When the children received their first communion, Rachel was invited to be present at the service and to wear a white dress.

As a Social Work Team Leader, Mary co-operated closely with Peter Absolon, one of the members of the clergy team, who set up a marvellous volunteer scheme called 'Hands', which still continues. Nearly 600 volunteers worked with the homeless and families with problems. Mary made many referrals to them. It was a one-to-one organisation where the helper and the helped were considered equal as partners. No do-gooding! Mary also helped Peter set up the Medway Action Committee for the Homeless. These were the late sixties and there was a lot of idealism and hope for progress. Mary always insisted although she was 'management' that she carried a small caseload to continue to be grounded. The area was in many ways more deprived than Hackney! Mary found the work very absorbing and satisfying.

Maureen McLoughlin, who was in charge, wrote to me about Mary's work: 'I first got to know your Grandmother when she was a part time team leader in the Rochester Division of Kent County Council Social Services Department in June 1972, when I had been newly appointed as the Divisional Director, and we were work colleagues for one year only because your Grandfather moved from being a member of the Strood Clergy Team to another appointment in the West Country. Your Grandparents visited me recently – the first time we had met up for over thirty years – and we found it hard to believe that we had worked together for such a very short time. Your Grandmother was an incredibly caring, thoughtful and supportive Team Leader of Social Workers who were facing some very difficult tasks, and I know they all grew to respect, admire and love her, not only for her professional support, but also for her concern and caring for their personal well-being. I rarely met your Grandfather on those occasions in a professional capacity, although I did meet him when I was invited to their home for a meal and enjoyed their unique warm hospitality. Where they have got the energy from to achieve all they have achieved in their lives, I can't begin to guess, but I have enormous admiration for all they have achieved and feel so privileged to know them.'

Family Life.

Perhaps this should have come first. Mary and Marcus always tried to make the children their top priority. Even so they were often out in the evenings and children were cared for by two lovely ladies, who were regular baby sitters – Jessie Waghorn and Brenda Paine. Both of them always brought some sweets for

Rachel and Jeremy and, although they were supposed to be asleep, were secretly rather pleased if the children came downstairs. My mother distinctly remembers creeping out of her bedroom, and delighting in two KitKats left out for them on the little sideboard ledge. Jessie was a great knitter and made cardigans for the children and socks for Marcus. Brenda's sister made a cake to welcome the family when they moved in.

Rachel and Jeremy in Granny Braybrooke's beautiful garden and with Grandpa Walker in Trafalgar Square

There was a quarry at the end of the garden, and my mother remembers playing there with Jeremy. One day when her Granny Marcia visited, they found a Bee Orchid, which was very rare. Granny immediately went to get her paints, and my grandparents still have the painting from that day. Jeremy and Rachel also discovered a deep tunnel in the quarry, going right into the hill. After their children showed it to them, Mary and Marcus were very worried about how unsafe it might be, and organised for it to be cordoned off, before later being blown up.

Time to Move on - *again*

The Team was experimental but gradually it needed a formal legal framework. In Marcus' opinion however, this distorted the way the team had operated. John was certainly the leader – but unlike many clergy he was not jealous and empowered others – so that each member of the team exercised leadership in his particular areas of expertise. The scheme, however, reverted to a traditional hierarchical structure of Rector and under him Team Vicars. John had decided it was time for him to leave. Under the new plan Marcus was to be responsible for two churches and when the Team Council turned down his request for some secretarial help, he realised that if he stayed, the work load would mean abandoning his wider commitments. Mary and Marcus decided it was time to see if God had other plans for them. When the family moved after their five years, a Ugandan Asian family was allowed to move in the same day – so Mary was saved some cleaning up!

9. Swainswick, Langridge and Woolley

In the summer of 1973 Mary and Marcus and family moved to a beautiful valley, just north east of Bath - you can see it as you drive towards Bath along the A46. Rose Hobday, who came with a coachload of parishioners for Marcus' Licensing wrote afterwards, 'It is a really beautiful place… I shall think of you as though you are on a permanent holiday'.

Thanks to the help of Tom Baker who was Principal of Wells Theological College when Marcus was there, and who was then Archdeacon of Wells, Marcus was invited to consider moving to the villages of Swainswick and Langridge. Marcus was asked to go and see the Bishop in Wells. They had a cup of tea, chatted for some twenty minutes and then the Bishop was worried that Marcus would miss the last bus back from Wells – no interview panel or long selection procedure. Mary and Marcus and the children then went to see the village and the house and to meet the churchwardens. Whilst the adults were getting to know each other, Rachel and Jeremy came downstairs and announced which bedrooms they had chosen. So that settled it.

The family moved in early July. Marcus went ahead to stay the night with a churchwarden, Jack Fisher (who was expecting him a day later) so that he could get the house a bit organised before the family arrived. The car was loaded up with a pet rabbit and guinea pigs (plus their cages) and a hamster. Jack Fisher must have wondered what they had let themselves in for. A colossal removal van arrived the next day far too big for the narrow lanes. There was a sharp turn into the Rectory drive, so the only way it could get in was by dismantling a dry stone wall – which was rebuilt when the van left. At least there were some beds and furniture ready for Mary and the children.

Rachel and Jeremy just had time to go to the school for a couple of weeks before the summer holidays. As the school adjoined the Rectory garden the children did not have far to go. The beauty of the coombe was a continual delight. The Rectory was a modern split level house with a lovely stone fireplace. There was a steep bank down to the lawn which was surrounded by tall trees. The garden was an ideal site for Rectory Fetes. It was an exciting day when a puppy, Rex, and a kitten, Harvey joined the family. Sadly, all too soon, Harvey was run over in the near-by lane, but Rex had a long life, moving with the family to Wells and then to Box. For some time, Rachel, who loved riding, pretended the gate to the Rectory drive was a pony: but this fantasy did not last for long. Eventually Mary and Marcus gave in to Rachel's longing to have a pony. The unused part of the church yard was fenced off, a shelter constructed and a pony ridden over from a nearby village to make its home in Upper Swainswick – many a mourner turned to Taffy for comfort after a funeral.

Soon after their arrival, the Queen came to Bath for a ceremony to mark the 1,000th anniversary of the crowning of Edgar as the first King of all England in Bath Abbey in 973A.D. Rachel and Jeremy were at the front of the crowd and the Queen stopped to ask them, 'How long have you lived in Bath?'

It was in Swainswick that Veronique, Roger and Odile's daughter, first met the family. She has written to me about this and their long friendship. 'I had heard a lot about Mary and Marcus. My Mum had showed me pictures of Rachel and Jeremy that Mary sent her, when I was about six. Mary was my Uncle Jean's pen-friend! As a teenager she stayed with my grandparents in Nancy. They took her climbing in the mountains, but Mary found this difficult because of her asthma. I don't think my parents went to Mary and Marcus' wedding but they met up before their wedding and my Dad said to Mary that Marcus was the perfect husband for her! The first time I met Mary was in Nancy around 1973. She had a bad back and needed to lie on the carpet for that – it was quite unusual for me to see guest in such a position!

Mary and my Mum decided to make an exchange for me with Jeremy. So Jeremy and Mary came to Tourcoing, in Northern France, in July 1978 for a week and Mary took me back by hovercraft (crossing the Channel only took half an hour!). I stayed in Swainswick near Bath for a fortnight. I was very impressed by Marcus, who took Rachel and me for a visit to London, including the Crown Jewels in the Tower of London. Mary became my English mother! Cuddling me! I was only 12! Then I came back twice to Wells and once or twice for short visits in Box. Once I went to Cambridge with Jeremy, to Mary's parents. Her father was very sweet! He showed us how to paint on the grass the tennis lines, in their garden. Mary's mother was very impressive with her cigarette and her loud voice. She had a strong personality!

Jeremy used to come skiing with us some times. Rachel came only once in Val Thorens. I remember she fell down and had a big black mark on her leg, quite painful, but hopefully nothing broken. (Actually, my mother still has swelling on her leg from this moment!).

Once, Mary took me to Westminster Abbey to the Dean's house! I was too shy to ask for sugar for my tea! I was very impressed to see Marcus as a priest and, looking at their pictures that he and Mary knew the Dalai Lama and so many interfaith people all over the world. I'm very impressed by their travels all over the world, the amazing amount of people they know everywhere, and the energy they have.'

The Parishes

There were two churches – St Mary's in Upper Swainswick and St Mary Magdalene in Langridge. Swainswick, a wooded settlement, was valued at 30 shillings in the Domesday Book so it is possible that a wooden building for worship existed there before the first simple stone church was built towards the end of the 12th century. The largest group of houses is in Lower Swainswick, which adjoins Bath. The houses in Upper Swainswick are mostly old and built of stone. Langridge is very spread out and there was another hamlet at Tadwick as well as some isolated houses on the A 46 and near the Bath racecourse. Later the small village of Woolley with its eighteenth century church, of which the architect was John Wood the Elder, was joined with the other parishes. During Marcus' time, the roof at Woolley church was replaced largely by voluntary labour by skilled parishioners. Much of the fund-raising from this was done by Bob Hedley who always called Mary 'Mrs Prayerbook.' He was – so he said – an atheist, so turned up five minutes late for every meeting to miss the opening prayers.

Initially the situation in the parish was not easy. Marcus' predecessor had left under a cloud and sold his story to the *News of the World*. He had some loyal followers who kept their distance, but it helped that Marcus and Mary were from completely outside the area and had not been involved in the disputes.

Afternoon Tea with Mary and Marcus

Norman Ashfield, the organist, wrote of Mary and Marcus, 'You came to us as we were divided: you leave Swainswick much more a living family, yet frustrated that we are scarcely likely to enjoy such times again. I have never seen anyone bond a parish together in fellowship in such a way.' He mentioned also the 'memorable retreats at Glastonbury and Lee Abbey.' These were happy years for Marcus and Mary who immersed themselves in the life of the villages. When Mary and Marcus first got there, the bells were being restored. Marcus helped haul one of the bells along the path to the church – mainly for the benefit of a photographer from the local press. 'Daddy, I've never seen you work so hard,' said Rachel.

'Daddy, I've never seen you work so hard!' – Rachel to Marcus.

Several people there and in other parishes have commented on the quality of the worship. Norman's mother, Muriel, spoke of Marcus' 'wonderful ability to make each service a complete whole phase of worship and continuity of thought.' Marcus has always wanted to choose the hymns himself and pays a lot of attention to the words – Mary then has to find a well-known tune for these often unfamiliar or recently written hymns.

Marcus and Mary spend a lot of time and care preparing their sermons, talks and prayers. Many people have expressed their appreciation. Joanna Pelly said, 'we were amazed and delighted by Marcus' sermons – always inspiring and instructive but "never above our heads" as well they might have been from someone with his knowledge and insight.' Jack Greenaway, who seldom missed a service at the Baldons - a parish we shall come to later – said, 'I never heard Marcus preach a bad sermon.' Many people too have much appreciated Mary's intercessions in church. Sir Alan Richmond, a regular member of Christ Church in Bath said to her in sincerity 'yours are the best intercessions that I have ever heard,' whilst other people have simply said, 'You really help me to pray.' From a young age I can remember that whenever I caught a fresh glimpse of my grandmother's jotted, handwritten prayers during the service, there would be a new crossing-out or an additional sentence squeezed in, as she adapted it to the global news of the day and to the congregation. And hearing the warm under-current of humour, a readiness to laugh and be hopeful in my grandfather's voice, made me feel early on that God too had a sense of humour.

Afternoon Tea with Mary and Marcus

My father Peter reflected, 'Marcus' sermons have a certain pattern about them. There will be clear relevance to the readings of the day, some element of the current news, a few casual references to meeting important people or travelling to far parts of the world all worked together to give a meaningful reflection that you can take away with you after the service and delivered in less than 10 minutes.'

They made many friends, including Mary and Nick Younger who at that time, lived at the top of the hill before they moved to Yorkshire: and then Tom and Fifi Charrington who succeeded them at Hill House. My Grandpa loved having intellectual chats with Fifi, who would always ask questions and challenge him. All the Braybrooke family were friends with the Shutters, along the road, and the children were allowed to go along to swim in their pool. Rachel and Fiona in particular were best friends, and when Fiona went to boarding school she often came to stay at the weekends. Other good friends were George and Joanna Cacanas, who went on several tours with them. Joanna wrote to me to say that 'Marcus really hides his light under a bushel, nothing flash or pushy about him and his quiet masques his good brain and huge capacity for uncritical understanding. He has turned up at crucial times in our lives such as the moment my father died and was there to quote "Go forth O Christian Soul." Mary and Marcus also looked in when, in his last year, I was needing help with my beloved George. Mary is full of fun with a bit of naughtiness sometimes, which makes her a joy to be with; she has the touch of the therapist about her too, with some practical and objective advice and comments. I wonder at their amazing disregard for their health difficulties which never stop them living in top gear, travelling widely and bravely. We love them both.'

There are many other friends in Woolley, Langridge and Bath whom they see occasionally and with whom they exchange Christmas cards. Sadly, the list grows shorter each year – but they still send over three hundred.

Best friends Rachel and Fiona running a stall at one of the many Rectory fetes.

Many parish events took place at the Rectory. Mavis Trask (née Clark), who had grown up in the village and was deeply involved in all that went on at the church said, 'I always think of the Rectory as my second home.' There were visitors from other parts of the world, especially relations from Australia. One of them is Joan Peacock, who kindly took me in when I travelled through the East Coast a few years ago. She wrote, 'My Cousin Mary is my precious English "Jewel". She is warm, caring and empathic towards others and has done so much in her career to help others. She has also been a wonderful support for Marcus in his interfaith work. I have been blessed to have Mary as my cousin. We were born 6 months apart, Mary in January 1935 and myself in July 1934, but on other sides of the world. We have followed similar professions; Mary the Social Worker and myself the Psychologist - both helping others to find a better life.

Afternoon Tea with Mary and Marcus

I was fortunate to be born into the Walker Clan. In Australia we had many cousins, but only two English cousins, Mary and Paul. While we were very proud to be part of the British Empire, we did not know our English cousins in our young years. I did not meet them until 1962 when I visited Uncle George and Auntie Phyllis in Cambridge on my honeymoon with my husband Ken Peacock. We loved the ambience of Cambridge and meeting my mother's brother and his wife. Later I visited Mary and Marcus in Bath which is such a beautiful medieval city. However my most wonderful recollection was meeting Mary with her warm caring personality. I thought she was the sister I never had!

Thirty seven years later in 1999 I visited the UK with my daughter Lisa and stayed with Mary in Oxford. It was such a joy to spend time with Mary and her beautiful granddaughters.

Mary and Marcus with Joan and Ken Peacock and one of their daughters

Mary and Marcus have made many visits to Australia and stayed with so many of the Walker cousins. They stayed with us in Melbourne in our Mt. Martha holiday home on the Mornington Peninsula and also with us in our home in Sydney in Pymble.'

The Bible Class

The village had an amazing Bible-class led by Audrey Green. On a Sunday afternoon the small cottage, where Audrey and her friend Olive Bates lived, was full of thirty or more teenagers. Each year they put on a Christmas pantomime and most years there was a residential weekend at Glastonbury. Besides the fellowship, many found support in their puzzling teenage years from Audrey's concern and support. They knew that whenever they turned up at the cottage, they would have a warm welcome.

In 2000, nearly sixty young people whose lives were touched by belonging to the Bible-class came back for a reunion, where they could meet up again and share their life-stories. One person had travelled all the way from Australia. After a service in church at which Marcus preached, there was a garden party at the Rectory, hosted by Revd John Bullamore and his wife.

Mavis Clark, Gwyneth Watts, and Rachel celebrating Audrey Green's birthday and Bible Class Reunion.

Mary told the *Bath Chronicle*, which published a picture of the young people with Audrey Green in the centre and Mary and Marcus on her left and right, that 'The Bible class was something which those involved could never forget. It was for young people aged between 11 and 18, but some people went on coming when they were twenty. Some have become very committed Christians and some haven't. What the class did was sow the seeds within people of the possibility of Christian faith.'

My mother Rachel remembers, "The bible class was unique—after traipsing from the church up the steep hill, we would squash into Audrey's cosy sitting room. I remember feeling quite shy around the older (and very good looking!) boys. One particular session, Audrey encouraged us to write down our fears on a piece of paper—mine was meeting motorbikes on the lane whilst riding Taffy, as it was such a dangerous road and if he met one he would turn on his haunches and gallop home. She promised that no-one would read them and explained that "our fears were safe with God." We then lit a candle and burnt the pieces of paper.

It was through the Bible Class that my grandparents met John Pritchard, who was later to be their Bishop in Oxford, and his lovely wife, Wendy. John writes,

'We've known Marcus and Mary from the late 70s when I came as a very green Diocesan Youth Officer to the Diocese of Bath and Wells and found an extraordinary Bible Class in Marcus' parish of Swainswick. Marcus kept an eye on me when I was an equally green vicar in Taunton and enabled me to go on a rather special residential course at St George's, Windsor. We kept in touch through the years so it was a delight to find them both in the Diocese of Oxford when I went there as Bishop in 2007. The friendship continued as enjoyable as ever. What defines them for us is their generous spirit, both gentle and robust, which embraces truth and goodness wherever it's found. They transcend the artificial boundaries that men and women love to erect and retain a wonderful enthusiasm for life and the discovery of new insights. It's also lovely to see how two people with very different personalities have forged and maintained such affection and respect for each other. I wonder if at times Marcus uses his deafness to have a little quiet.

One of the most surprising things to me has been Mary and Marcus as a humble and unpretentious couple, coming from a convinced Christian heart having such a huge reach to communities of faith across the world. They have been involved in many highly significant ventures and seem to know everyone with any engagement in interfaith concerns.

Bishop John Pritchard and Marcus in 2006.

Sunday School

Besides the Bible Class, more than thirty children crowded into the downstairs rooms of the Rectory for the Sunday school, run by Mary. Mary once got some of them to do a survey asking members of the congregation about why they came to church. One person said, that if they were asked again, they would stop coming to church. As Mary says, 'many regular church-goers feel embarrassed to talk about their faith.' Usually the children started in church or sometimes for the whole of a family service. At one Harvest Supper, the very supportive organist, Norman Ashfield wrote a 'psalm' sung by the choir which included the verse,

'What though the church be filled with chirping of children,
At thy rebuke, O Marcus, both vestry and belfry shall be silent.'

Rachel recalls Sunday school always being lively and fun, and one particular favourite activity was Mary teaching the children how to make beautiful candles from melted down wax in water.

Some weekends away together for the adult parishioners were held at Brunel Manor near Torquay and at Lee Abbey. These were a great way of developing real fellowship. Langridge had some brilliant fund raising events – including a bumper harvest festival at Bath race-course. Marcus' suggestion that there was cider to drink was welcomed – a previous rector had been a strict teetotaller. There was another harvest supper dispute which nearly tore Langridge apart – should there be apple pies or apple and blackberry pies. With the wisdom of Solomon, Marcus suggested there could be a choice!

For much of the time Marcus was in charge of the training of Lay Readers in the Diocese. This meant quite a lot of travelling around the diocese to discuss with candidates what would be helpful for them and to arrange for tutors. The theological studies were demanding and Marcus had to assess their essays.

Bishop Frank West, Bishop of Taunton, was the warden of the readers. Three or four times a year the sub-wardens and Marcus met with him at the Bishop's beautiful old Rectory at Dinder, near Wells, where Beryl West laid on a splendid meal. On one occasion, Frank West called at the Rectory when Marcus was out. Rex just that moment had been sick and the Bishop cleared up the mess.

Marcus and Mary were also involved in many aspects of Bath life. Mary was a magistrate and social worker and did a year's course at Bath University. While at Swainswick, Marcus was elected as Chairman of the World Congress of Faiths – at 39, he was the youngest person to hold that position. He set up a WCF Education Committee which, as reported in the *Guardian*, was one of the first bodies to call for teaching all children about the world religions and not just Christianity. It also raised the questions about the provision for children of immigrants who were Muslim, Hindu or Sikh – (the Butler Education Act made special arrangements for Jewish children); and whether Assemblies could only use Christian material; and about the provision of vegetarian school meals. In time bodies like the SHAP Working Party and RE Council took up these issues.

Mary and Marcus also took the lead in trying to apply interfaith insights to social needs and with Paul Weller arranged conferences on how faith communities and health workers could share insights on how best to care for Older People and for the Dying. John Prickett, who was a good friend, edited some useful books on these subjects, in which Rabbi Hugo Gryn, Vice-chair of WCF, was greatly interested.

Afternoon Tea with Mary and Marcus

Marcus also spent a three month sabbatical in the Holy Land at Tantur Ecumenical Centre. Revd Tony Cato had kindly offered to help during the time Marcus was away, but the day after Marcus had left, sadly, Mrs Cato died. This meant that Mary had to take charge while he was away. During his absence she also declined, without asking him, a suggestion that he might be Principal of Lincoln Theological College. When I asked my grandmother to explain further, she replied, 'I said 'no' to Lincoln because we had only recently moved, I wasn't interested in him climbing the clerical ladder! I don't approve of hierarchy. I liked Bath and did not fancy moving to Lincoln and the children had just settled in their new school. I imagine I must have mentioned it in phone calls!' And my grandfather was his usual peaceable self, 'I don't think I minded very much. It had happened by the time I was home, so it was no longer an option and would have been unfair to the parish. It would have been a good step up the clerical ladder, but I have had a far more interesting life'.

Rachel recalls, "I went with Mum and Jeremy to Tantur to visit Dad. We timed it to be just before my 12th birthday so that I would get a half-price aeroplane ticket (my parents always search for a bargain!), and we wanted to be there for Holy Week. Being in Jerusalem for the Palm Sunday procession is very vivid in my memory, and visiting Bethlehem, the Sea of Galilee and the Dead Sea brought the Bible to life for me. We often played volleyball at Tantur, and I remember Mum falling over and injuring herself (a common trait on holidays!)."

A Magistrate - Bath bench

Whilst they were in Swainswick after a couple of years Mary's name was put forward by Swainswick Parish Council to be a magistrate. After a very intensive interview, which she recalls being 'Much worse than for any paid job,' Mary was selected in 1976 to sit on the bench in Bath and spent 16 very interesting years in Juvenile and Adult and Family courts, usually one afternoon a week. She was allowed some time off from her part time work to do this. There was quite a lot of training and Bench meetings as well. The Bath bench was friendly and fairly relaxed and there was good support from the Clerk of the Court and his staff with some enjoyable social functions. Mary found it fascinating coming to decisions in the retiring room with two others who might not be at all like minded. It was hoped that decisions were unanimous but sometimes it was two against one! She attended the Crown Court in Bristol from time to time with another magistrate sitting with a Judge on Sentencing. She remembers with satisfaction one sitting where she and her colleague disagreed with the Judge and he had to give in! Mary chaired the court after two or three years and was involved with the Probation committee. Everyone had to take a turn on the Fines committee: not so popular!

Bath University

Mary, as we have seen, started her social work as soon as she gained her degree in Sociology. Increasingly, however, employers required their staff to have a professional qualification in social work. On moving to the West Country, Mary applied to do a new postgraduate course in Applied Social Work at Bath University. After a year she was accepted. In the meantime she did some lecturing on Sociology at the Bath Technical College.

'But what about the children?' some of the parishioners wondered. Margaret Foster, who was a wonderful animal lover (and a great teacher of animal care for Rachel), and who became a life-long friend, supplies the answer. After a morning service in October 1974, she says, 'Mary followed me down the church path and as we chatted by the church gate, Mary asked me if I might be able to help by cleaning the Rectory twice a week, so that she could go back to University to get the qualification, which all social workers were by then required to get. I asked the Play school where my son, Timothy, had been, whether they would take my daughter Alison, who was just over two years old. "Yes," they said, "if she does not wear nappies." She didn't, – so I started at the Rectory.

'Cleaning included taking their lovely dog Rex for a walk. When they moved to Wells, I went there once a week to help. This now sometimes included feeding Rachel's horse, Shaman, as well as walking the dog. And then when they moved to Box, I followed them there. Oxford was a step too far for me!'

Another link was that when Rachel got Shaman, Alison became the owner of Taffy – Rachel's first horse – who lived to be twenty-six years old. Marcus and Mary, who still keep regularly in touch with Ray and Margaret, say that 'without having someone who was so understanding and dependable, life would have been impossible. When later we moved to the Baldons, Janet and Arthur Cullen were equally unfailing in their support.'

Rachel and Jeremy were mostly healthy children, though Jeremy did develop asthma like Mary. Like all children they did have some accidents, though luckily nothing too serious. Jeremy once put a button up his nose, and ended up in A and E but no amount of prodding could dislodge the button. The following day it appeared through his mouth while playing cricket. On a different occasion, Jeremy accidentally opened the car door and fell onto the road on the way home from school in Frindsbury. Luckily Mary was driving slowly, though he did cut his head. Rachel cut her forehead badly and narrowly missed her eye when she walked into a barbed wire fence whilst collecting eggs at the Vernon Harcourts' farm. She's not sure if the eggs survived!

Taffy on the Rectory Lawn

Rachel also broke her wrist trying out a pony to buy. The pony called Pixie was very lively and bolted. Rachel fell off as Mary and Marcus watched in horror. Another trip to A and E with a very muddy Rachel. Needless to say, they didn't buy the pony! During heavy snow, when it wasn't safe to use the bridleways, Marcus carefully shovelled a large square of clear grass on the lawn, so that Rachel could exercise Taffy. In the midst of a drought in the summer of 1976, Grandpa would take buckets of the bathwater for his flowers, after every member of the family had bathed in it. From that summer to this day Mary and Marcus have shared bath water.

Mary studies at Bath University

The Social Work course that Mary was undertaking required a lot of study and essays – some of which their good friend Joanna Pelly typed. This was demanding for Mary and the rest of the family, especially when Rachel and Jeremy developed viral pneumonia, but thankfully recovered well.

There were also practical placements, with an adoption agency in Bristol, at a mental health unit with disturbed children or ones with learning difficulties and at the Royal United Hospital Bath, where Mary later was offered a part time job. One of the professors at the University was Bob Holman, who came to talk about his studies of poverty at a parish meeting. Mary said to him afterwards, 'Should you put it into practice as well as write about it?' In 1976 he resigned his professorship and helped to found the Easterhouse Project in a deprived area of Glasgow. He was to become widely known for this and his calls for social justice. The *Guardian* described him as 'a visionary who lived his dream.''

Hospital Social Worker

In the following years, Mary worked in many community hospitals, including Westbury, Warminster, Trowbridge, Bradford-on-Avon and for a long time in Paulton hospital and St Martin's hospital in Bath. She was very blessed in that when Marcus' work required a move, she switched to the nearest hospitals - all the time employed by Wiltshire County Council. She later worked at the National Hospital for Rheumatic Diseases ('the Mineral') in the centre of Bath and visited younger people with physical illnesses in the area.

On one of her trips to visit a new patient in Warminster she was hit head-on by a car from the other side of the road and ended up in the Royal United Hospital with various injuries. Mary was touched that the lady she was visiting (a remarkable person with muscular dystrophy who was deeply religious) was the first to send her a get well card and they had not even met! Marcus was at a conference in Frankfurt at the time so Rachel and Jeremy both quickly came from the Isle of Sheppey and Southampton to be with her to sort out everything. Mary had not wanted the conference interrupted, but Marcus was upset that he was not told the news until he reached Frankfurt Airport and also because he did not know how badly she had been injured. Mary was overwhelmed by the visits and cards she received. Revd Professor Clifford Burrows, who was part of the Ministry Team at Christ Church was particularly helpful as was Professor Donald Nicholl, author of the book *Holiness*, who was leading a parish weekend.

Paulton

Mary worked at Paulton Hospital for ten years. It was one of the jobs she most enjoyed. Paulton Hospital was founded in 1872. In 1972, the hospital celebrated its centenary. 'The hospital is not just 100 years,' the Chairman of North East Somerset Hospital Management Committee said, 'it is one hundred years not out.' Until the mid-nineteenth century, most hospitals were in larger towns, which meant that those living in villages often could not get treatment. In 1859, the 'Cottage Hospital' movement began when Dr Albert Napier founded a hospital at Cranleigh in Surrey. Cranleigh, of course, was where Marcus grew up; where his mother worked as a volunteer for many years; and it was there that his father spent his last weeks.

By 1865 there were 18 cottage hospitals and 180 by 1880. The Paulton hospital, as recorded by a centenary booklet, *Paulton Memorial Hospital, 1872-1972*, was founded in 1872 by Colonel and Mrs Mogg. The Bishop, at the opening ceremony, said that this development showed that God had brought good out of the terrible evil of the Crimean War, thanks to the work of Florence Nightingale and many others.

Mary was closely involved with the community and set up a lunch club to enable all the professionals to meet informally and have useful talks. The most amusing one was on incontinence by a very forceful nurse who had everyone doing exercises! There were a lot of chest problems and pneumoconiosis because Paulton had been a mining area. When Mary worked there the hospital served approximately 40,000 people. The hospital had a Maternity Unit, two acute wards; geriatric wards and a geriatric Day Hospital, as well as busy Out-Patient Clinics with input from consultants of Bath's hospitals.

The report that she wrote, as she was leaving, gives a good picture of her work. 'I took over Paulton's acute beds in 1979 which then numbered 28 and included six surgical patients - as well as covering other units elsewhere. Previous Social Work input had been limited to a half day a week and there were some anxieties about mileage claims if I visited the hospital more than once a week!

Afternoon Tea with Mary and Marcus

'Shortly after starting work the then-Matron asked me to help develop the Maternity Service which had previously had no input. Enjoying a variety in my work, I was glad to do this. The acute beds kept me very busy though the pressure on beds was not as acute as it is to-day. I was given time to make adequate arrangements for discharge from hospital.

'We arranged Ward Meetings on a Monday morning, between the Occupational Therapist, the Physiotherapist, the Ward Sister and myself, to formulate multi-disciplinary care plans. Some patients were already known to the local community but many new ones were referred and passed on for domiciliary and/or Social Work support.

Most was short-term work but I gradually began to offer a service to the physically handicapped and their families and to the dying patients and bereaved relatives, following many through into the community when they were not known to the Area Teams. Communication with Midsomer Norton Social Services and Frome Social Services was always excellent and supportive - as was that with Keynsham Social Services.'

'A sad and challenging situation,' Mary said, 'arose with one patient who had taken an overdose and was diagnosed as brain-dead. She remained on life support for several years and I was with her and her mother when she died peacefully.'

Mary realised that it would make sense for her also to cover the geriatric patients at the hospital, as many overlapped and particularly the Wansdyke patients at St. Martin's Hospital. As a result she met regularly with the geriatricians, Michael Rowe and Rebecca Dunn. The doctors - about 26 in all - were nearly all very supportive and helpful. Each year a pantomime was organised with most of the staff taking part. Mary has some lovely videos to remind her of those days. She always loved acting and singing and felt it brought the workers together as well as giving the patients a laugh. Marcus was allowed to attend too.

Farewell to Mary after ten years working at Paulton Hospital.

When Mary eventually left Paulton and St Martin's to work at Bradford-on-Avon, there was a great farewell party. One of the consultants, Dr Michael Rowe, wrote to me about Mary's work: 'I haven't seen Mary or Marcus for many years but we still enjoy their Christmas greetings and accounts of their adventures. I worked with Mary at St. Martin's in Bath and at Paulton hospital from the time I was appointed as a consultant geriatrician in 1979 until Mary left Bath. I met Marcus only in her company. Mary was wonderfully down to earth and a joy to work with; so matter of fact in dealing with staff and with patients. She would stand no nonsense, prevarication or excuses for not getting on with seeking opinions and providing services to patients. Manipulative relatives more than met their match. All firm advice dispensed, however, with lots of laughs and yet authority as prejudices and received non-wisdoms were debunked and dismissed. We had a lot of fun and achieved a lot in modernising the service.'

April Hammond, writing as a person with disabilities and as a former social work client, said of my grandmother, 'Just a brief illustration of Mary's impact upon me is the fact that I am now involved in the training of social workers at the local college. I often use your grandmother as a model for the initial social work intervention and what they now refer to as "the use of self" in the profession. She never had any clipboards, briefcases or black stockings; nor did she talk about "processes" or "risk assessments", just a well-thumbed notebook, an old blue raincoat and the time to listen. I think this description may be your perfect title, if you are focusing on her career. I have a long success story to relate which I often use when training social workers at the local college.' April's parents, Chris and Roy, wrote in a Christmas card to Mary, 'We have said many times you are still the best social worker she has ever had and we thank God for your getting her out of Shaftesbury Court. She has been able to blossom and make a life for herself.'

April Hammond

Farewell

It was a shock to the family when Bishop John Bickersteth asked Marcus to be Director of Training for the Diocese of Bath and Wells. They were happy in Swainswick and had many friends there. Despite their initial reluctance to move, the Bishop was insistent. A particular problem was to find somewhere for Rachel's horse. The Bishop had a long discussion with Rachel and found a vast field where Taffy was very happy, and a few months later Shaman. Taffy was also the first horse for fifty years to occupy a stable at the Old Deanery where the family lived.

The parishes were sad to see Mary and Marcus and the family leave. Audrey Green, who ran the remarkable Bible Class, said, 'Marcus was a perfect pastor, he couldn't have been better.'

Afternoon Tea with Mary and Marcus

Kitty Champion of Woolley said that Marcus had made their link with Swainswick, after nine hundred years with Bathwick, easy, and had saved the church from redundancy and oversaw it's restoration. 'We sometimes thought', she wrote, 'he is the best and too good for us'. Warm tributes were also paid to Mary for her great contribution to the life of the churches and the villages and many people said how much they would miss Rachel and Jeremy.

Gay Moore wrote, 'I have lived in Woolley since 1971 and Martin since 1982. We knew Marcus through the Church, and Mary through the hospital where I worked as a physiotherapist and she worked as a social worker (quite the best one I have ever met). 'When I think of Marcus and Mary, I think of their energy, philanthropy, adventurous spirit, humour and the fact that whatever they do, they do it really well. It seemed that they must have more hours in their days because of the enormous amount of things they managed to pack in.

'We share their love of India. One day we were on a cycle rickshaw in Madurai when we suddenly saw them in the street. We went back to their hotel with them and Marcus invited us to join them that evening at a meeting of Christians and Muslims. There were some very interesting and friendly discussions and at the end we were all invited to a studio for a group photograph. I think the Muslims thought we were important theologians as we were with Marcus and Mary. I'm afraid we did nothing to disillusion them so the group photo appeared in the World Congress of Faiths Magazine.

'The most surprising thing about them is how many people they have met. They met both the Pope and the Dalai Lama. I asked Mary whom she liked better. The Dalai Lama she said - but perhaps I am being indiscrete, (sorry).'

L. to R. Mr Naziruddin, Mr Clotworthy, Mrs Moore, Dr P. B. Ahamed Kabeer, Mrs Mary Braybrooke, Rev. Marcus Braybrooke with standing, Dr Kabeer's sons Zaheer

10. To Wells Again

Marcus' new job in Wells was Director of Training for the Diocese – a 'Two-in-one training job', as the *Bath and West Evening Chronicle* described it. It involved persuading clergy that some in-service training might be helpful. 'My task,' Marcus says, 'was also aimed at helping lay people share more fully in the life of the church and be more confident in expressing their faith in their everyday working lives.' Mary was to find the arcane ways of cathedral life fascinating – Marcus found them irritating. Besides the Bishop, the Baha'is of Mendip arranged a welcome party for the family.

Initially the plan was for the family to live in Vicar's Close – but then they were offered the residential part of the Old Deanery. The office of Dean of Wells dates to the middle of the 12th century. The earliest part of the Old Deanery was built during the start of the 13th century, but there were extensive alterations in 14th and early 15th centuries. Towards the end of the 15th century the north range was added and also many stone Tudor roses. It is said that Henry VII slept in the Deanery on one occasion – probably on the top floor as that was the safest place – the room is now a store room. Further alterations were made in every century.

Mary outside the Old Deanery

In the seventeenth century's Civil War, Dean Walter Raleigh – a relation of Sir Walter Raleigh - who was a staunch Royalist, was murdered there. (Rachel wrote about this for her 'A' level history exam). By the end of the nineteenth century, the successive deans were finding the costs of maintaining the building, which they had to meet from their own resources, were prohibitive.

In 1947, Dean Malden leased some of the building to the Diocese as an administrative centre. As administrative work always grows, so the Diocese took over more and more of the building, some of which was used by the staff of the Board of Education. The Braybrookes were the last family to live there, and Rachel and Jeremy loved to climb the tower, from which there were amazing views of Wells and Glastonbury Tor. Mary and Marcus' bedroom was large enough for the table tennis table to be set-up occasionally so that the children would take friends up to play.

There were two beautiful meeting rooms on the first floor, which were used for Rachel's and Jeremy's eighteenth birthday parties and one of the store rooms on the second floor was used by Jeremy for his carpentry. A disadvantage was that the heating was set to office times – so on a cold evening Marcus would sneak to the offices to turn it on again. They were also provided with rather dangerous gas heaters. The Wells Dramatic Society had a room to store costumes and sometimes the Assistant Diocesan Secretary, who was a leading member of the Dramatic Society, would be heard up on the third floor – at first the children thought it was a ghost. There was also a Clergy Shop, which had gowns and morning and evening dress given by clergy wives when their husband died. Marcus still has some of the clothes he bought there.

There was a walled garden. From the south side, the house looked onto the green and the cathedral, although sadly for the whole time they were there the West End was covered by scaffolding. There were also stables, which had not been used, since before World War I. With careful diplomacy the Wells Floral Society were persuaded to move to another store room, so that Rachel's horse Shaman could have a stable. Canon Samuel Cutt always had a carrot with him when he walked by. The Dean agreed that Shaman could be led across the Cathedral Green – provided there was a bucket in attendance.

Bryony and Paddy with Mary in the Old Deanery Garden

Jeremy, who had not been too happy at Beechen Cliff, his school in Bath, settled quickly at the Blue School, the local comprehensive school. He had some good friends and did very well there. He also had a Saturday job at a local greengrocer – and brought home unsold fruit and vegetables.

The whole family and especially Jeremy became good friends with Bob and Theresa Fyffe who came to be Youth Chaplain in the Diocese - Jeremy had earlier told the interviewing panel that he was the best choice. The Diocese was persuaded to buy a video camera – in those days the batteries were large and heavy. Bob and Jeremy made good use of this, including filming a surprise 'This is Your Life' to which they had invited many of Mary and Marcus' best friends. It was a wonderful and happy surprise – although Mary wished she had tidied up the house. Rachel rushed home from Exeter to make up the beds and help with the food.

Rachel had been doing very well at the Diocesan school, but the Blue School did not suit her. After two years, when she had got her O Levels, she moved to the technical college at Chippenham – some 25 miles away. The course she wanted to do would qualify her as a Riding Instructor with the necessary business skills and training in grassland management, and also required working for 'A' levels.

Somerset County Council, however, was not prepared to pay for her to do this. Mary and Marcus worked out that it was cheaper to pay for a mortgage on a small house in Wiltshire – which would mean the course was free – than to pay the fees. It was also a small investment towards a home when they would retire. Later, as we shall see, the cottage in Box was to become the family home. For two years, however, there were two homes and during the week Mary and Marcus often slept in different houses. At first Marcus helped look after Shaman during the week until he (Shaman not Marcus) was wrongly accused of having trampled on a lamb and was quickly moved to Woolley. When on one Monday morning Rachel forgot her riding boots, Marcus arranged for them to travel to Bath by bus.

Growing Up in a Vicarage

Many well-known people, including David Steel, Gordon Brown, Jon Snow and Theresa May, grew up in a vicarage or a manse. Although the Old Deanery was not a vicarage, this is perhaps a good point at which to pause and ask my mother Rachel and my uncle Jeremy, what it was like growing up with a Vicar for a Dad and a social worker and magistrate for a Mum.

Rachel says, 'As I get older I realise that living in a vicarage as a child was a privilege. It has taught me to relate to people of all ages with differing backgrounds and religious beliefs. It has also given me a solid foundation for my own Christian faith. I had a happy childhood, and I particularly have fond memories of Swainswick. Mum and Dad were loving and caring parents and despite their busy schedules, they were both very thoughtful and found time for Jeremy and me. Jeremy and I played well together as children. We became engrossed in imaginary games of "cars and roads", farms, Sindy and action man, and bikes became buses! I occasionally kicked a football, or played cricket, but more often than not poor Jeremy was encouraged to play horses and canter over jumps on the lawn!

I also loved playing with my dear friend Fiona (Shutter) who lived along the lane. We had sleepovers, swam in her pool, played with our Guinea pigs, and walked our dogs by the brook. We started an animal club in Audrey Green's summerhouse. I also enjoyed playing with my cousins. Frances and I shared a love of horses, though I saw less of Bob and Tim as they were older. Philip, Peter and Patrick were good fun to be with. We mostly met at Kersell. Once, when they took me punting in Cambridge, I fell in and everyone laughed (except me!).

I was mostly happy to go to church and enjoyed the Sunday school and Bible class, but occasionally I wanted to ride my pony instead. Dad was actually more tolerant of this than Mum, but I was told under no circumstances to ride near the church on a Sunday!

I enjoyed both my primary schools, but being a vicar's daughter at secondary school was a bit tricky! At the Diocesan School I was called "Prayerbook" instead of "Braybrooke" and if I swore my friends teased me and pretended to be shocked! It was embarrassing when Dad took assembly, but the head-teacher was fond of him and asked him regularly. Vicarage life inevitably involved moving house several times in childhood. For me, at the age of 14 the move to Wells was not easy. I found it difficult to settle at the Blue school as subjects I thought I understood were taught very differently, and I had some problems with bullying. Not wanting to upset my parents, I didn't tell them.

Mum and Dad entertained regularly, and had many meetings at the house. Homeless men to Lords and Ladies were welcome at the Rectory and offered a plentiful spread of food. Afternoon tea was a particular favourite. (Such an appropriate title for the biography, I'm sure you agree!) Mum is an excellent cake maker and Jeremy and I delighted in "licking out the bowl" and arguing over the spoon of a delicious chocolate cake mixture when we were little!

'We have had many funny moments together. At one particular party Mum was tired and when people arrived they just stood in a circle not communicating and the atmosphere was flat (unusual for their parties). So Mum said loudly, "Shall we all play ring, a ring o' roses?" Then we both escaped to the kitchen in hysterics. Another time, Mum and I got the giggles in Dorchester Abbey. A lady vicar announced the service was in a cream leaflet, and Mum turned to me and said far too loudly, "It's not green, it's cream!" I said she'd misheard but she didn't hear me. She mentioned it again until we were both in uncontrollable laughter, and we just couldn't stop despite the stares!

'We had many memorable family holidays, in Great Britain and abroad', Rachel recalls. Dad became an expert at packing our tiny Renault 4, raising his hands in exasperation as Mum would appear with just one more bag! Particular highlights for me were visiting Israel in Holy week, Bermuda to see the Shutters, Europe, India, and my four trips to Australia to get to know our beautiful family down under. More recently, I much enjoyed a cruise on the Danube with Mum to celebrate her 80th and my 50th – even though the weather was very, very hot.

It was special to me that Dad prepared Peter and I for marriage, and took our wedding service. Also that he baptised all four of our daughters, Kathryn, Helen, Sarah and Anna. Mum and Dad are wonderful grandparents and have always been supportive and shown a real interest in each of the girls' lives.' (As one of the aforementioned girls, I couldn't agree more).

To my grandparents themselves, my Mum wrote, 'As a couple you work amazingly well as a team you really are soul mates yet different personalities. Dad you are incredible. You can go from preaching the most thought provoking sermon to picking up horse poo. Always humble and always helping everyone. Mum, I love it that we are best friends and can talk about anything. We are very close, yet we have quite different personalities. I tend to worry about what people think of me, yet you have a lovely confidence and say what you think!'

Jeremy, Rachel's brother and my uncle, also shared his memories of their childhood.

'It is not until I was an adult that I appreciated how different it was to grow up as a Braybrooke – whether it was living in the Rectory or the Old Deanery there was a constant stream of visitors seeking out Mary and Marcus. Not just parishioners but friends from India, America, Australia, France and many other countries came to share food or stay for a few days. With them came interesting gifts, lively conversations or new routines. Our house was always welcoming to everyone. Mary was an expert at rustling up food and would quickly make tea and scones for unexpected guests. I remember initial concern when a homeless man asked to use our toilet and he didn't emerge for some time. We soon found out that he had washed all his belongings and as a thank you then cleaned all our windows.

Beyond our home many adventures took place when we went away on holiday as a family; as children sleeping on luggage racks on the overnight sleeper to Scotland or 'borrowing' friends' houses in Kent, Cornwall or Wales. In time we became more adventurous travelling to Israel, New York, Bermuda and Australia. Mary and Marcus certainly allowed us freedom and gave us confidence – how many parents would leave their teenage children in Australia and let them make their own way home with a two night stop-over in Hawaii?

Confidence to travel started early. When very young I was put on the National Express Coach to Cambridge to be met by grand-parents, later I was allowed to travel alone to France and Holland. However, on the ferry to Holland I spent most of the journey trying to convince the authorities that I had not run away from home! It hadn't occurred to us that a teenage boy travelling without money and not knowing the address I was going to might raise questions. I only knew that Marcus was going to meet me in Holland. (It was the day of Charles' and Diana's wedding).

As adults we have continued to share more adventures including altitude sickness in Tibet or an earthquake in Gujarat. Marcus and I, not knowing the severity of the earthquake debated whether to try contacting home from Gujarat to let everyone know we were safe or whether we might cause worry if it had not been reported. As with so many experiences it took great perseverance over many hours to get a telephone call through, only to then find out it was international news and everyone was anxiously waiting to hear from us.

Afternoon Tea with Mary and Marcus

More recently I have introduced my own family to the joys of travelling with Mary and Marcus. Amazingly most of the trip to Australia and Hong Kong went smoothly; only needing to find one emergency doctor for Mary in Northern Queensland. However, Mary and Marcus did almost cause the flight home to be diverted. Swigging their trusted TCP they were oblivious to the anxiety caused by the unusual smell in the cabin – as anxious flight crew looked for the source of the smell we had to quietly explain it was just their preferred 'tipple'!

Growing up as a Braybrooke has been a unique experience and a tribute to Mary and Marcus that they allowed me freedom whilst always being willing to provide support and encouragement'.

But now – back to what Mary and Marcus were doing in Wells.

Director of Training

Director of Training was a new post. In part, it was felt that some clergy were 'stuck' and had not kept up with a changing world and that others were isolated and needed more support. Because the number of clergy has been declining, and therefore the linking of parishes, the aim was to encourage laity to take a greater share in the leadership and worship of the church. This was not just for practical reasons, but reflected the theological insight that that lay and ordained together made up 'the people of God – a royal priesthood.' (1 Peter 2, 9). The job also involved helping clergy to see the need for in-service training (the annual allowance was less than £100 per head!) and then to suggest suitable opportunities. Marcus was particularly glad that, with the strong support of the Bishop John Bickersteth, the Diocese agreed to make money available for clergy to have a sabbatical: three months for personal renewal study once in a lifetime. Those who took advantage of this found it of great help. Marcus also worked closely with the Bristol University Extra-Mural Adult education programme offering courses on theology and world religions.

Marcus quickly discovered that the clergy were afraid to say what they really thought to the laity and the laity were hesitant to say what they thought in case the clergy were upset. So he arranged a variety of courses and study days to look at the then lively contemporary theological debate. He invited several controversial figures such as John Robinson and John Hick to speak – and often people picnicked in the garden of the Old Deanery. Many people when they came to the Diocesan offices would look in to be welcomed by Mary with tea or coffee. Marcus also started a group to study the paranormal and gave support to the Ecumenical Teaching Order which provided lay-people with material to study theology together. This was to be a precursor of the 'Bishop's certificates,' which are available in many dioceses.

Amongst Marcus' responsibilities was the in-service training of curates in their first three years of ministry. Marcus encouraged the curates to develop a specialist area of study, but the primary concern was relationships, especially of curate and vicar and, even more tricky, curate's wife and vicar's wife. Curates and their wives did not always find it easy to adjust to their new roles and this could create tensions within the marriage. Marcus, with Mary's invaluable help, therefore, arranged a number of residential weekends for curates and their wives – all clergy then were male.

Marcus' new position was a Diocesan job, which meant a lot of travelling, and he missed the close link with a church and its congregation. Occasionally he was asked to take a mid-week early communion service at the Cathedral and took some part in the life of St Cuthbert's, but the hidden tensions in the congregation meant he never felt relaxed leading worship there. He took some services in local villages and across the Diocese. For a time, during vacancies, Marcus was acting Youth Officer and Director of Education. As youth officer, with Jeremy, he arranged for a small church tent at the Glastonbury Festival, which had started in the nineteen seventies and, was still quite a modest event. Several people stopped to chat and a few people came to an early morning communion service. Jeremy, with his children, still goes each year to the Festival.

Afternoon Tea with Mary and Marcus

ACCM Selector and Examining Chaplain

Mary was also very involved in the selection of Clergy. She was invited to be one of the national ACCM (Advisory Council for the Church's Ministry) selectors, whose job it was to help candidates discern whether they were being called to ordained ministry. At a conference in 1980 the candidates were interviewed in the selectors' bedrooms. It was, however thought to be rather improper for Mary – a woman – to interview young men in a bedroom – so the bed was removed.

Mary was asked to give a talk on 'The Christian Layman's Role in Modern Society.' She suggested that it was more appropriate for her to speak about the 'Laywoman'' or 'Layperson's role.' She noted that in the 1960's 'would-be priests were mostly involved in matters of social concern, which they saw as their most important Christian witness' – others have said that their emphasis was on 'The Kingdom of God' rather than 'the Church.' Roles were confused, both in terms of clergy as compared with social or health workers.

Some nurses see a clergy visitor as 'a nuisance, interfering with ward life etc.' (in those days clergy had easy access to any patients and virtually all chaplains were C of E or R.C.). Mary also wondered whether hospital visiting should be by the hospital chaplain or by the parish priest, especially if the person was a church member. She emphasized the need for clergy to train lay leaders. She stressed that 'our Christian commitment involves us in every aspect of life and seeing people as a whole. The lay committed Christian person is often in a better position than the priest to know what people really feel. We are called to different vocations, but we all work for the same Lord Jesus Christ.'

After the conference, an ACCM secretary thanked Mary for 'her splendid talk' and for 'adding to the cheerful, good humoured atmosphere and making the whole thing such fun,' continuing, 'It was the best conference that I have attended.'

Being an ACCM selector was important and demanding work. When Mary's term of office ended, Bishop John Bickersteth thanked her for sharing in this vital task. 'I dare to express the gratitude of the whole church as well as of the diocese.' He then asked her to be one of his Examining Chaplains, who had the task of deciding whether a candidate should be recommended by the Diocese to go to an ACCM selection conference. She worked closely with Canon Samuel Cutt, who was a near neighbour, a great friend and an excellent cook (and also a brilliant preacher). After he retired and moved to Peterborough, Mary and Marcus would go to visit him at his nursing home whenever they were in the area.

Besides all this, Mary was also a pastoral tutor on the Aston Training Scheme, which helped possible ordinands, who lacked the required educational qualifications, by providing a distance learning programme arranged by the Open University, and by offering pastoral support. In a book published to mark the tenth anniversary of the Aston Scheme, Mary said she felt at least with one candidate that her 'social work skills were essential.' The students, she said, found the course very demanding and she felt that more flexibility was required. Some of the candidates were rather resentful that they were required to take the course, as they felt that had learned more in the 'university of life' than some clergy who had spent two or three years at a college. One of her candidates wrote to Mary saying, 'I very much appreciate your help, friendship and guidance. I am grateful to the Lord for the ways he has arranged this.' The Principal of the Aston Scheme also said how grateful he was for the care and concern she had shown to her students.

The Wells Peace Group and a Peace Gathering in Edinburgh

Jeremy and Mary were very active in the Wells Peace Group. When Bruce Kent, then chair of CND, came to Wells, he took a great liking to Mary (of course!). Marcus went to Peace Group meetings when he could.

Because of this involvement, Bishop John Bickersteth asked Mary and Marcus to represent the Diocese at an ecumenical Peace Gathering in Edinburgh. The day before they went north, David Sheppard (cricketer and Bishop of Liverpool) had given the Dimbleby lecture and spoke about the 'two Britains' – one prosperous and the other struggling. Listening to it in the 'comfortable' Britain of The Old Deanery, Wells, it was startling to spend the next night in a high-rise building on a decaying new estate on the outskirts of Edinburgh. During the drive from the station their hostess - an outspoken deaconess in the Church of Scotland - told them that if they heard a fight at 2 am they should keep their windows shut and their lights off. The week before she had been woken up by a wife throwing her husband down several flights of stairs, followed by his false teeth! 'Needless to say,' Mary recalls, 'during our last night, we met through her, a lonely, alcoholic old man, a baby of 18 months, whose home had been burgled, who was brought to sleep in our bedroom and we heard a violent quarrel outside! The Deaconess had not had time to discover that I was an experienced social-worker and unphased by what was happening.'

'The peace of the world, which was the main theme of the Gathering for Peace, seemed far away from more immediate problems of peace within families and communities, just as it must seem to the hungry and racially oppressed of much of the world.'

The Gathering, which was attended by several hundred people from all over the world, was arranged by the Edinburgh Council of Churches. Most of the time was spent in small groups, of which the members belonged to many Christian Churches and of very varying backgrounds. Exhibitions arranged by many peace organisations were on show in the various city churches as well as displays of Chinese dancing, mummery plays by Quakers and workshops.

Marcus was asked to speak at a gathering of the local Sharing of Faiths committee and on Easter morning to preach at St. Mark's Unitarian Church - a rather challenging place in which to preach about the resurrection. At the service there were members of the Corrymeela Choir from Northern Ireland, which included both Catholics and Protestants, and there was also a Buddhist in the congregation, so it was a really ecumenical occasion.

They made many new friends and renewed some old friendships. On Good Friday they took part in a silent Act of Witness Cross walk through Edinburgh ending up on Calton Hill with a beautiful view of the city and the environs. The police were polite and helpful and the traffic did not seem to mind being disrupted. Marcus was reminded of a Korean Christian at the Vancouver World Council of Churches Assembly, which he had recently attended, who had told him that during a similar Walk of Witness on Good Friday in Korea they were attacked by the police as they marched and were flung into prison. Mary wrote, 'We could not help wondering if we would be prepared to face the suffering that the Way of the Cross demands and is certainly required in the search for peace.'

A Tour to India

Time in India was an important influence on Marcus. Mary was uncertain about whether she wanted to go there when the time came for the second World Congress of Faith tour to the sub-continent, but was glad she had. Mary wrote in *World Faiths*:

'I wasn't really sure I wanted to go to India. Would the heat, poverty and dust be overwhelming? In spite of much second-hand knowledge from Indian friends and from my husband, I wasn't sure I could cope. Now, I wouldn't have missed the trip for anything.

Afternoon Tea with Mary and Marcus

We were away for only two weeks and two days but it seems like a year, so alien was the experience from any previous venture. In spite of a proud and independent attitude, the welcome from the Indians was very warm. One lasting memory is of being surrounded by staring, inquisitive, and sometimes demanding, Indian faces. Materially it is impossible to forget that we have so much in the West and many of them so little. Yet they have much to teach us about acceptance, about family love and hospitality - and some of them about the way of non-violence. Slowly, very slowly things were beginning to improve.

Within a few hours of our arrival in Delhi, at a reception at the Gandhi Peace Foundation, we met a great variety of religious people, Hindu, Sikh, Baha'i, Muslim and Christian - all concerned for peace and for the improvement of social conditions. We were given a tremendous welcome from the Sikhs wherever we went and took part in a seminar at Khalsa college in Amritsar. At Amritsar we were also much moved by a visit to the Golden Temple and the deep sense of worship there.

At Rishikesh (where the Beatles went) we had an interview with a Swami at the Divine Life Society - an orthodox Hindu group. Then we saw an impressive clinic for leprosy patients who were busily occupied, with what remained of their hands, making beds, weaving and producing splendid cloths for sale.

Whilst others went for an audience with His Holiness the Dalai Lama up in the mountains, a few of us stayed in Amritsar and saw round two hospitals. One was run by a magnificent humanist, a place for "incurables" and the dying, rather like the work of Mother Teresa. No-one there is ever refused admission and though conditions were very primitive, there was love and compassion. The other hospital at Tarn Taran is run by the Church of North India, formerly by the Anglicans, for women and children, with maternity, surgical and medical wards. It was rather like some of our neighbourhood hospitals - but not so sophisticated - and was not full because many were in the fields harvesting.

I cannot begin to describe all we did and saw. Highlights were a visit to the Taj Mahal, as impressive as its pictures, and other fine Moghul architecture; houseboats and *shikara* (a sort of gondola) on Lake Dal, near Srinagar in Kashmir. I have a picture of Marcus in one of the *shikaras*, helping to deliver suit cases.'

At the Shalimar gardens in Srinagar.

The tour was reported in the *Wells Journal* by Michael Chamberlain He wrote that 'Mary Braybrooke, a hospital social worker, said: "I shall nev'er forget the look of pure delight on the faces of some children to whom I gave a packet of Smarties, one tiny sweet seemed to produce such joy." The group spent some time with the Brotherhood in Delhi, an Anglican or now Church of North India – religious community, which was founded in the nineteenth century by Edward Bickersteth, a great uncle of Bishop John Bickersteth. They also shared in the morning service at All Saints church in Srinagar. The church had twice in recent years been burned down by Muslim mobs. "It was a sad reminder", Marcus said, "of the bitterness that religious differences can often cause and why encouraging understanding and friendship between members of different religions is so important."'

As Mary mentioned, many of the group made the long trip from Amritsar to meet the Dalai Lama, a Patron of the World Congress of Faiths. 'When they got to Dharamsala,' Michael Chamberlain wrote, 'Marcus' heart sank as he stood outside the Dalai Lama's home in the hillside village of McLeod Ganj. Together with his party of 34 people he was told that His Holiness's private secretary was ill and no arrangements for a visit had been made. Then, after a few minutes, security checks started, hand bags were searched and everyone was frisked. "I realised, then, we were going to see His Holiness, but the official said 'just for a few minutes," said Mr Braybrooke.'

Marcus and the Dalai Lama

"We were shown into a large sitting room and soon the Dalai Lama was talking about the need for spiritual values.' Only religion can give inner peace not medicine and drugs', he said. But he roared with laughter when I told him there were four psychiatrists and three other doctors in the group. The Dalai Lama explained how vital it was in a world made one by modern communications for people of all faiths to understand each other and to work together for peace. 'Such friendship with others,' he said, 'made one a better member of one's own religion.' Nearly an hour passed before we took our leave."'

Active Liberals

No longer in a parish, Mary and Marcus felt free to take a more active part in politics – supporting the Liberal Party. They became good friends of Alan Butt-Phillips, who was prospective Liberal candidate for Wells, and his wife Christina Baron, who was also standing for Parliament and is now a member of the Church's General Synod.

In May 1982, as the *Western Gazette* reported, the Liberal leader David Steel spoke at a Garden Party held at their home at 9 Cathedral Green. It was the time of the Falkland War and David Steel called for a full parliamentary inquiry into the Falklands crisis. "When it is all over, Parliament must get a full inquiry on how the messages to the Foreign Office were ignored. We must also look around at the readiness of our allies in Europe to export arms to unstable countries." Afterwards Mr Steel was taken on a conducted tour of the Cathedral. On a similar occasion Paddy Ashdown also spoke there and Jeremy Thorpe, who had come to see

Afternoon Tea with Mary and Marcus

a friend, made a private visit to learn about interfaith activities. Mary has remained loyal to the Liberals. Marcus, for at least the last 15 years has been a member of the Green Party and delivers leaflets when there is an election. He thinks every Christian 'If we want real change, should belong to some party.'

Church Life in Wells

Mary also contributed a lot to church life in Wells, especially as a member of St Cuthbert's – the city's parish church. She started a youth club, to which some young people from both the Blue School and the Cathedral School came. She asked them what qualities they would look for in a new clergyman, the answers included 'good at listening', 'willingness to go to pubs' and 'a Citroen Dyan with a CND (Campaign for Nuclear Disarmament) badge on it.'

Marcus was not at ease with church life in Wells. Almost as soon as he moved there, the Archdeacon's wife harangued him about his 'heretical' theology. Because he preached at churches across the Diocese, Marcus did not feel fully involved in the life of St Cuthbert's and found the atmosphere in the vestry before a service was tense. The congregation he got to know best was at the nearby village of Coxley. Occasionally he celebrated at an early mid-week communion service (there were 39 retired clergy in Wells competing for the privilege). Canon Samuel Cutt also regularly asked Marcus to preach at the Cathedral.

Marcus made some good friends with a few people who were more interested in what the church was doing in the world than in the sometimes petty disagreements about ritual. Mary, as always, was quick to make friends and enjoyed life in Wells – a city whose beauty both remember with gratitude.

Leaving Wells

After about four years in Wells, Marcus and Mary went back to Tantur, near Jerusalem, where Marcus had spent his three month sabbatical. The Rector, Donald Nichol wanted him to join the staff and establish a peace academy. There was a long six months, whilst Donald tried to negotiate with Notre Dame University in the USA - the main financial backers of Tantur – who continued to prevaricate. Eventually Marcus felt he could wait no longer. Jeremy was finishing at the Blue School and instead of being directly answerable to Bishop John Bickersteth, with whom Marcus always had happy relations – a ministerial committee was to be set up – with a different approach to training - to interfere with Marcus' work. Soon after saying no to Tantur, Marcus, to his great surprise, was approached about becoming Director of the Council of Christians and Jews. The Diocesan Secretary, prophetically, said that if he took the job, he would never get back on the clerical career ladder.

Having grown up regularly interacting with my grandparents' many friends from all across the world, and perhaps therefore taking for granted their open mindedness and empathy with all people, it sometimes catches me off guard to consider what they sacrificed. For a country parish vicar to be openly engaging with leaders of other religions, and listening to them rather than trying to convert them, it is no wonder that Mary and Marcus were accused of being 'heretical'. I don't doubt that there are many moments across the years in which they have faced hostility and criticism for their nonconformist views. My grandmother has a boldness and the confidence to say exactly what she thinks, which I think comes in part from being totally comfortable in her own skin and full of worldly experience. My grandfather is a quiet renegade. He sees, listens and thinks, absorbing the world around him, and gently changes it by responding with love. Their shared good humour also helps—we joked once that Marcus "couldn't even convert a PDF".

Goodbye to the Diocese

When Marcus and Mary moved on, the Bishop, John Bickersteth, wrote a warm message of farewell in the Diocesan News. 'Marcus Braybrooke has served with great distinction in this Diocese as a parish priest, greatly loved by those in the Bath area, and latterly for the past five years as Director of Training. In all this work (which he reflects on below) he has kept his vision and scholarship, and gained the respect and affection of large numbers of people up and down the Diocese, clergy and lay. We wish him every blessing in his important new work with the Council of Christians and Jews and are glad that his base is not far away so that we may be able to see him about the Diocese from time to time. + J.B.W.'

Marcus also wrote some interesting reflections on his work. '"Aim at the higher gifts" Paul said, but "put love first." On the Continent the word 'formation' is often used to describe the growth of Christian character. The ambiguity of Christian training is that secular models of education, training and management skills cannot be applied to Church life without *metanoia* (transformation). What Christian people most need is to accept more deeply the grace of Our Lord Jesus rather than develop specialist skills, although we are not to bury our talents. Take the use of time. Is it a matter of deeper prayer in which we order our priorities before God or using the managerial skills of time management? Shared ministry requires managerial skills of leadership and delegation, but should also reflect our theological model of the Church and the nature of Christian authority.

Training requires self-knowledge which is a spiritual discipline. We have therefore tried to encourage both individual clergy and parishes to identify their own needs. This provides the motivation necessary for them to seek the right training to meet those needs. Rather than Diocesan schemes backed by external authority, we have tried to encourage self-motivation for training. It is encouraging therefore that a steadily growing number of clergy are taking advantage of a wide range of training opportunities and that funds are available for this. More and more parishes too are having conferences, quiet-days, missions and house groups. Shared ministry is increasing and laity are demanding more say in parochial policy and taking their share in pastoral work.

Yet whilst church life needs to be well ordered and efficient, the Gospel is compelling because it is true. We cannot shirk the difficult task of reflecting on and seeking to communicate our experience of God's love in Christ, and applying this to the problems of the world. So training has to include a variety of study days and evening classes.

Just as Christian growth cannot be arranged, but waits on God's grace, so too with dialogue. Members of different religions can be brought together, but only God makes possible a meeting of hearts and minds. Increasingly Jews and Christians, moving beyond past suspicion and prejudice, are waiting to share the deep treasures of faith. There is a vast amount of common study to help us understand the first centuries of this era in which both Christianity and Rabbinic Judaism took shape. Together Jews and Christians, in the light of the Holocaust, are reflecting on human nature and on how the reality of God's mercy can be affirmed in the face of such evil. Together they affirm the reality of God and moral values in a world which, if it denies them, will destroy itself.

Dialogue, like training, is, in a sense, subversive of existing religious institutions. Both seek to equip God's people for the new world that is coming to be. So easily we retreat into the familiar rather than following the Spirit into the unknown - and for that above all we need God's grace. I am grateful to the many people across the Diocese who have shared in the work of training and Christian growth and who have given their friendship to Mary, Rachel, Jeremy and myself. I shall value your prayers in my new work as Executive Director of the Council of Christians and Jews.'

11. Box and CCJ

Because there was no house with the job of Director of the Council of Christians and Jews, the family settled in the tiny cottage in Box. This meant Marcus had a long daily commute, although there was a good train service from Chippenham, but it also allowed Mary to continue working for Wiltshire Social Services and serving as a magistrate in Bath. Rachel was by then training as an Occupational Therapist at St Loye's College in Exeter and lodging in term time with Mary's Aunt Joan Rowsell, although she was often away on clinical placements around the UK, and organised her final placement to be in Australia.

Jeremy, after a year's globe-trotting ('in which I gather he grew his hair long, but no one has yet shown me the photographic evidence'), started at Southampton University, studying medicine. With the children away so much, the family coped with the lack of space.

Because Marcus was working in London, Mary and Marcus were apart quite a lot of the time. Besides some time together in the evenings, they would also every other Friday meet at Slough station (how romantic!) and drive to Cranleigh or Cambridge to see their parents.

The Council of Christians and Jews

The Council of Christians and Jews (CCJ) was formed during the Second World War to bring together Jews and Christians to affirm the moral values that they shared; values which had shaped European civilization and which were threatened by the Nazis and their deadly anti-Semitism. The Presidents included the Archbishops of Canterbury and Westminster, the Moderator of the Church of Scotland, the President of the Free Church Council and the Chief Rabbi. CCJ exists to promote understanding and co-operation between the two faiths. Many people assumed that Marcus had joined CMJ - the Church's Mission to the Jews.

Marcus was asked to a meeting at Sidney Corob's office in Mayfair. He thought it was to be told what the job might involve but found there were perhaps eight people there to interview him. The recently appointed chairman was Donald Coggan, former Archbishop of Canterbury. Marcus found him a great person to work with. Mary used to look after him at conferences and he called her 'Mother.'

Marcus' appointment was reported in the church press. *The Tablet* noted that some Christians now had a better understanding of Judaism and that there were good personal relations between the leaders, but it went on to say: 'The need now is for spiritual contact between the two faiths, but one of the difficulties is that Orthodox Jews have a deep suspicion of all theological discussion and fear, after long experience of Christian missions, that the deeper purpose of dialogue on the Christian side was to convert Jews to Christianity.'

CCJ was in poor shape at the time. The previous General Secretary had been asked to clear his desk and leave. The Administrator, Leonard Goss, who was Jewish, had assumed he would get the job and made no effort to welcome Marcus. When he first arrived in the office there was not even a chair for him to sit on and a few weeks later the locks were changed without telling Marcus, so when, after an overnight journey back from a meeting in the North he arrived early, he had to take shelter in a hotel. They did establish a *modus vivendi* and sadly Leonard died very suddenly at the end of the year. His widow Mildred stayed on as a very knowledgeable and hard-working secretary. A Roman Catholic deacon, Graham Jenkins was a great support and Marcus often stayed at his home.

When Marcus started there was not much money (there never has been) and very little programme. It was, however, a time when the churches were just waking up to the Church's dramatic new appreciation of Judaism. This included recognising that Jesus was a faithful Jew; that it was the Romans who put him to death; that God's covenant with the Jewish people had never been revoked and that they were still a people of God. The Parting of the Ways between Rabbinic Judaism and the Early Church was as much for historical reasons as theological ones. A major concern was to resist all forms of anti-Semitism. Mission and Israel were highly controversial issues.

Marcus did a lot of travelling, lecturing and writing. Clifford Longley, who had a deep interest in the subject, was at the time Religious Affairs correspondent for *The Times,* so there was good coverage of CCJ in the media. CCJ was a member organisation of the International Council of Christians and Jews so each year Mary and Marcus attended the annual Colloquium. It was on their way to the first Colloquium that they first met Sir Sigmund (Sigi) and Lady Hazel Sternberg. Sigi was coming down an escalator which was going up – he was always able to achieve the impossible. He and Hazel were to become good friends and in the nineties he and Marcus with Sheik Zaki Badawi founded the Three Faiths Forum – now the Faith and Belief Forum. Marcus also took part in some of the dialogue meetings arranged by the World Council of Churches.

Each year there was an annual conference at Hengrave Hall – an Elizabethan house set in a large garden near Bury St Edmunds – run by Catholic sisters. At the time accommodation was still in dormitories. An important initiative that Marcus and a good friend Rabbi Tony Bayfield took was to set up the Manor House Dialogue group. They invited seven or eight clergy and rabbis, who were open to serious discussion of the theology of each religion, to meet two or three times a year. Several participants, such as Baroness Julia Neuberger and Bishop Richard Harries, became well-known.

I met with Rabbi Tony at a small café in London, to ask him about his experience of the Braybrookes. Over coffee, he mused: 'I met Marcus first in 1983. He was just about to become the Executive Director of the Council of Christians and Jews. I had just come up from a period of ten and half years as a congregational Rabbi in Weybridge and Surrey, to establish a new Jewish religious educational and cultural centre in Finchley. I can't remember precisely why our paths first crossed but we instantly found we had a great deal in common. First of all, we'd both been to Magdalene College, Cambridge – though your grandpa had been there long, long, long before me because he is so much older', he joked, adding, 'I often say this in his presence and he grins knowingly'.

'We quickly spotted the incongruity between both of us for our different reasons, having been to the most reactionary college full of hunting, shooting and fishing types. In and around the 1960's not only did they not even contemplate letting women into the place, but your ability to row was more important than your scholarly ability as far as the college was concerned. I was the grammar school boy. I studied law...' he paused, his eyes twinkling, 'but the step from criminology to rabbi work was almost indiscernible!'

'The first thing we had in common was this shared rather ironic academic background. The second was that we were instinctively liberally minded - particularly in a theological sense. I was already of the view that God is infinitely larger than any religion, and that the idea that God would entrust the whole of His Truth to any one group of people, at any one time, was an astonishing piece of hubris: the idea that we could comprehend the whole of God's truth was just absurd. I had spent ten and a half years with a congregation in Weybridge and Surrey, which was not a Jewish area. I spent the whole of my time doing PR for the Jewish community. I gave talks without number. It's summed up by one – to the wives of Woking or something similar, and I drove up one dark night, got out the car and there was a woman standing outside. I asked her for directions, and she looked at me and said 'Are you the Rabbi?', and I said 'Yes'. And she then said 'Not what I expected. Not what I expected at all', and walked off.'

I asked Tony what he thought she had expected. 'Black hat, beard, probably forked hooves and a forked tail as well!', he laughed, continuing, 'This was deepest, darkest Home County, but even so, the idea developed, and I spent a lot of time explaining who we were and being polite and occasionally doing Bible studies and other things but I'd reached the point where I needed something more than good relations, superficiality, and polite cups of tea. I quickly gleaned the fact that your grandfather, though coming from an apparently different place – coming from abroad and from India – was also coming from the same place.'

'And the next thing we shared was a desire to talk at a serious level and to see where that goes. And the final thing, though I don't think either of us would have been able to articulate it at the time, was that we didn't want to just talk about the theology of Christian/Jewish relations. We wanted to talk theology. And I think we both recognised very soon that in a mixed group of like-minded people, be they Christians or Jews, we could actually talk more openly than we could in a group of our own colleagues, because we were tied into the institutional, and the dogmatic and the doctrinal. And what we did, I think beginning in 1983, was to set up a group, basically 8 Christians and 8 Jews, none of whom were there as representatives, but as different people, all interested in the enterprise. And although we couldn't have articulated it right at the beginning, what we came to see was that if you have a small but consistent group, meeting not very frequently, but regularly, over a period of time, with no agenda other than what happens in the group itself, you build friendship and trust, and in those circumstances you can begin to share. And actually it's there that by exploring somebody else's faith you come to understand your own much better. I think the metaphor might be that what you're trying to create is not a huge park, but you have a number of gardens. And by going into the other person's garden and being able to appreciate it, you go back into your own garden having learnt – well, something about gardening. And you're much better able to appreciate and to recognise the weeds in your own garden.'

'We met for 10 years; a two day residential and several single days a year, and when we intuitively knew that the group was coming to the end of its natural life we decided to do a book. It was called *Dialogue with a Difference* and it was published by SCM Press, because another member of the group Reverend Dr John Bowden, who was very influential and very important to Marcus, was, as well as being an Anglican priest, the chief executive of SCM press. Under him SCM expanded and there were so many Jewish books in his list. We both loved John. He died in 2010 and we miss him enormously.'

As we chatted, we discovered that John and my grandfather had both introduced Tony to Alan Race, whom I had the pleasure of meeting in Salt Lake City during the World Parliament of Religions. Tony continued, 'Out of Marcus' and my work together, emerged a method of doing dialogue. One can only really do it in that consistent, regular friendship.' Rabbi Bayfield was later approached by the chairman of the Council of Christians and Jews, Bishop of Manchester Nigel McCulloch, who said 'The book you did with Marcus has been enormously influential and we would like you now to do its successor'.

Tony explained, 'The new book had a new group – slightly bigger, sixteen of us, and we broke them into eight pairs and took eight cutting edge dialogue subjects and then the first pair produced draft papers. They read them and then the group discussed it, and then out of that discussion the first pair revised and rewrote, and the second pair did their papers revising and building on the work of the first pair. This went on for three years, revising and revising. The process of the writing of the book mirrors how you do dialogue. You sit down and you talk and you listen, and you're prepared to be given a very uncomfortable time by some people. Though interestingly, the Christians gave the Christians a much harder time, and the Jews gave the Jews a much harder time. That's the process and your Grandpa is equally as responsible for that. I don't think that even in the States there is an exact parallel of how you do it.'

In that process we became good friends and I met Mary, who I think is one of the loveliest people anyone could hope to meet. She gives the first impression of being a lovely, kindly, sweet-tempered humorous lady, all of which she is, but actually behind that is a very fine mind, enormous moral strength and great determination. She's been more than just a rock to Marcus. She is a partner in the truest sense of the word,

Afternoon Tea with Mary and Marcus

and he wouldn't have achieved without her becoming the publishing house that he is today. In his work he ends up quoting from reformed Jewish liturgy. Remarkable.' Having discussed responsibility within religion, Tony commented, 'Marcus doesn't airbrush Christianity. Our colleague John Bowden said the most important thing is self-criticism. And Marcus would accept that. The religious claim to be humble but they are not, and they are not nearly as self-critical as they should be.'

Finally, I asked Tony what he believed should be the next steps for Interfaith work. I mentioned that when my grandmother first told me of her teenage idealism and of the celebration club she hosted in her garden and her dreams to change the world, what surprised me was actually her contemporary realisation that the world had not changed as she had hoped. Her frank and honest admittance of disillusionment took me by surprise. Tony responded that prophetic tradition 'provides you with a degree of direction, but that's all and then it's a gradual process, step by step.' He continued, 'I agree with Mary that one of the characteristics of the abyss that the Western world went through between the election of Hitler and the death of Stalin is that it's no longer clear that we're making progress. And I don't think that it's a given that good will win out. But you have to do what you can. And I console myself with the fact that although evil often lives on and the good we do is often interred with our bones, I believe that God somehow redeems the good and the just and the compassionate - the tiny acts of goodness and compassion in our lives. So that some of the time I don't believe in the futility of what I do. I believe my own theology. But I am deeply suspicious of utopianism, which is another form of human arrogance: that we can make a blueprint. Plato was quite a clever bloke but he wasn't always right. And there's a phrase in contemporary Jewish theology – *tikkun olam*, which means repair of the world.

And I believe that all we can do is repair – patch and mend the world and make it work a little bit better. And I think Jews have been through too much actually to believe in any more than that. And yet I would add that the most important thing of all is to maintain hope. That part of the core of religion is hope, and if Jews can continue to hope in spite of everything, then anybody can.'

It was a pleasure to meet with Tony, and to discuss in depth the weight of his working relationship with my grandfather during these periods of his life.

An important initiative that Marcus took was arranging a meeting of the Joint-Presidents of CCJ (pictured here). Marcus had been surprised when the Chief Rabbi, Dr Jakobovits, told him that he would really like to spend time with the Archbishop. They had sat together on the platform at public meetings, but had never had a proper conversation. Eventually a date was found that they and Cardinal Hume and the other joint Presidents – the Moderator of the Church of Scotland and the President of the Free Church Federal Council – could meet. Then late on the Sunday before, Marcus had a telephone call from the Archbishop

to say that the funeral of the Duchess of Windsor had been arranged for the same afternoon and if he was not there, *The Express* would say that the Church had not reconciled itself to Edward's Abdication. Eventually, some months later, another date was found and the meeting was so cordial that it is now an annual event.

Afternoon Tea with Mary and Marcus

Marcus also took on the editing of CCJ's journal *Common Ground* from his good friend Rabbi Harry Levy. Bernard Resnikoff, Director Emeritus of the American Jewish Committee in Israel, said of the journal: 'There is a consistent pattern of balance…and thankfully an absence of tired platitudes. The editor takes on prickly issues in his editorials with such sweet reason and tidy adjectives that we here, respectfully, refer to him as the "gentle provocateur."' Thanks to the initiative of Elizabeth Maxwell, the format of *Common Ground* was transformed into a glossy magazine with pictures in colour – but with as much serious content as ever.

A special occasion was when Marcus was asked to preach at the Civic Service, held to mark the inauguration of a new Lord Mayor of Westminster. The reason for the invitation was that the service was always held in Westminster Abbey. On this occasion, the Lord Mayor was Jewish - so it was felt Marcus was unlikely to offend members of either faith.

When Marcus had to retire from CCJ because of ill- health, Lord Coggan wrote, 'It was a good day for the Council of Christians and Jews when Marcus Braybrooke became its Executive Director. He brought to its work considerable parish experience – always an advantage - for in this work one meets all sorts and conditions of men and women; a knowledge of theological colleges and their staff and students and intimacy with the World Congress of Faiths. He brought also great personal gifts. Quietly spoken, with a ready pen and an engaging sense of humour, he was soon at home in the realm of Jewish-Christian relations. With good team co-operation, the work of CCJ became increasingly well known, articles appeared in journals and participation with the International Council was strengthened.'

India's Grief

During the time Marcus was at CCJ, Jeremy spent some of his gap year in India where for a time he worked at a cancer hospital near Kanyakumari. He was in India when Indira Gandhi was assassinated. Although this book is mainly about Mary and Marcus, Jeremy's letter to them is so interesting that it's worth quoting;

'Well, haven't things been happening in India! For me it has been a fascinating experience to observe a nation mourn the death of its leader, but I'm glad I am not in a big city where there has been a lot of trouble. I learnt of her assassination within five minutes of her death and by the time we left the hospital two hours later all the buses had stopped and all the shops shut. In the evening as we drove around people were just standing aimlessly in groups whilst others were just sitting on their doorsteps. A genuine air of sadness in this region was very apparent.

'The next day we went to a clinic in the hills and on the journey there were several groups marching peacefully in single file with black flags. All the other flags were by this time at half-mast and many black flags flew from the buildings. At one point a group had blocked the road with stones (despite heavy police presence everywhere) and were none too keen on letting us continue but because we were in an ambulance they eventually let us through, having tied a black flag to the vehicle. There were also a lot of pictures of Mrs. Gandhi displayed everywhere draped in flowers.

'The drive up into the hills was one of the most beautiful journeys I have been on. First we drove through rubber estates and coconut plantations and then as we got higher we entered a jungle region and the road degenerated into a track. It needed every bit of our four-wheel-drive vehicle to get up what was the worst track I have been on.

'When we reached the clinic that the International Cancer Centre holds every week in a remote tribal village there were only a few patients, because most of the regulars assumed that we would not come due to the assassination. The clinic consisted of two rooms - a store room for patients' records and a consulting room. The consulting room contained a small table, a chair and a stool. There was no privacy at all, with people wandering in and out, and children watching through the door and window. This sort of medical care is what is really needed. There is no doctor for 20 miles and no transport apart from a bicycle. It is really good that the International Cancer Centre bothers to travel 50 miles to hold the clinic.'

Jeremy went on from India to Australia, where he worked for a time, saw a lot of Mary's relations and circumnavigated the continent.

1986: A Difficult Year

1986 was an *annus horribilis.* Mary's parents came to live with them in Box and both died later in the year. Their much-loved dog Rex also died. Marcus' mother was knocked off her bicycle and was in hospital for a time, so his Dad needed support. Both Mary and Marcus, who was commuting to London, had demanding jobs. In the midst of trying to help others care for needy relations, Mary found she herself was now caring for her parents. Later she wrote about her experiences in *Community Care.* Her moving article, 'Strength out of Suffering,' which has been used in the training of palliative care workers deserves to be quoted in full.

'In the middle of setting up a group to help carers of relatives with senile dementia, I was also caring for my dying parents. As a result I gained deep insights into myself as a professional social worker, as a patient's relative, and as a daughter. Overall, the experience was positive. Yet, despite being surrounded by a loving, caring family, and by considerate professional colleagues and some dear friends, there were times when I felt I could no longer cope.

My parents, both in their eighties, had lived in their comfortable house in Cambridge for 60 years. For the past few months we had arranged domiciliary assistance, [such as a home help every morning, mobile meals, a social worker and neighbours calling, and a night nurse from the British Nursing Association.] We also held a case conference with the GPs and various support services.

My father, who suffered from emphysema, had been fully caring for my mother for the past three years, as she was gradually dementing. He was an intelligent man with many interests which he had to curtail. Nonetheless, he felt this was his duty and found it hard to accept outside help, though he also felt slightly ashamed of my mother's illness and thought that his friends would find it hard to understand her dementia. He gradually took over the cooking and housework. From Christmas 1986 my mother refused to leave her bed on some days and her physical as well as mental health grew worse. Her doctor found she had cardiac asthma following a bout of severe breathlessness.

My father's health also deteriorated and he had increasing chest infections. He had difficulty in sleeping and complained of headaches and unpleasant nightmares. He would sit with his head down, finding it difficult to make decisions. Antidepressants were prescribed. At Easter my parents came to stay with us for a week's holiday, after an invitation from Marcus who had driven down to Cambridge after work to see them. We were surprised that they accepted, as they hated leaving their home. There followed almost three weeks of no sleep for the whole household. At the end I felt like a zombie, with pains round my eyes and head. My husband realised well before I did that my parents would not want to go home after a week. I spent much of that first week continuing to set up the support services in Cambridge, fearful that the familiar home help would be lost if they were away for too long, and using my professional skills to arrange what I thought was necessary.

Both my parents needed help with dressing, washing, going to the lavatory and getting downstairs and needed reminding where the rooms were. During the night my mother wandered a bit, but my father was constantly in and out of bed through the night and very restless. We had some funny moments as well as much anxiety. My mother followed my father everywhere and was very jealous of my care for him. She was also quite aggressive with me and angry when I made suggestions that she might like to wash and so on. I became quite emotionally involved with some of the things she said, which I would never have done as a professional. She also showed her humour, including informing our GP that he conceived twins because his wife wore black frilly knickers!

At midnight, about ten days' later, the telephone rang to say my husband's parents were both being admitted to hospital because my mother-in-law had suffered a heart attack. At the same moment as the telephone rang, my father fell out of bed - which happened again during the next few nights. We called out the GP who treated his cuts but took no other action because he thought my parents were only with us on holiday. During the next week I worked when I could. My colleagues were sympathetic and understanding; kind friends came to sit with my parents when there were meetings I could not miss so that I could carry on with my medical social work. In the next few days we became increasingly anxious about my father. He was walking into doors on the left-hand side, eating very fast and his food fell off his plate on the left-hand side. He seemed unaware of what he was doing most of the time, becoming increasingly confused and disorientated. He also became very angry with my mother and told me several times that he could no longer look after her, nor did he want me to look after her, and that she ought to be in a home.

This was all out of character. The GP called in a geriatrician, whom I knew through work, and my father was admitted to hospital the following evening on a ward which I myself worked on so that many of the staff were known to me. He spent the next five or six weeks in hospital, and was given loving care and every attention in spite of his falls and confusion.

Nevertheless, I became increasingly anxious about him and broke down when visiting because of not knowing what was the matter. Various tests had revealed nothing except his emphysema. Eventually, a scan revealed he had an inoperable brain tumour. My reaction was of relief because I knew he would not have long to suffer and that he would not have wanted to go on as an invalid, being unable to cope. I found the uncertainty more exhausting than knowing the diagnosis. I was asked by the consultant to make a decision with my family about whether he should be told and whether treatment should be palliative or more aggressive.

I have never wanted to talk to so many people so much in my life. I needed to work things through with the help of others. I realised the immense value of having someone to listen sympathetically and, perhaps for the first time in my life, I realised that as a professional social worker there was indeed a great deal that could be offered to people in similar situations.

Telling my father that he had an inoperable tumour was dealt with during the next few days, and I had much support from the consultant in doing this. I had no doubt that my father should be told, thanks to both my professional and personal knowledge of him. He gradually took the news in and was determined to make the most of what time he had to live. In fact, he taught many of the nurses a great deal about being positive towards dying and death. The nurses said afterwards how much they had appreciated this.

Sharing care with the ward staff was complex - perhaps more so for me because they knew me in other capacities. I wanted the very best for my father, yet I wanted complete co-operation from the ward. I did not want him to be treated any differently from anyone else, but it was hard both for the nurses and for me not to give or be given some special individual treatment. In some ways it was more difficult for the staff because they were anxious that I should find everything well done. Therefore, they were sometimes over-sensitive that I might be criticising when I was asking, say, for a bedpan.

Afternoon Tea with Mary and Marcus

My father was given a room on his own and we made it his room with all his photographs and cards. We gradually evolved a system whereby we all helped in his care. We took him to the lavatory, dressed and undressed him when we were there and fed him when necessary. The little individual needs that were catered for helped him considerably; for example, having his tea without milk.

His greatest anxiety, apart from constipation, was that he should not be a nuisance to anybody. He said he wanted to die with the least inconvenience to anyone. He also spoke movingly about a dream he had. I had put a picture of his parents up in front of him on the wall and he said that one night he dreamed his mother's arms were stretching out to greet him. He never rang the bell for a nurse to come to him because he did not want to trouble them. Likewise, he did not complain at all when he developed shingles, which must have been excruciating.

My father had three objectives before he died. It was interesting that he allowed himself to die after these had been achieved. The first was that his wife should be settled in a nursing home, because he did not want me to look after her. The second was that before he died my daughter should go to Australia where all his relations lived. The third was that he should go back to Cambridge to say goodbye to his friends. During this time my mother was at home with us for another week. She gradually became more and more confused, refusing to get out of bed. When she became incontinent of faeces, which I found in the drawers of our daughter's bedroom where she was sleeping, I realised I could no longer cope with looking after her.

She was wandering into our room at night, refusing to go to bed, and I knew that we would break if we went on like this indefinitely. I also knew that my father was anxious for her to go elsewhere. I managed to find a vacancy in a local nursing home, but when the time came to take her to it I was unable to do so and had to leave this to my husband and daughter.

The guilt I felt afterwards remained with me, though she settled well and was happier than she had been in our own home. My father visited her in the nursing home, and my brother took him to Cambridge to say goodbye to his friends and see his garden. On many occasions when we had him out to tea he said he had never been happier in his life and that to be surrounded by love and kindness was the most important thing in the world. I found it particularly helpful to hear him articulate his attitude towards his dying so well, an attitude which I had rarely encountered professionally as people are frightened to express their feelings at this time. It made me feel it would be helpful to encourage people to talk more than we often do, and to help people to see that this can be a positive experience in their lives. I was by this time exhausted and my doctor signed me off sick for a month. I went away for a night on my own by the sea.

After a week I returned to work because of shortage of staff and because I was feeling better. My father was also living longer than I had expected. One or two people had mentioned that he was only likely to live two weeks: but it was now four or five weeks. Giving a time to relatives as to how long a person may live can be very harmful, and in my experience, now personally as well as professionally, nearly always is. I remember one client who lived two years longer than she was given by the doctors. Her relatives were continually expecting her to be dead and, indeed, wished her dead nearly all those two years which made life very painful for her. Professional counselling about this could have helped to enable both the positive and the negative feelings to come out.

My husband and I (with our dear dog Rex) spent the last three nights at the hospital. We were in and out during the night and my father asked for us several times. My husband read prayers and psalms with him, and he seemed very peaceful and much comforted. He slept quite a lot but had bouts of consciousness. He was now on regular diamorphine and did not seem to suffer any pain, only discomfort from the leg bag for his urine. He died on a Monday morning at seven o'clock. I was with him. Marcus had set off for work in

Afternoon Tea with Mary and Marcus

London, but as he was about to get on a train, over the loud speaker he heard a message to go to the Station manager's office.

It was the changeover of night and day staff, so they were busy. The last night had not been easy because it was clear to me that the staff, whom I did not know, could not understand the reason why we wanted to be with my father and I almost felt we were in the way.

The only sister in charge of the hospital was called after the death, though I remember it took me some minutes to find anyone to tell them that my father had died, and I found that very lonely. I helped the sister to take off his pyjamas after he had died and watched as he was washed and laid-out. It was very moving. I was grateful that throughout his illness I had been allowed to share his nursing and to participate fully in what was happening. I was glad my brother came to share that day with me. As the day staff came on many friends came in to offer their sympathy, including the consultant and my social work colleagues. I found this very helpful and I was much moved that two consultants, the senior house officer and the ward sister all attended his funeral the following week.

Many of the staff said that the positive attitude of my father towards death had helped them in their care of other dying patients. He insisted on giving presents to those who had cared for him himself, as he thought he would rather do this before he died than leave it for me to do after he had gone.

In the last weeks I became very tired and quite accident prone, especially when I was driving the car. I also felt very vulnerable and found it hard to make decisions. I nearly always wanted to burst into tears at any acts of kindness.

I had an absolute need to pour out all the problems to everyone in a way that I had never felt before, and I had never envisaged that I would really appreciate so much the help that I was given. I was also prepared to listen to advice and to ask for it. In a strange way, at times I found myself being objective as a professional social worker, looking at myself and observing my own reactions with interest. My mother died exactly six months later. Again we were with her as she was dying and when she died. She became more lucid and admitted her fear of dying. I think she basically died from a broken heart at losing her husband, though many times she felt he was just down the garden.

The care and support of the nursing staff - and particularly one who burst into tears as my mother was dying - again proved helpful and supportive. During the six months, I had guilt feelings that I was not looking after my mother myself. As with my father, I wanted the very best for her but not to seem too interfering.

Though all this happened a year ago, I still mourn my parents and I still have vivid, though usually happy, memories of their faces as they died. I remember their long lives much more now and am gradually thinking of all the childhood memories as well as the most recent ones. I have not found that the pain of their loss has diminished, though I know it was inevitable. I am grateful that I was allowed such a positive experience of their deaths as well as their lives.

Looking back I see that the caring was done on a team basis, between the professionals and the relatives, and that each of us had our part to play. It has made me more open in discussions with my own clients and more confident that what I have to offer can be of help.

Several points emerge. First, healthy grieving is a much longer process than is often realised. Effective counselling needs to acknowledge that there is a gap which cannot be filled and that people need to talk months and years after the event, particularly at the time of anniversaries. Recovering cannot take place until this loss is recognised. Second, there is a real gulf between those who have a genuine religious faith, believing that this life is part of a wider whole. Many in the caring services operate with a secular framework. Third, time should be made to be sensitive to patients' real needs, especially those who do not ask. Fourth, I question whether enough is done to mobilise the resources of relatives and visitors in joint caring of patients. The involvement of the professional in expressing emotion is helpful. If this professional is not afraid of emotions it may help others concerned to express theirs.

As Henry Nouwen says in *The Wounded Healer*, if the professional has acknowledged his own pain he can make the experience of weakness a means of strength and offer that experience to others who simply face a bleak suffering they cannot understand.'

* * *

Whenever I revisit this beautifully written article, it moves me to tears.

It is worth noting that George's wish for Rachel to be in Australia when he died was fulfilled; she had a very close relationship with her grandfather, and on the morning of his death she was on a beach north of Sydney with his sisters Grace and Ruby, and Joy—Mary's first cousin—and together they raised a glass in his memory and shared their mourning.

12. Christ Church, Bath

Soon after taking on the directorship of CCJ, Marcus also became an unpaid minister at Christ Church in Bath. The church had an unusual history. Toward the end of the eighteenth century Archdeacon Daubney visited Bath, then a fashionable social hub, and was shocked that the poor people did not go to church. Their excuse was that they could not afford the high pew rents charged by the churches. Archdeacon Daubney, therefore, launched a national appeal for funds to build a new church – it was to be the first not to charge pew rents.

It was a 'proprietary chapel,' which meant that it was not part of the parochial system but controlled by a body of trustees with a 'minister' rather than a vicar or rector. At the time there were a number of such proprietary or 'peculiar' chapels – Westminster Abbey is a 'royal peculiar' – but most of them have now been absorbed into the parish system.

This is what the Archdeacon and Diocese were keen to do with Christ Church: but with its 'Liberal Catholic' tradition the congregation had no wish to be taken over, perhaps 'converted', by the surrounding evangelical parish church. One member of the congregation liked to quote this verse of a hymn:

> *Christian, dost thou see them*
> *On the holy ground,*
> *How the troops of Midian*
> *Prowl and prowl around?*

The hymn continues 'Christian, up and smite them…' but it did not quite come to that. When the Diocese insisted on going ahead with the merger there were so many protests to the Privy Council that the scheme was rejected, and the church continues to thrive. These discussions were going on all the time Marcus was 'minister' there. When the decision to merge was made Marcus, who was in India at the time, had to ring up the Diocesan office to find out what had been decided. No one had the courtesy to let him or the vicar of the neighbouring parish know the result of the so-called Pastoral Committee's deliberations.

Margaret Heath was well aware of the difficulties and she and her husband Sir Mark were, like many others, a great support to Mary and Marcus. Margaret recalls, 'Mark and I moved to Bath in late 1988 and went church tasting. We liked Christ Church best, although at that time your grandparents were in Australia. At the back of my mind I might have heard about him from the late Murray Rogers in Hong Kong. When the Braybrookes returned Marcus visited us at home and we took to him at once. His wide interests, humour, modesty and love of people were very striking. His kindness attracted people who were not easy to the church and he was very patient and tolerant. There is a strong evangelical element in Bath Anglican church life and unfortunately many were opposed to our liberal attitude at Christ Church. Interfaith relationships were not approved and I think Marcus was given a very tough time . . .

'This diocese, once Bishop George Carey, who had made Marcus a Prebendary (or Canon) of Wells Cathedral, had left to become Archbishop, simply did not begin to understand Marcus' world-wide status, ability and wonderful qualities. It was suggested that Christ Church was a 'chapel of ease' to Walcot St Swithin's. We fought and won a battle to prove that, in fact, Christ Church was a proprietary chapel run by a board of Trustees, who appointed the priest in charge. Marcus decided to leave us so that personalities would not be involved in this dispute. There were tears in the congregation when he announced he was off. He and Mary had made life fun for their congregation. We had had entertainment at harvest suppers; a parish weekend (Mary beat me at ping pong, need I say?); visits to other churches and activities which got us together happily. Marcus was officially medically unfit but he did an immense amount of work, backed by Mary. He introduced high-powered visiting preachers and ran a wonderful church.

'When he left he was appointed to the little pilgrim church of St Mary Magdalene. Fortunately for the Braybrookes, the stone which Bath had rejected was warmly welcomed by the then Bishop of Oxford. Oxfordshire's gain was our loss.

'Twice Mary borrowed my former home for parties, which I enjoyed a lot. One was her farewell to Bath magistrates and another for Marcus' local 70th. Mary had a strange added link that as a social worker in Cambridge she had had to appear in court when my mother was on the bench. We both have strong Aussie connections, too. Marcus and Mary have kindly invited me to several of their parties, always very interesting, and I went with a friend to see Marcus getting an award at Lambeth Palace.'

Despite the difficulties Mary and Marcus have happy memories of the years at Christ Church and speak with great affection of many members of the congregation. As Marcus had a full time job at the Council of Christians and Jews, he had very limited time during the week to devote to Christ Church, but was well supported by the Revd Professor Clifford Burrows; his predecessor, Revd Ronald Broakes; and, for a time, by the Very Revd Tom Baker, who had been his Principal at Wells Theological College. Tom lived for some of his retirement in Bath and often came to Christ Church. Three (Lay) Readers, Tom Slade, Sarah Sheppard and Cyril Selmes were also very active. But the 'clerical team' did not dominate. Instead real emphasis was put on developing 'a peoples' ministry.' In his training job Marcus had been keen to encourage lay people to take a far more active role in the leadership of the church. It was an attempt to take seriously St Paul's teaching that the whole congregation is a 'royal priesthood', and to get away from the besetting clericalism of the church and the impression often given that priests are more important than anyone else.

Christ Church gave Marcus a chance to put this into practice. The hope was that each member of the congregation would see that they had a vital contribution to make to the whole community and feel valued because they did so. Without a full time vicar, the congregation trebled in size – partly boosted by Anglican refugees from the many extreme high Catholic and low evangelical churches in Bath.

Most of his clerical brothers were unsympathetic to Marcus' 'modernist' views and very critical of his invitation to a Rabbi and later an Imam to preach at the church. Marcus recalls that at the first chapter meeting he attended the clergy were angrily attacking the radical book of essays, *The Myth of God Incarnate*, edited by John Hick. After a time Marcus asked where they had managed to get copies, as the SPCK bookshop that he rang up said they had not yet got any. It transpired that none of them had actually seen, let alone read, the book! Marcus was also one of the few clergy in Bath willing, in certain cases, to marry divorcees in church, which was against the rules of Synod, but not illegal - thanks to A P Herbert, an M P who insisted that the law of the land, which allowed divorce, was superior to the law of the Church. These rules were not changed until 2002. In his view, it is the couple who make the marriage which the priest blesses – so a 'Blessing Service' instead of a full Wedding makes no sense theologically. He always said at the start of the wedding service that 'The Christian ideal is lifelong marriage, but the Gospel also tells of God's forgiveness. We all fall short, in different ways, of the ideal Christian life.' He found it annoying that clergy who refused to conduct a marriage for divorcees themselves referred couples onto him. He also discovered that a member of the congregation who felt called to be a priest was not even considered because his wife's previous marriage had ended in divorce. Marcus wrote about this to the *Church Times*. His letter generated quite a debate and soon the rule was changed. (At one time those who were illegitimate were not allowed to be ordained.)

Besides an active congregational life, the church was used for lectures and concerts – including some of the Bath Festival concerts which were broadcast by the BBC. One of them was attended by Prince Charles. For a

Afternoon Tea with Mary and Marcus

time the University chaplain Vaughan Roberts and his family made Christ Church their spiritual home and in term time some students came regularly to the church. A number of residential away weekends were arranged at Lee Abbey, Glastonbury, Ammerdown and Brunel Manor, near Torquay, which did much to deepen fellowship among church members. The Ammerdown weekend was at the time when there was much public alarm at the spread of AIDS. A few days before the weekend, the Warden of Ammerdown telephoned Marcus to say that besides the parish group, there would also be 'a gay retreat', led by Marcus' friend Rabbi Lionel Blue, (pictured here) who was well known for his amusing and profound BBC Radio's 'Thoughts for the Day.' When Marcus told this to the people who had booked, only two people withdrew. The rest of the group enjoyed making friends with the other guests at Ammerdown.

If fellow Anglican clergy were difficult, Mary and Marcus made good friends with neighbouring Free Church ministers and took an active part in ecumenical programmes. The highlights were a Good Friday 'Walk of Witness' in the centre of Bath and a Christmas Day lunch, held at Kingswood School. Some three hundred people came, some were homeless, others would have been spending Christmas alone and many people enjoyed helping. The music was of a high standard. Some members of the choir were originally from the West Indies and there were special services on the Independence Days of Jamaica and Barbados.

Bradford-on-Avon

Mary's work at Bradford-on-Avon was particularly rewarding. Wiltshire, at the time, was developing a new scheme to help bridge the gap between health and social services to benefit patients. Politicians today have at last realised that this is a good idea, but now it is to save money. It is a pity they do not ask those who are doing the work. Mary once wrote to congratulate a choir member of a previous church, who became a Cabinet Minister. He replied that it would be good to hear 'her worm's eye view,' but he never asked for it.

Mary, one of the first experimental link workers, was based at the Health Centre and the nearby St Margaret's Surgery. *Link,* the Newspaper for Wessex Health Staff, had an article about Mary's work, with a lovely picture of Dr Richard Snow, one of the GPs, listening attentively to her. Mary told the reporter, 'My work isn't about what I want or what the GP wants but what the person wants. Sometimes this conflicts with what the carers want and there is a lot of compromise and reconciliation involved.' Mary, the report says, worked closely with carers, voluntary agencies and the local hospital and brought an imaginative approach to the work. One example was Mary's use of money from her small budget to buy a freezer for an elderly client to store precooked meals, and this made it possible for her to stay in her own home.

Steve Richards at Mary's farewell in Bradford-on-Avon, 1994.

Jill Tremellen, the Wiltshire facilitator, said, that, 'For a number of patients the scheme has meant the difference between staying in their home rather than going into residential care. It has also broken down barriers between professionals who are now actually working side by side.' When Mary retired from her position with Wiltshire County Council, the Director of Social Services thanked her for her work over so many years and said, 'I am especially grateful for the pioneering work which you have undertaken as a link-worker. I have benefited from your thinking and I am personally very grateful to you for developing link-working.'

One patient wrote to Mary, saying:
'Thank you very much indeed for visiting me, and for staying for such a long time. I was exhausted, and fear that you were, also. For me it was a wonderful meeting, I have never had such a helpful, understanding conversation, ever. I have often been very tired, regularly, in fact, but when you left I felt so pleased and grateful, and, overcome by speaking naturally and not altering my words to try to meet the other person's requirements.

Occasionally, lots of years ago, I would meet someone socially and have some rapport. Since I have been restricted, I have been without true talking, and I am still overcome by meeting you. I wish that I could be looked after by you, but I know that that is not your job; I hope that we will perhaps meet once in a while before your year is up. I look forward to the family support people, and have also put a card in the bookshop window asking someone to take me to Tesco's when they go, and to do the hard bit at the cash desk which I cannot do ... I am regularly in trouble when I shop locally ... Every time I go out alone is a gamble, but, there one is, 'out' is vital to me. I wish Dr. Snow would ask you to see my separated husband, in all the world you would be able to ease him as no one else could.

I hate Christmas, it gets worse every year. There are lots of us nervous wrecks, who dread Christmas most severely. This is supposed only to be a thank you letter. I am most hugely grateful to you, and count myself very fortunate to have had your visit'.

Rachel and Peter's Wedding

A highlight of the time at Christ Church was the wedding of my parents, Rachel and Peter Hobin on June 24th 1989 – within a few days of Mary and Marcus' Silver Wedding. As Peter is a Roman Catholic, he had to get special dispensation to be married at Christ Church. It so happened that the priest, Fr Michael House, was the brother of Marcus' brother-in-law Patrick. They were delighted that Michael was allowed to share in the service.

It was a beautiful day, and the bride was even more beautiful. She was driven to the church from a friend's house in the famous Royal Crescent in a pony and trap accompanied by Jeremy, who gave her away (a most appropriate role for a brother!). At the end of the service, Marcus did a quick change from his surplice to

Afternoon Tea with Mary and Marcus

Morning Dress, so that he could accompany Peter's mother Hilda out of the church. Mary recalls that Rachel looked stunning with her handsome husband Peter beside her, and there were lovely bridesmaids.

Just married – Rachel and Peter on June 24th 1989.

After the service, everyone was offered a drink and some sandwiches. George Bunkin, one of the Church Wardens, besides congratulating the bride and groom, also proposed a toast to Mary and Marcus, in honour of their Silver Wedding. The reception was held at the gorgeous Rockery Gardens in Bath on a very hot summer's day – the owner of the restaurant was dismayed that his profits would be small because most of the guests wanted water not wine. Marcus remembers that Mary looked very beautiful in a lovely blue dress that she had bought in Sydney when they and Rachel were there earlier in the year. My grandmother later wore the same dress at the wedding of my sister Sarah, in 2017.

Peter, who, I am told, made an excellent speech, recalls Marcus saying that 'if Rachel looked after him half as well as her horses, he would be a very lucky man.' Having grown up in a happy household with a family that has included several dear horses over the years, I can attest that my grandfather predicted correctly.

I asked my father recently to share his thoughts about my grandparents. 'My first memories of Mary and Marcus are from a house warming party hosted by Rachel in William Smith Close in Cambridge. Rachel had recently started working as an Occupational Therapist at Addenbrookes Hospital and I was in my final year at

Afternoon Tea with Mary and Marcus

Selwyn College studying Chemical Engineering. I distinctly remember having separate conversations with Mary and Marcus at the party. Both of them were genuinely interested in what I was doing and my background, particularly my Catholicism, Marcus in a gentle and supportive way, Mary in a more challenging, questioning and provocative manner! Retrospectively, I can see that I was in some way being interviewed for suitability as a boyfriend, despite the fact that I think that it was only the second time that I had met Rachel(!). I can imagine that I was "discussed" after the party, but clearly no vetoes were issued as we started dating shortly afterwards.

'I remember Rachel and I being invited to a CCJ reception in London just before we were married, where I met Sigi Sternberg. This was my first encounter with the Jewish community which I found to be very welcoming. More recently, nearly 30 years on, I attended an extremely well attended prestigious fundraising dinner for the Faith and Belief Forum (previously Three Faiths Forum). I was struck by the fact that Marcus was recognised as the last surviving founder of the Forum as Sigi and Sheikh Zaki Badawi had passed away. I found it remarkable how much progress has been made by the Forum which only started in 1997, particularly the way that it is making a real difference to young people, likely to be future leaders, through their ParliaMentor leadership programme. For me it is inspirational on two levels; on the one hand clearly demonstrating that with energy, commitment and teamwork so much has been achieved, yet with the positive interfaith experiences that so many young people have been and are being given it is likely even more remarkable progress will be made in the next 30 years.

'Marcus and Mary (and also Rachel) are quite forward thinking and somewhat impulsive, and often just want to get on with doing something rather than thinking about it. This is quite different to my natural instincts which are to spend significant time thinking and reflecting before making a decision. This made my proposal to Rachel quite challenging as I very much wanted to maintain some element of control (!). I did my thinking and reflection about deciding to ask Rachel to marry me in as much of my own time as possible including spending over an hour in the bath on holiday in Wales before asking her the next day at the top of Snowdon. We chose a ring in Chester and then went to Box where I followed Marcus into the garden shortly after arriving to formally ask for permission to ask for Rachel's hand in marriage, which he gave before quickly checking that I had actually already asked Rachel. Mary was both very surprised and delighted, together with being a little put out that she hadn't seen it coming quite yet (mission accomplished from my perspective!). It was lovely to have Marcus marry us at Christ Church in Bath and then 27 years later for him to marry Sarah and Chris Parsons in Brighton in 2017' – pictured below.

Angina

In 1986, Marcus came home from London with sharp chest pains – the beginning of the heart problems that meant he had to retire from CCJ and full-time ministry in the church. Looking back, Marcus recognises that he had been working too hard – and over taxed his health. CCJ was a stressful job – Terry Waite described it as 'one of the most difficult jobs in the Church of England.' The commuting from Chippenham was tiring (catching a train at 6.45am and back about 7.00p.m. or often much later) as well as caring for a church.

To have his career cut short and to cope with the financial loss, although Marcus received a small clergy disability pension as well as invalidity benefit, was difficult. More than ever the family depended on Mary's hard work and her earnings. Marcus has gone on 'working' but has not been paid for ministerial work since 1988 (except for occasional services) and all his interfaith work has been on a voluntary unpaid basis. Uncertain health, however, Marcus says, 'helped me to rely more fully on God's grace – I often prayed, "God if you want me to do this, you will give me the strength I need."' The illness also gave a certain freedom and Marcus realizes that he would not have been able to do so much interfaith work and writing – or have been so free to say what he most deeply believed. A rabbi friend – also a doctor – said to Marcus soon after his heart problems were diagnosed; 'Don't become an angina cripple.' He hasn't, but he admits this has often meant trying to hide how he was actually feeling – maybe saying 'I feel a bit tired' - when there were chest pains. He was afraid that if he said too much Mary would be even more worried and she and the doctors would try to stop him doing what he wanted to achieve. He says 'I have discovered the truth of God's promise to St Paul, "My grace is sufficient for thee: for my strength is made perfect in weakness."'

For a few years after his retirement from CCJ, Marcus continued as minister to Christ Church. When he left Basil Sheldon, the secretary of the Christ Church Trustees, paid a lovely tribute to Mary 'You have endeared yourself to us all, and this bouquet expresses the affection in which you are held by the congregation and our gratitude for what you have done for Christ Church. It cannot have been easy for you, while having a fulltime occupation, but for seven years you have thrown yourself whole-heartedly into the life of Christ Church.' Basil then expressed his sadness that Marcus, who had doubled the congregation, was leaving. Besides mentioning other qualities Basil said that Marcus 'was an outstanding preacher not afraid of a touch of humour, a carer for his flock, an innovator, and he made services both interesting and enjoyable.'

Magdalene Chapel, Holloway

For the next couple of years Marcus was chaplain of Bath's Magdalene Chapel in Holloway. The origins of the Chapel, which was cared for by Bath Abbey's monks, are obscure. Towards the end of the twelfth century a small hospital for people with leprosy was founded close to the Chapel and maybe it ministered to them. Towards the end of the nineteenth century the Chapel became the responsibility of the Bath Municipal Charities and still is so. The beautiful old chapel had a peaceful atmosphere which encouraged quiet and prayer. It was there, I am told, that I was baptized. From various relations' stories I have built up a picture of my baptism. The overriding memory mentioned is that of my older sister Kathryn throwing a plastic toy cow into the font, and later repeatedly dipping her finger into our mother's wine glass for a taste.

Magdalene Chapel, Holloway, Bath

13. Interfaith Pioneers

It is time now to say a little about Marcus' and Mary's long efforts to encourage friendship between people of many different faiths. If you want to know even more about this, Marcus has written and edited over forty books: all thoughtful, considered and fascinating. He does little to promote his excellent writings - in fact after talks or meetings Mary is far more likely to mention that they are available for purchase. My personal favourites include *The Bridge of Stars: - 365 Prayers, Blessings and Meditations from around the World*; *Beacons of The Light - 100 Holy People who have shaped the history of humanity*; and *Peace in Our Hearts, Peace in Our World - A Practical Interfaith Daily Guide To A Spiritual Way of Life*.

The Interfaith Movement

Marcus' initial involvement in interfaith work was, as we have seen, as an officer of the World Congress of Faiths and then as Director of CCJ. Over the years, he and Mary have had links with many other interfaith organisations across the world. Mentioning them all involves a lot of names, but explains why Marcus has been called 'the Dean of the Interfaith Movement.' He has himself given a good account of this interfaith work in his recent *Faiths Together for the Future: The story of the World Congress of Faiths and the growing global interfaith movement to heal the world*.

Before describing this work, however, let Rabbi Ruth Broyde Sharone introduce this 'Interfaith Couple', when, as she wrote in *The Interfaith Observer*, she had 'High Tea with Marcus and Mary':

'The English landscape rushed by the bus window, lush green hills alternating with roads that twisted and turned through leafy glens. Excitement welled up in me, the possibility of resolving a mystery: Why is the Rev. Dr. Marcus Braybrooke, a retired Anglican parish priest living near Oxford and the author of more than 40 books on interfaith engagement – the acknowledged 'historian' of the interfaith movement – known to so few, even within the interfaith movement itself? . . . Today I was going to tea at the home of Marcus and Mary Braybrooke, hoping to shed some light on the mystery . . . Even at the global conferences, which he often attends, Rev. Braybrooke keeps a low profile. In part, Marcus' natural modesty means he doesn't seek out the limelight. You have to seek him out to find him, and I was about to find him.

When I got to the bus stop where he had promised to meet me, I spotted him immediately – a bespectacled, ruddy-cheeked Englishman, congenial in every manner. Marcus was wearing a tweed jacket, v-neck sweater, and tie, a picture-perfect Oxbridge intellectual straight out of central casting.

At the Braybrooke cottage, Marcus's wife Mary came out to greet me and immediately made me feel at home. Photographs of the family were prominent everywhere in the living room, and their charming caramel-coloured poodle, appropriately called Toffee, sat quietly in Mary's lap during the interview, as well-versed in interfaith etiquette as the rest of the family. Together for nearly 50 years, Mary and Marcus have two children and six granddaughters. She is his interfaith partner, they both emphasized. In fact, Mary was exposed to interfaith prayer services before she met Marcus, as a teenager attending Unitarian interfaith services in her church. "We thought it was the most natural thing to be working together with people of other faiths for justice and peace," she says. "Decades later interfaith services suddenly were considered a novelty," she points out bemusedly. "In the fifties we also studied world religions, but many people today believe that was a much later development."

Marcus traces his interfaith initiation to the sixties, when, after graduating from college, he studied in India with Hindu professors and lived with Hindu families. The year was formative for him, he confesses, especially visiting a leprosy clinic for the poor, run by a Hindu doctor with the help of a Christian from Sri Lanka and a local Muslim. "When I saw in India how religions could come together to help the less fortunate, I was profoundly affected by that interfaith model," he recalled. "I also found it extremely refreshing and unexpected that the Hindus in India spoke about direct experience with God, at a time when 'God is dead' was a catch phrase among Western Christian theologians." As a student, Marcus noted that "the academic student of religions may be content with exterior dialogue." But his mentor, Fr. Murray Rogers, taught that the "exterior dialogue" needed to be accompanied by "interior dialogue" so that listening to people of another faith, observing their spiritual practices and studying their scriptures "should go hand in hand with inner reflection or dialogue with the Lord."

After being exposed for many years to the idea of "respect for the other," the main mantra of interfaith engagement, Marcus developed his own theory called "Mutual Enrichment." In it he claims that respect for the other is not enough. Interfaith engagement at its best, he proposes, leads to "Mutual Irradiation" – an approach reflected in his *Peace in Our Hearts, Peace in Our World.* "Mutual Irradiation." His choice of words and their capitalization point to his belief that something of great import can take place in the interfaith process. Indeed, he suggests that, when interfaith engagement is at its best, cellular changes will occur and the people involved will never be the same.

"Interior dialogue is not a matter of comparing religions or trying to prove the superiority of one's own faith," Marcus underscores. "Mutual Enrichment both deepens and broadens one's faith." He quotes Christian missionary C. F Andrews, a friend of Gandhi and Rabindranath Tagore, who said that through deep contact with other faiths, "Christ has become not less central but more central and universal: not less divine to me, but more so because more universally human."

In recent years he has given special attention to relations with Islam and counts many Muslims as his friends. "If only we could have responded to the terrorist attacks on the Twin Towers and elsewhere with spiritual rather than military force, how different the last decade would have been," he conjectures.

"The violence of those who acted in the name of Allah was so unlike all that I had learned of Islam, from friendship with Muslims, from reading the Qur'an and above all the inspiration of the Sufis, that I continue to find it sad to see Islam so misrepresented in the media," he notes, and tells a story. "Some years ago a Muslim explained to me that the inner conflict within the world of Islam is between those who say 'God is most great' and those who say 'Islam is most great.' There is a struggle for the soul of Islam. So as a Christian I have felt it right to do what I can to help people discover the true Islam. As has been said, the question today is not so much *which* is the true religion - but what is *true* religion? Is religion life-giving or death-bringing?"

Marcus Braybrooke's prose is poetic and lucid as he explores complex subjects with a directness and eloquence that has to be read to be appreciated. In a field where many use quotes for substantiation, Marcus uses them for elucidation and inspiration. He has been profoundly impacted by the people he has met during a lifetime devoted to interfaith activism, and the personal experiences he accumulated, with his wife at his side, have informed his writing as much as his scholarship.

It was time for high tea. We sat down to tea and a table piled high with treats: a walnut cake that Mary had baked for the occasion, as well as chocolate cake, scones, English muffins, butter, and homemade jelly. In short, a sweet, high-caloric bacchanal. It was a typical and colourful English ritual, celebrated for centuries. For me it was the last lap of my treasure hunt. Marcus Braybrooke, an exceedingly humble man of letters, was no longer a mystery to me. An important scholar, chronicler, and a grass roots activist and delightful raconteur all rolled into one, he will undoubtedly continue to enrich the global interfaith community, however many know him by name.'

Afternoon Tea with Mary and Marcus

The Growth of an International Interfaith Movement

But before we continue with the interfaith movement and the Parliaments of Religion, with which we started the book, we need to back-track to earlier gatherings and adventures. In these Mary and Marcus have both shared, and through them made friends with people of many religions in different parts of the world. To encourage the growth of an interfaith movement, they say, depends upon good working relationships with key-workers in these organisations.

The Temple of Understanding

One of the first organisations with which Marcus forged links was the Temple of Understanding. This was the vision of Juliet (Judith) Hollister who hoped that just as the leaders of nations came together for summit meetings, so should religious leaders. The Temple's first 'Summit Conference' was in Calcutta in 1968.

When Marcus was invited in 1970 to the Temple's Second Summit Conference, a practical difficulty was the cost. The conference was at the grand Hotel Intercontinental in Geneva. Marcus' friend Heather McConnell who edited the WCF journal *World Faiths*, asked one of her friends in the hotel trade whether he could get them a special reduced price. 'No hope' was his answer, 'they wouldn't give a discount to Jesus Christ himself.' Nonetheless, Heather wrote a letter to the hotel manager explaining that this young priest wanted to come but could only pay for it by pawning the church candle-sticks. They got in at half price! Even so they went to a nearby café for a croissant and coffee to save money.

The Conference was a remarkable occasion, not least because of a memorable service in St. Pierre Cathedral, which is known as the adopted home church of John Calvin - one of the leaders of the Protestant Reformation - in which people of many faiths offered prayers. (Would Calvin have approved?).

Besides meeting Juliet Hollister, Marcus also met Finley Peter Dunne, who was the Executive Secretary of the Temple. In 1985, he and his wife Evelyn, who was quite frail, visited my grandparents at their home in Box, following the Ammerdown meeting of interfaith organisations, of which more later! He wrote a warm letter thanking them for their wonderful care – 'meeting us at Bath, coping with our luggage, the delightful visit to your home in Box and the great extra delight of visiting Wells Cathedral.' Thanking them for their role at the Ammerdown gathering, he said that Marcus 'should be knighted' and Mary 'should be sanctified.' Sometime before, Mary and Marcus had visited the Dunnes in their home at Kitty Hawk in North Carolina, where the Wright brothers made the first controlled powered airplane flights. The ocean was nearby and Mary was keen to swim, but it was so rough that Peter insisted she stayed on land.

To keep up the link, Mary went to the 1974 Temple of Understanding Summit at Cornell University, travelling with Archbishop George Appleton, former Anglican Archbishop in Jerusalem, and Sir Zafrullah Khan, a former minister in the Pakistan government. The Bath Chronicle in their report noted that 'the couple work together as a husband and wife team promoting interfaith co-operation. The Rev Marcus Braybrooke is staying at home for this conference to look after the couple's young children.' (It was not, as one parishioner thought that Mary had left her husband!). She also spent a few days with Marcus' sister Susan in New York, where the Watergate enquiry was dragging on and there was considerable fear because of the high level of crime. Susan's flat had five locks.

Over the years, Mary and Marcus made good friends with others associated with the Temple, including Jim Morton, who was Dean of the Episcopal Cathedral of St John the Divine in New York, where he asked Marcus to preach on one occasion; Kusumita Pedersen; Alison van Dyk; Professor Seshagiri Rao, who became co-editor with Marcus of *World Faiths Insight* and William Stansmore. Marcus was later to receive a 'Lifetime

Afternoon Tea with Mary and Marcus

Achievement Award' from the Temple in 2010. A special memory was meeting Archbishop Desmond Tutu's daughter, Mpho Tutu – pictured here.

World Conference on Religion for Peace

The Second Assembly of the World Conference on Religions and Peace (WCRP) – now known as 'Religions for Peace' – was another event to which Marcus was invited. It was held at Leuven (Louvain) University in Belgium. He found much of the procedure irksome as resolutions were debated clause by clause. He has three special memories. One was of talking with the Venerable Thich Nhat Hahn, a Vietnamese Buddhist peace-worker, who was to become admired across the world. The second was a visit to the First World War battlefields and the memorial at Ypres. The third was of a visit to Breendonk which had been a concentration camp in the Second World War. There they were shown a punishment cell, so small that a person could not stand upright. On the blue plaster an unknown prisoner had sketched with a finger nail the figure of the victorious Lamb of God (see the Book of Revelation) - an affirmation that goodness is stronger than hatred.

Subsequently, Marcus worked closely with Dr Homer Jack, the first Secretary General of WCRP and with his successors, Dr John Taylor and Dr William Vendley, as well as with members of WCRP (UK), especially Jehangir Sarosh.

The World Council of Churches

In the seventies, the World Council of Churches (WCC) began giving increased attention to the relationship of Christianity and other world religions. This was a very controversial subject as many Christians held that only those who had faith in Jesus Christ would be saved and go to heaven. Others who had responsibility for encouraging dialogue with people of other faiths, especially, Stanley Samartha, John Tayor, Wesley Ariarajah and Hans Ucko, who all became good friends, were helping Christians to recognise God's love is for all people. Marcus was invited as an observer to the World Council of Churches' Assembly in Vancouver in 1983 – staying first for a few days with a very welcoming Canadian family. He especially remembers the worship tent that was the vibrant heart of the gathering and, most of all when at about midnight, Archbishop Desmond Tutu, who had unexpectedly been allowed to leave South Africa, appeared and vividly described the cruelty of *apartheid*.

World Thanksgiving

It was at the WCC gathering that Marcus first met Peter Stewart, who invited him to a 'Thanksgiving Breakfast.' Later, Marcus helped Peter arrange a Thanksgiving gathering at Westminster Abbey and went with him to Northern Ireland. He and Mary also went to Dallas to share in conferences at the World Thanksgiving Centre – mentioned already at the beginning of this book.

My mother remembers from her childhood that there was a popular soap opera on TV called 'Dallas', so if she or Jeremy answered the phone, they would call out, 'It's the man from Dallas.'

Afternoon Tea with Mary and Marcus

I was very pleased to see the centre's chapel on our way to the 2015 Parliament of the World's Religions. I found it to be a very special place, and was delighted to be given a poster by Peter Stewart, whom we visited when we were in Dallas, of the 'Golden Rule' painting by Norman Rockwell. It depicts a group of people of different religions, races and ethnicities, with the caption "Do Unto Other as You Would Have Them Do Unto You". A copy of it had hung in my grandparents' bathroom for as long as I could remember, and I was touched to have been given a copy of my own.

Time in Dallas gave Mary and Marcus the opportunity to visit his half-sister Angela Galloway and her husband Joe Marshall and their sons, Josh and Matt, at their lovely home in Irving. On one occasion, they hosted a party in the Braybrooke's honour – as reported in the Irving Journal. When we stopped on the way to the Salt Lake Parliament of Religions, Marcus was asked to give a lecture at the University of Dallas.

Mary and Angela

The World Day of Prayer at Assisi

Peter and Betty May Stewart, John Taylor and Judith Hollister with Mary and Marcus were among the small group of interfaith leaders invited to the first World Day of Prayer for Peace at Assisi in in October 1986. Major religious leaders, including the Dalai Lama and the Archbishop of Canterbury, joined with the Pope to call for peace, unity, and interreligious understanding. The Pope closed the meeting with the call, 'Let's keep spreading the message of Peace and living the spirit of Assisi.'

As a child, the need to choose favourite things seems important – favourite colours, animals, numbers. I decided early on that Saint Francis of Assisi would be my favourite saint, and although that's probably not the recommended way to interact with the teachings of historical saints, he has remained so. I remember my grandparents giving me a small, beautifully painted ornament, which I still treasure, depicting Saint Francis holding the paw of a large grey wolf. To hear them tell the story of how Francis made peace between local villagers and a creature normally depicted as villainous, but which had long been my favourite animal, was a source of great inspiration to be kind and to love nature.

The World Day of Prayer for Peace began with a welcome by Pope John Paul II at S. Maria del Angeli. Participants then processed to the town of Assisi where faith groups met for their own prayers before assembling to offer their prayers outside the Basilica of St Francis. At the end, olive branches were distributed and all exchanged handshakes or embraces as signs of peace and friendship. According to the programme, the leaders were 'together to pray', whereas, Mary wrote afterwards, the Holy Spirit transformed it into an occasion in which everyone – leaders and people – 'prayed together.'(The distinction is that you can be present while other people pray but still assume that only your prayers will be heard by God.)

Mary also remembers that a Buddhist monk at the evening meal said how the Pope had given him bread and water. He felt as if he had received Holy Communion. On the next day the interfaith representatives met with Cardinal Arinze, the President of the Pontifical Council for Interreligious Dialogue. Mary was impressed that his scarlet socks matched his biretta.

On their way to Assisi, Mary and Marcus had been looked after by followers of the Indian teacher, Sai Baba. On the way back they travelled by train with Peter and Betty May – but suddenly they all realised that they were going in the wrong direction and would miss their plane. As the train drew into the next station they saw there was a train at the opposite platform heading in the right direction – so they hurried out, walked across the railway line and got onto it as it started to move. Marcus says that rumour had it that Peter Stewart was late for a plane so drove onto the runway and stopped just in front as it was preparing to move!

Interfaith Meetings at Ammerdown

Some members of the World Congress of Faiths, which is one of the oldest interfaith organisations, rather resented newer groups. Marcus suggested WCF should not picture the creation of a massive world organisation, like the World Council of Churches, but take as a model the Peace Movement or the Campaign against Land Mines, which was a coalition of nearly 800 organisations.

To try to strengthen the sense that various interfaith organisations were partners, Marcus persuaded WCF to convene a meeting of representatives of international interfaith organisations at the Ammerdown Conference Centre near Bath in April 1985. To emphasise the spiritual nature of the gathering, participants were invited to spend the first hour in silence in the centre's beautiful chapel. The gathering concluded with an interfaith service at Christ Church - the church in Bath, where Marcus was the minister.

In April 1988, a second meeting of international interfaith organisations was held, again at Ammerdown. The main outcome was a call for 'worldwide celebration of the centenary of the World Parliament of Religions.' Marcus was asked to convene a planning body - an *ad hoc* group – which became known as the IIOCC – the 'International Inter-religious Co-ordinating Committee'.

Nothing would have been achieved without the generosity and dedicated hard work of their two good friends David and Celia Storey, who were treasurer and secretary. Marcus had known David at College and they had met on occasions since then. After a meeting in Chichester at which Marcus was asked to speak, David and Celia very quickly became excited by the plans for 1993 and soon found themselves immersed in an enormous amount of work to make it possible. The group had no funds and no budget, but just enough faith. WCF also had its own sub-committee to relate to this work, which often met at the London home of Sheila Wilson.

Afternoon Tea with Mary and Marcus

Australia, WCRP, and India

In 1989, Mary and Marcus, with my mother Rachel, who was taking a break before her wedding in the following summer, set off for Australia. They hoped to strengthen links with the World Conference on Religion and Peace by attending its fifth Assembly in Melbourne. In discussions there it was agreed that Bangalore should be the venue for a joint event to mark the 100th anniversary of the World Parliament of Religions, which had been held in Chicago in 1893. There were also preliminary discussions about establishing an International Interfaith Centre to co-ordinate and research the work that was going on worldwide. It was agreed that Oxford would be a suitable location.

On the final day of the WCRP Assembly participants were bussed to Mornington Beach in time for a sunrise silent vigil at the start of the Third World Day of Prayer for Peace. The figure of St Francis had been brought from the First World Day of Prayer at Assisi and placed at the edge of the sea, where waves gently lapped it and children splashed and played around it. After breakfast, there were prayers from many religions and as the day got hotter the Anglican Bishop of Melbourne asked people to keep their prayers as short as possible and said, 'I expect the Almighty will also be pleased.' Mary, Marcus and Rachel used some of the time in Australia to catch up with other members of the family.

Auntie Ruby and Uncle Stan Batey with Mary

The Brahma Kumaris.

On the way back they stopped in India, with a few days in the beautiful city of Udaipur and a visit to the Brahma Kumaris World Spiritual University at Mt Abu – they had already worked with the BKs for several years in the UK. My grandparents recall that 'Rachel was so attractive to young Indians' that they had to keep a watchful eye to ensure there was not another 'Jewel in the Crown' incident, so when a waiter at the hotel invited Rachel to climb a nearby tower and in the words of an old song – 'Mother (and Dad) came too.'

Mt Abu, in Gujarat, is a beautiful hill station, set around a lake – a favourite place for honey-moons. The road twists and turns up the mountain. Quite soon the door of the bus fell off and for the rest of the journey two young men held it shut. Mary and Marcus had already worked with Brahma Kumaris (BKs) during the 'One Million Minutes of Peace' campaign. The focus of the BKs' work is teaching meditation and the value of silence. A special place for meditation is Baba's rock – the founder of the movement, Dada Lekhraj Kripalani, who later took the name Brahma Baba. In the evening one can watch the sunset over the mountains of bordering Pakistan. Rachel shared a room with Lilian Carpenter – whose husband was Dean of Westminster and President of WCF, both of whom became great friends.

There were many retreats and meetings that Mary went to at the Global Retreat Centre. Before the start of one of them, Mary and Marcus invited the group to their home for tea. One of the guests was the Anglican Archbishop of Cape Town, the Most Revd Dr Thabo Cecil Makgoba, who signed their visitors' book and afterwards he wrote to thank them 'immensely for the hospitality and the great time I had with you. I congratulate you on getting together such a powerful but humble group of people for reflection and dialogue.'

Date	Name	Address	Comments
26 July 2011	+Thabo CapeTown	20 Bishopscourt Cape Town 7708	Lovely company + delicious eats, thanks
7/26/11	Chung Ok Lee	431 East 57 St New York NY 10022	Beautiful to get together informally
24/7/11	Liz Corrigan	BKWSU London	Lovely start to the retreat
25/7/11	John + Verdy Pritchard		

International Association for Religious Freedom.

When Marcus first joined the World Congress of Faiths many leading members were Unitarians, who had close links with the International Association for Religious Freedom, which was founded a few years after the 1893 World Parliament of Religions. The first IARF Congress that he attended was in Holland in July 1981 – and over lapped with the wedding of Charles and Diana. He was joined there by Jeremy, although as already mentioned, the Customs Officers in Holland had hesitations about admitting an unaccompanied 15 year-old, who had little money with him. IARF was very supportive of efforts to bring interfaith organisations together and Marcus worked closely with Diether Gehrmann, and later with Bob Traer.

After one meeting in Frankfurt, as he waited for his plane at the airport, his name was called over the loud-speaker. He was told to ring the IARF office, and was then given the bad news that Mary had been hurt in a car accident, which has already been described. IARF had no more details. Marcus recalls, 'I could not get hold of any of the family before my flight was "closing."' He remembers the desperate hurry to get through immigration and catch the bus back to Oxford – no mobile phones then. Thankfully, the accident was not life-threatening, though it was bad enough.

Preparing for Sarva-Dharma-Sammelana

After all the preparations for and excitement of Rachel and Peter's wedding and their own silver wedding, Marcus' attention focused on preparations for 1993, 'The year of interreligious Understanding and Co-operation.' So that he could focus on this, in 1991 he resigned as Editor of *World Faiths*. Revd Dr Clinton Bennett, who became acting editor, wrote a generous tribute to Marcus, whom he called 'Interfaith Man,' who had built up a network of friends throughout the world who greatly value his insight, his deep commitment to his own faith and who shared his vision of a better future for the whole creation. 'It was this vision,' he added, 'which helped to inspire the decision by four international interfaith organisations to designate the centenary of the World Parliament of Religions as "The Year of Interreligious Understanding and Co-operation."' Clinton then quoted what Marcus himself had written about his hopes for the year: "Many people believe that the survival of life on this planet depends upon our realizing our oneness. For a just and peaceful world, we must replace competition with co-operation. We can only tackle the problems of war, poverty, homelessness and the environment if we think and act on a global scale.

'Awareness of ecological issues, together with the sad and sordid events we have just witnessed in the Gulf - the result of nothing other than greed (on both sides of the conflict) - again remind us that the human race must develop better ways of reconciling its differences. If religions, most of which cherish peace, and seek to create human societies in which the needs but not the greed of all are adequately met cannot contribute to the process of making peace a reality, they should declare themselves irrelevant and archaic.

The resolution of rival truth claims and the pursuit of theological debate may very well be important in eternal terms but if, whilst we argue about the nature of Revelation or about the character or existence of God, people are killed or maimed, made homeless or starve to death, God must weep as we fail to live by the creeds we preach. The year 1993 will offer us creative opportunities to practise what we preach, both to celebrate what the interfaith movement has achieved since 1893 and also to "renew our efforts to build a better world."'

Preparing for 1993

Preparations for 'Year of Inter-religious Understanding and Co-operation' involved writing letters and articles and helping to plan events in Britain and the joint gathering in Bangalore, which was named Sarva Dharma Sammelana – a Sanskrit title meaning 'people of faith coming together.' Several meetings of the planning committee (IIOC) were held at the welcoming home in Chichester of David and Celia Storey. After another meeting in New York, hosted by Fr. Luis Dolan, a small group, including Marcus, went to see the Secretary General of the UN to ask for his support. He replied, 'Of course, I give you my full support – but I can say nothing.' This was because of the Communist block's opposition to any religious programs at the UN. By the start of the new Millennium, the UN was able to host a meeting of religious leaders in the General Assembly Hall of the UN building, although Marcus, who attended as an observer, felt many participants' priority was to affirm their own importance.

'Trying to get the four international organisations – each with their own agendas – as well as the local supporters to work together for the event in Bangalore was not easy,' Marcus says. 'Another difficulty was that many interfaith workers in South India were champions of the marginalised *dalits* and had no wish to dialogue with the high-caste Hindus who were leaders of some of the interfaith organisations. The most serious difficulty was the outbreak early in 1993 of communal violence between Hindus and Muslims. There was a real question whether it was safe to go ahead and whether anyone would risk coming. In February, at a key meeting in Bangalore, our local organiser gave the Japanese group a tour of the beauties of the garden-city – and soon afterwards we heard that the Japanese would come.' Later, one Japanese lady, who had been afraid to travel to India because of communal troubles, said Sarva-Dharma-Sammelana was 'a foretaste of paradise, with the blue skies, beautiful flowers, butterflies and everywhere smiling faces.'

Jopie Boeke, Celia Storey, with Mary and Marcus at the opening of Sarva Dharma Sammelana

Afternoon Tea with Mary and Marcus

Sarva-Dharma-Sammelana

Sarva-Dharma-Sammelana was a gathering of six hundred people, of many faiths and from many countries, at the Ashok Hotel in Bangalore. There is a full record in *Visions of an Interfaith,* edited by David Storey.

When Marcus, Mary and Jeremy arrived in Bangalore, they found that nothing had been done to tell the media. Fr Roger Lesser who had served in India for many years, however, had good contacts. In less than 48 hours it was arranged for the opening ceremony to be shown on All-India TV, but having 'the press office,' Marcus says, 'in our bedroom made it hard to take a siesta. And even to go to the loo!'

The primary purpose of Sarva Dharma Sammelana was to bring together interfaith activists to see how they could be more effective, and the programme was shaped around discussions rather than set speeches, which was not the Indian pattern. When Celia and Marcus were on a preparatory visit to Bangalore, they suddenly decided that the governor of Andra Pradesh should be invited. They went and joined the crowd outside his office and got to speak to him. At first he was hesitant when they talked about 'religion' – the cause of communal tension – but when they mentioned 'spiritual,' his face lit up and he agreed to come to the opening ceremony. As the dignitaries were about to process in, Marcus realised that the Governor's attendants were surprised that he was not the first to enter – so Marcus said to the Governor 'at state services in Britain, the Queen always comes in last.' At the ceremony the Governor kindly invited everyone to a reception at Raj Bhavan – which evoked memories of life under the Raj.

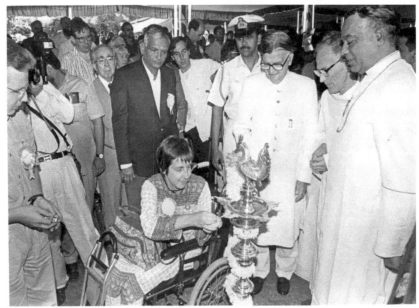
Cherry Gould lighting the lamp at the Opening Ceremony

Equally delicate was who to invite onto the platform to light the lamp at the opening ceremony. Celia had visited one swami who said he would only come if he was the only person on the dais. Late on the evening before it all started, Marcus decided to ask their friend Cherry Gould, who was in a wheel chair, to be the first to light it. She was wheeled in by Jeremy Braybrooke and again tensions dissolved.

The whole conference was set in a context of prayer and meditation. Indeed in the hotel garden, where many events took place, there was a tree under which Gandhi used regularly to spend time in meditation when he was in Bangalore. The conference began with a joyful and prayerful Opening Ceremony. There were three programmes; one involved intensive small group work; the second consisted of visits to a large number of local religious centres; and in the third programme, there were seven workshops on key issues, such as 'Education for Understanding' or 'Service and Solidarity'. In the evening there were cultural programmes, some hosted by local communities. These allowed many of the citizens of Bangalore to share in Sarva-Dharma-Sammelana. The final ceremony, arranged by the younger participants, was also an uplifting occasion and Marcus was given a white silk scarf, sent by the Dalai Lama. 'My own lasting memory,' Marcus says, 'was of the warmth of the friendships and the sheer enjoyment of the rich variety of people all of whom were committed to working for a happier world.'

Vivekanda's Rock and Delhi

Just before the Bangalore event, a gathering was arranged at Kanyakumari, by the World Fellowship of Inter-Religious Councils, in which a good friend, Fr Albert Nambiaparambil, had played a leading part for many years. The rock, at the southernmost point of the Indian subcontinent is where Swami Vivekanada, a prominent figure at the 1893 World Parliament of Religions, dedicated his life to 'My God, the poor of every land.' My grandparents travelled with others on the ferry to the Rock. It was crowded and hot and Mary almost fainted. Her doctor son, Jeremy, came to the rescue and tried to get her back as soon as possible to the hostel where they were staying. A Baha'i cleared the crowd aside so that she could be the first to get onto the ferry. The taxi driver was a Muslim. Then about an hour later, there was a knock on the door and a Parsi lady, who was a friend, was there, holding a large brown envelope. 'I think you left this on the rock, do you need it?' In the envelope were their tickets, passports and traveller's cheques. It was, Mary says, 'a wonderful example of human kindness and caring.'

From Bangalore, Mary, Marcus and Jeremy headed to Delhi and, besides a visit to Gobind Sadan arranged by Mary Pat Fisher, there was a Day Centennial Meeting in Delhi at which Dr Karan Singh, a former member of the Indian government and Chairman of the Temple of Understanding, presided. The highlight was a speech from Shri P V Narasimha Rao, the Prime Minister of India, who stressed that India's constitution gave equal respect to all faiths. Next day Marcus was pictured with the Prime Minister on the front page of several Indian newspapers.

Tokyo

That evening, Mary and Marcus flew on to Japan. 'There was a typhoon brewing and the plane lurched about,' Mary says. 'Marcus slept through it undisturbed, while a delightful Indian doctor kept me company. When we got to Tokyo everything was flooded, although in the sunshine, the water soon dried up.' On the following day, Marcus – the only person from outside Japan to do so - was asked to speak at a major Japanese gathering. The Abbot of a monastery showed him the 1893 conference badge given to one of his predecessors.

They have many other memories of Japan. Mary and Marcus with members of IARF were invited to a ceremony at the Ise Grand Shrine, for which special clothing (pictured here) was required. In the pilgrims' hostel men and women – even if married - were in separate dormitories. When Mary asked if she could come and say goodnight to her husband, the other men asked if she wanted them to leave, but she relayed that a good-night kiss does not have to be private. With some of the 'rather large ladies from America', Mary had a Japanese hot bath. This involved completely undressing and having a shower designed for much smaller ladies than Mary and her companions. Unbeknown to the ladies, Marcus noticed quite a number of Japanese lads outside the building – hoping perhaps for a live peep-show.

Mary and Marcus also travelled on a Japanese Bullet Train to the Tsubaki Grand Shrine. When an attendant noticed water was dripping onto the floor – it was from a bottle in their luggage on the overhead rack – they said nothing. (Their excuse was that they did not speak Japanese!).

The brief visit to the beautiful Tsubaki shrine was memorable. The Tsubaki Grand Shrine is one of the most important Shinto shrines in Japan, although it has never been associated with State Shintoism, which was a militaristic perversion. Indeed, the priest was in hiding throughout the Second World War. His son, Yukitaka Yamamoto, about whom Marcus has written in *Beacons of The Light*, was conscripted into the army, and having seen the full horror of war, dedicated himself to work for peace, especially in his leading role in IARF. Revd Nikkyo Niwano, the founder of Rissho Kosei kai, was also a leading member of IARF. Nikkyo Niwano spoke for Yukitaka Yamamoto and other Japanese religious leaders, when he wrote, 'A world of great harmony will appear when all nations, all races, and all classes come to live in accordance with one truth, so that discrimination among them vanishes, discord and fighting do not occur, and all people work joyfully, enjoy their lives, and promote culture'.

Yukitaka Yamamoto especially valued the discipline of *misogi harai*, or water purification. He revived the full ritual in 1959 and practised it on a regular basis. For the *misogi*, a person puts on a loin cloth and a headband. After exercises to shake up the soul and other rituals of purification, one enters the waterfall to commune with the *kami* (spirits). One then takes the weight of the water on the back of the neck, allowing it to cover the body and wash away impurities. At the same time the bather shouts out 'Purify my soul – wash my soul – purify the six elements of existence.'

When Mary and Marcus visited the Tsubaki Grand Shrine, they were privileged to be invited to take part in the *misogi* purification. Mary, who substituted Christian prayers, particularly remembers the sense of oneness with Nature that she experienced. Marcus, who had not been well earlier in the day, was more concerned with surviving the cold water.

Chicago

It was then on to Chicago for the World Parliament of Religions. As in 1893 participants again stayed in the Palmer House hotel. A lot of time was spent waiting for the dilatory arrival of the elevators (or lifts) which were presumably also one hundred years old. Still, the waiting was a good time for meeting new people and Marcus had his first close encounter (literally) with a 'White Witch' in the jam-packed lift!

For Mary and Marcus, tired after their journey, the happy chaos of the Parliament, which was already in full swing, was overwhelming. Ma Jaya Sati Bhagavati, who founded the Kashi ashram and who had vigorously opposed the prejudice endured by many sufferers from AIDS, vividly described the scene: 'At first, it was like a huge playground, I put my hands together and greeted everyone I saw. To my happy surprise they all answered in their own way, some bowing, some smiling in return…. The grand lobby, stately and elegant, became a garden of rare and exotic flowers, the diaphanous robes and gowns blossoming upon satin sofas. The robes and gowns were not like mine. The accents, expressions, and speech patterns were foreign. The ideologies, theologies, and spiritual beliefs had little in common. But paradoxically, as the children at the plenary sang, "We are one family."' Mary and Marcus were soon surrounded by friends – no doubt, desperately trying to remember where they had met them.

Emphasis on the many personal encounters should not hide the carefully planned programme, energized and inspired by Dr Daniel Gómez-Ibáñez. For three afternoons, Marcus was invited to the Assembly of religious and spiritual leaders, who met in what is now the Art Hall, which had been used for the 1893 Parliament. Assembly members sat at tables of seven or eight, presided over by a facilitator. One distinguished leader whispered to Marcus that 'It's like being back at junior school.' He was subsequently asked 'to hold court somewhere else' because so many of his friends came over to greet him and interrupted the deliberations.

Discussions at the Assembly focused on what became known as 'A Declaration Toward A Global Ethic,' which was an attempt to highlight the moral values shared by the world religions and a call to people everywhere to promote: a culture of non-violence and respect for life; a culture of solidarity and a just economic order; a culture of tolerance and a life of truthfulness; and a culture of equal rights and partnership between men and women. A topic also gaining traction in more recent Parliament of Religions has been about commitment to respect for the environment. It is interesting that the Declaration was not a message from leaders telling other people what they should do, but a document that they signed to indicate their personal commitment. The signatories invited 'all people, whether religious or not, to make the same commitment.' Attempts have been made to show that these are not just personal commitments, but should also apply to the 'Guiding Institutions' – for example: 'Are politicians and the media all committed to promoting a 'culture of tolerance and a life of truthfulness'? The Declaration has occasioned a lot of subsequent discussion. With Peggy Morgan, Marcus edited a work book, *Testing the Global Ethic*, for use by teachers. The Prime Minister, Tony Blair, faxed a message of support, which was read at the launch of the book.

The Closing Plenary of the Parliament was an open-air event, on a warm, late summer afternoon in Grant Park, and was attended by nearly 30,000 people. It was preceded by an afternoon of music. The final session was delayed for nearly an hour waiting for the arrival of the Dalai Lama, during which Marcus, who was one of those invited to offer a prayer, sat next to Cardinal Bernadin. My grandparents recall that 'he was a special person'. Soon after the Parliament, he was diagnosed with cancer. At almost the same time he was accused of sexual interference with a young seminarian – soon a headline story in the American press. Cardinal Bernadin, after the man had admitted the accusation was false, went to see and forgive him. On a subsequent visit to the USA, when Marcus was staying at a monastic guest-house, the little book that the Cardinal wrote just before he died was there by Marcus' bedside. It is a book he still treasures. It was a memorable final ceremony and Mary, with their good friend Hal French, happily joined in the dancing with which it concluded, as she waited for Marcus to emerge from back stage. It was then back to Box for a few days before the move to Marsh Baldon. Before we follow them there, it needs saying that they were also fully involved in special events in Britain.

1993 in Britain

The first task was to make people aware of the year. To many, it was a surprise to learn that the interfaith movement was a hundred years old. Marcus' history of the interfaith movement, *Pilgrimage of Hope* - published in February 1992 in Britain and the USA - provided a solid historical account of what had happened and had been achieved. He also prepared a simple study guide which became quite popular and - a rare event for WCF - made a profit. There was some national publicity. *The Independent* had a series of articles on inter-religious relations and the year was mentioned by some speakers on BBC Radio's 'Thought for the Day'. In the autumn of 1993, BBC 1 showed an excellent series called 'Faith to Faith' - the first programme focused on the Chicago Parliament.

There were a lot of local events and Mary and Marcus were often asked to speak at them. Yet, although the emphasis of the year was on local activity, a major national launch was held to create public awareness of the Year and to encourage and inspire those planning local events. The planning committee, chaired by Lord Ennals, was itself an example of inter-religious co-operation. Hardly anyone missed any meetings and they were remarkably harmonious. Marcus has written a full account, in *Faiths Together for the Future,* of the launch, which was held at The Brahma Kumaris' Global Co-operation House in London on January 27th, 1993. It was a day-long event in three parts. The morning was fairly formal; the afternoon was spent in

Afternoon Tea with Mary and Marcus

workshops and the evening was a cultural celebration. Speakers in the morning included Bishop Trevor Huddleston, known for his long campaign against apartheid, and Edgar D Mitchell, the Apollo XIV Astronaut, who spoke movingly of the sense of the oneness, beauty and fragility of planet Earth as seen from space. That image had been shown at the start of the proceedings. To create a link with the 1993 Parliament, a lively dramatisation of the 1893 Parliament was presented by Jane Lapotaire, Clarke Peters and Robin Ramsay. At the end of the morning, children from the local Barham Junior School carried in a great globe, but on a stretcher - the world was dying and required urgent care. As the children started to rescue the world they sang, led by Marneta Viegas, Michael Jackson's 'Heal the World', while an enormous 'One World Quilt of Unity', made by a group in Milton Keynes, was raised as a backdrop to the stage. The morning was punctuated by the Water Ceremony. On the stage, there was a fountain. Two members of each faith were asked together to bring a gift of water and to say a prayer. For some the water came from a special source. The Christians brought water from the river Jordan, the Hindus from the river Ganges, the Muslims from Zamzam. Some of the prayers specifically related to water. The Christian prayer was from the Roman Catholic baptism service. From the Qur'an there was a verse about God making all things from water. Because of suspicions that interfaith was really a new amalgamated faith, some care was taken with explaining the significance of the ceremony. The programme said: 'Each religion has treasures to share with all people. In the ceremony, representatives of each World Faith will say a prayer and offer its treasures in the form of water. The water may symbolise the cleansing of the scars of conflict, the bringing of refreshment to the thirsty or the renewal of hope for a just and peaceful world where nature's bounty is valued and not polluted. The mingling of the waters symbolises how from their own rich and diverse sources faiths can come together in the service of humanity.'

The evening, introduced by Clarke Peters, included moving readings by Hayley Mills and by John Cleese. Tibetan children from the Pestalozzi Children's Village and other children sang and danced. Late in the evening Sheila Chandra sang 'Sacred Stones', which blended in a wonderful and moving way Eastern and Western traditions of sacred music. It was a fitting climax to the day. Mary, Marcus and Jeremy then had the long drive back to Box, although they had been further delayed by Marcus being interviewed for TV. The day served its purpose. Over eight hundred people participated on a working day: many of whom were later to arrange local events. Some had travelled from Scotland and Wales. Some religious leaders had come from the South of France. To make sure the year did not just peter out, a Service of Thanksgiving and Rededication was held in the West London Synagogue. The service included a sermon by Bishop Tom Butler, then Bishop of Leicester, and a reading of the 'Declaration Towards a Global Ethic.'

Subsequent Parliaments of the World's Religions.

Mary and Marcus have vivid memories of all the subsequent meetings of the Parliament, including the Salt Lake City one, which I mentioned at the beginning. There is not space to describe them in detail, but at the second Parliament in Cape Town in 1999, Mary and Marcus specially remember also the visit to Robben Island where Nelson Mandela was held prisoner for so long, and a tour of one of the townships. Subsequent Parliaments have been held in Barcelona, Melbourne, Salt Lake City (as you know!) and Toronto.

In addition to being a very important year for interfaith, 1993 was also the year of my birth. I am pictured here, at the family home in Farndon disagreeing with my grandmother!

14. The Baldons and Nuneham Courtenay

Almost immediately on their return from their world tour, Mary and Marcus moved to their new home in Marsh Baldon. So now it was unpacking, beginning to get the garden in order, starting work in a new parish and trying to make the dream of an International Interfaith Centre, which had been discussed in Bangalore and Chicago, a reality. Mary, at first, during the week stayed near Bath, as mistakenly, she thought she was too old to get another job. Marcus approached the Bishop of Oxford, Richard Harries, whom he knew well because of their shared interest in Christian-Jewish dialogue, to ask if there was 'a house for duty' position - whereby a priest is provided with a house but no stipend (pay) in return for part-time care of a small parish – near to Oxford. Richard said that such an arrangement might meet the needs of the Baldons – one of the parishes in the Dorchester-on-Thames team ministry - where there was a vacancy. The Rectory needed quite a lot of work. The Diocese agreed to some improvements, although Mary and Marcus themselves paid for most of them, as they hoped many visitors from around the world would come and stay. Sadly, the large garden had been abandoned during the inter-regnum and taken over by a fine crop of nettles, but it was quickly put in order – Marcus having bought a ride-on lawn mower. In due course Rectory fetes were held there and part of the 'glebe' was fenced off for Rachel's pony. The house became a warm and welcoming home both to parishioners and my sisters' and I have special memories of time spent there.

I am on the left, with Kathryn in the middle, Sarah on right, with baby Anna in the middle

My younger sister Sarah, for example, says, 'Staying with my grandparents has always been wonderful, whether as a child or more recently, whilst working late shifts and early shifts, when I had the offer of a nearby bed and great company. As a child, I discovered that Grandpa made brilliant hot chocolate and grew the best spinach, which he would always dish up for me with butter when I came to stay. Grandma, I soon found out, always knew where the snacks were. I also remember how warm the bathroom was (because to them nothing is worse than being cold when getting out of the bath!) and Grandma repeatedly telling me to make sure I dried myself properly – especially under my arms. Although I don't know what adverse effects I thought would occur should I not dry myself suitably, this advice obviously stuck with me, as my husband recently pointed out when I give him the same advice when he gets out of the shower!'

Afternoon Tea with Mary and Marcus

The Parish

Mary and Marcus have many happy memories of their eleven years in the Baldons and Nuneham Courtenay and the kindness of so many people in the villages. Marsh Baldon clusters round a very large green. Toot Baldon is more scattered and Nuneham Courtenay cottages are either side of a main road. The countryside is beautiful and it is a constant surprise that the villages are only a few miles from the centre of Oxford. There are old churches in both Marsh and Toot Baldon; the nineteenth century church in Nuneham Courtenay has been closed for a while but there is a chapel at Nuneham Park, which is in care of the Churches Preservation Trust. At the same time that Mary and Marcus moved to the villages, the Brahma Kumaris, whom they knew well, established the Global Retreat Centre at Nuneham Park.

Despite their other commitments, they both gave a lot of time to village life. Besides the usual services, there was a regular monthly fellowship to discuss current issues, a contemplative group, healing services and the NB (Nuneham/Baldons) group for older people. They were wonderfully supported by the churchwardens, Hugh Sandilands and Dr Ron Hewitt and their wives, Veronica and Sonia, and by Graham and Sonia Hobbins, Peter and Nicola Barclay-Watt and Jennifer Morton and too many others for me to name them all.

The NB Group

Mary and Marcus made many friends in the villages. Many people appreciated their ministry. Sheila Barrett wrote to me, saying, 'Marcus' and Mary's coming to the village of Marsh Baldon made a huge difference to me. Prior to their arrival I had approached the local vicar when my daughter was planning her wedding. Although I had moved to Nuneham Courtenay after she had left home she still wanted to marry in my local church. The vicar refused. I felt that I had let my daughter down. Thank goodness for Marcus, who is such an open, warm and welcoming man. My daughter had a wonderful wedding in Toot Baldon. The evening of the rehearsal the village had a power cut but when we arrived at the church it was alight with candles that Marcus had lit. It was truly beautiful.

Afternoon Tea with Mary and Marcus

'The first time I met Marcus was when my granddaughter asked if she could be baptised. On the way to our appointment Lauren asked "do you think he will be a kind man Nana?" When we arrived at the door, the first thing I saw was their Welcome sign, and very welcome we were made to feel. We both agreed on the way home that Marcus was, indeed, a very kind man. The encouragement and belief he had in Lauren played a very important part in Lauren's confidence and I will always be extremely grateful and feel blessed that he came to Marsh Baldon when we needed him. Mary too has been a good friend and a great support and we usually go together to the local book-club.'

To Mary and Marcus' delight, quite soon after their own move, Rachel and Peter moved from Cheshire to Harwell – less than half an hour away. They have many happy memories of visits to Farndon to see Peter and Rachel and their growing family, Kathryn, Helen (myself), Sarah and Anna, but were glad to be spared the long journey. My father Peter has said, 'Bringing up four very young children was both physically demanding and tiring as well as very rewarding. Marcus and Mary were so supportive in very many ways. They gave us breaks as a couple to recharge our batteries. They invited us all to join them on time-share holidays to Spain and Torquay. They looked after the other girls when Rachel and I had to concentrate on Sarah when she had a kidney operation at the age of 2 and when Anna was born 2 months premature. When Helen was nearly two, she was significantly underweight. As the symptoms were confusing the paediatrician Marcus researched the symptoms and correctly identified the cause (drinking too much apple juice!). They have always been incredibly generous and full of love.'

Mary and Marcus were also delighted when Jeremy and Amanda moved to the Baldons. Jeremy was specialising in cancer treatment at the Churchill Hospital in Oxford. At first they lived in Marsh Baldon, but later moved to an older house in Toot Baldon, where Lizzie - the first baby of the new millennium to be born in the village – and Christina (in 2002.) were born.

They were married at Toot Baldon church on the 30th of August 1997. Bob Fyffe, who had been Youth Chaplain when the family lived in Wells, shared in the beautiful service, which included communion. The reception was held at the Village Hall, which Amanda had made very attractive.

Amanda and Jeremy on their wedding day

My grandparents were glad for Jeremy when he became a consultant at the Bristol Royal Infirmary (but sorry to bid the family farewell). At least they moved to Somerset - an area they know so well first to Blagdon and then to East Horrington, near Wells. Jeremy, now lead oncologist at Bristol Royal Infirmary, is also doing research at Oxford and is on the Nice Committee.

For over a year Mary continued working in Bath – coming for weekends and, occasionally, mid-week to the Baldons. Various friends in Somerset welcomed her to stay with them. When a social work job was advertised in Oxfordshire, Mary was convinced that, because of her age at fifty-nine, she would not get it – but was persuaded to apply. Sylvia Kenyon, who became a great friend and went on some of their tours, was working at the Churchill Hospital. She says that when Mary enquired about a job, she said, 'I'm rather old.' Sylvia replied, 'So am I.' Mary was offered two jobs and continued working until 2009. It took longer for her to be transferred to the Oxford bench of magistrates.

Lizzie and Christina in the Baldons, before they moved to the West country

Mary was a regular member of the Baldon's Book Club (whilst simultaneously belonging to the Oxford and the Clifton Hampden Book Clubs!) and continues to belong to it after the move to Clifton Hampden.

Lesley Schillinger, a nearby neighbour, says that Mary, 'who was hugely loved by my whole family, always had something insightful to add – sometimes naughty (we got up to all sorts!), sometimes moving. She is always inspirational'. Lesley also has a lovely story about Marcus, who asked her seven year old son Bruno to read in church. He said yes, but then had second thoughts. 'I told him to tell Marcus that he was just too shy to do it. Bruno looked at me in astonishment and said, "no, Mummy, - who could possibly say 'no' to Marcus?" He did the reading and enjoyed it, but best of all he didn't have to disappoint Marcus.'

Mary as the fairy Godmother

Ron Hewitt and Mary in costume.

Mary was also a star in the Baldon Players' plays and pantomimes, often acting alongside Ron Hewitt. I have any fond memories of helping her to learn the lines by reading out all the other parts, while she peeled us both clementines. She has always made every role she's taken memorable, from when she played a posh and fusty patriotic wife—who held out an umbrella and cried out dramatically "We are British!" in *The Boyfriend*, to when she played the much more comforting role of the fairy Godmother in *Jack and the Beanstalk*. Sarah and I also joined in as fairy dancers for that pantomime, though I remember worrying that a couple of verrucas on my toes would fall off into the feet of my tights during the performance. I recall how loudly the audience laughed when my Grandmother magically reappeared multiple times during one scene and eventually gave an exasperated sigh: 'I don't know whether I am coming or going'

The Millennium.

There was a real sense of optimism at the start of the new Millennium. Tony Blair said, 'What struck me at the various events was this real sense of confidence and optimism. You just want to bottle it and keep it.' It is now almost impossible, after 9/11, the wars in Iraq and elsewhere, the financial crisis of 2009, and now Brexit arguments, to begin to recall the sense of hope as the Millennium approached. There was a real sense that the world was becoming more peaceful and caring, both for the poor and the environment.

At first, government plans had little place for religion. One cabinet minister, reputedly, said, "What's the Millennium got to do with religion?" Church leaders were quick to say that there was a strong connection: but how to express this in a way that was sensitive to the growing size of other faith communities? After much discussion it was agreed that the Millennium Dome should have a faith zone, which proved to be rather beautiful, with displays about the world religions and a beautiful circular space for meditation – an oasis of peace amidst all the activity in the Dome. A group of advisors from different faiths assisted those responsible for imagining and planning the faith zone, but Archbishop George Carey suggested to the planners that Marcus should be an unofficial advisor. As a result Marcus was offered tickets for the opening, which he attended with Mary, Jeremy and Amanda. As the arrangements for the opening were very muddled and some people were not sent their admission tickets in time, everyone was offered a free return visit – in fact Mary and Marcus went back a couple of times with members of the family. When they arrived at the Dome, like everyone else, they were rather lost, but soon met Peter Gabriel - a friend from Swainswick days - who had composed some of the music. When they took their seats for the Opening Ceremony, they found they were sitting next to the section where the Queen and members of the Royal

Afternoon Tea with Mary and Marcus

Family were seated, as well as Tony and Cherie Blair. Three days later, there was a beautiful interfaith ceremony in the House of Lords, to which Mary and Marcus were invited and at which Tony Blair spoke. There were also local celebrations, and as mentioned Lizzie, the first baby of the new millennium to be born in the Baldons, led the local procession.

All too soon, the horror of the attack on the Twin Towers changed everything. In his book, *A Heart for the World,* Marcus quotes some of the religious figures who deplored the US government's response to 9/11. The Dalai Lama said, 'If we could love even those who have attacked us . . . we would become spiritual activists.' Archbishop Rowan Williams said, 'If we act in the same way as our enemies, we imprison ourselves in their anger and evil and we fail to show our belief in the living God, who always requires of us justice and goodness.' Incidentally, the distinguished theologian Hans Küng in his Foreword spoke of Marcus as 'a witness of our times,' noting that the 'book is especially precious in a time when many people tend to despair.'

The Kidney Unit

Not only was Mary young enough still to get a new job – she worked for another nineteen years. From 1994 to 2000, she was employed by Oxfordshire County Council Social Services to work at the John Radcliffe (JR) Hospital. Then after some locum jobs, Mary was back at the Churchill Hospital, where she was employed by the National Health Service as a Kidney Support Adviser or Renal Social Worker. She worked at the Churchill Kidney Unit until 2009.

A nephrologist said that having a social worker was 'the icing on the cake.' One doctor seeing her back there, asked for a refund of what he had just given towards her JR retirement present! At this farewell gathering she was given three beautiful roses, which have flourished in the garden. Dr Chris Winearls, who was head of the Kidney Unit spoke of Mary's 'humanity; compassion; humour; realism; humility – bordering on the saintly.' He also mentioned Mary's 'common sense' to which Mary replied, 'The trouble, Dr Winearls, is that common sense is not that common anymore.' He also said that 'Mary was always ready for a robust argument', but she and Marcus were 'non-proselytising Christians.'

Mary and Dr Winearls

Mary made an amusing speech on how social work had changed, she said, 'I started as a child care officer and remember that when I went shopping with our daughter, aged 3, we had a row about buying a pair of shoes. She wanted flimsy pink ones whereas I wanted her to have good strong Clarks ones. She said 'I don't care very much for you'. I answered 'I don't care much for you either,' to which she answered, 'You have to, you're a child care officer. Mary added 'When I worked in hospitals, the original name for the role was 'Lady Almoner.' The story goes that someone said one day. 'Tell me, Lady Almoner, how is Lord Almoner today?'

'Sometimes I have to discuss with patients whether they want to continue with dialysis – if they don't they will die in a short time. In one discussion I asked what the husband thought. He replied, 'Well it's up to the wife. I shall miss her of course.' Her final story illustrated the misunderstanding that can happen between agencies. She was working with a family with lots of problems. The man was quite depressed. His one love was playing his organ, but he needed to get it repaired. I asked the probation officer if he could help. His reply was 'You shouldn't be encouraging him to play with his organ!' The probation officer obviously had a one track mind!' Paul Harden, one of the consultants with whom Mary worked closely, especially at the Great Western Hospital in Swindon, wrote to thank Mary for her 'companionship, support, fun and dedication over the last seven years'. 'It has been a real pleasure to work with you and you will be greatly missed by many staff and lots of patients.'

Besides her work with clients and doctors, Mary gave a number of talks. She was always a lively speaker. Her contribution to one conference about renal failure was evaluated by all the students as 'the best of the day.' She wrote an article on 'What I tell my patients about benefits and entitlements' for the *British Journal of Renal Medicine* (Winter 2008). She gave a paper in Prague on the 'Need for education on other cultures in a kidney unit' for EDTNA (The European Dialysis and Transplant Nurses Association). She also gave a paper to an international renal conference in Spain on 'Organ Transplants', which was published in the *British Journal of Renal Medicine* and in *Faith Initiative*.

The Oxford Bench

Soon after leaving the Bath bench Mr Stevens, her Clerk, put forward Mary's name to join the Oxford bench but somehow the Oxford bench papers got lost and Mary eventually received a very formal letter assuming she had never been a magistrate and saying how difficult it was to be accepted etc. However all this was eventually resolved and Mary joined the Oxford bench where she remained until she had to retire at 70. Mary much enjoyed these ten years although found Oxford at the beginning more formal and much larger than Bath, and felt a little lost until she got to know other colleagues. She did mainly adult courts and was saddened at her last sitting before she retired that she sat with two colleagues with whom she disagreed and had to announce a decision to send an 18 year old to a Youth Offenders Institution. She could not persuade her colleagues to change their minds. It was interesting that Mary was a social worker and a magistrate. She always managed to differentiate her two roles. Firstly, as a social worker she was naturally supporting her client in sorting out his/her problems but as a magistrate whilst appreciating the situation of the defendant she knew she was representing the community and looking at justice for all concerned, especially the victims. Since retiring she has taken an interest in Restorative Justice, which was supported by the Thames Valley Police, and links up with Marcus' writings on the different dimensions of Forgiveness. Mary continues to campaign on many issues and supports a wide range of charities.

Being a Justice of the Peace, Mary says, 'has been one of the most interesting jobs and responsibilities I have had. It meant meeting many people from all backgrounds. Chairing the Court was a challenge, keeping the defendants and also the solicitors and public in order. When she retired she gave a speech at the last formal dinner of the Oxford Bench. As the other retiree talked about cricket, Mary told the story that when she and Marcus were courting and he took her to the Oval to see the West Indies. Afraid she would be bored and took her knitting. The West Indies batting was too exciting to think of knitting!

Mary with John Smith, Chairman of the Bench

Afternoon Tea with Mary and Marcus

A Woman of Oxford

In 2004 Mary was chosen as one of a select group of 'Women of Oxford' – people who had made a significant contribution to the life of the city. When interviewed by the local paper, Mary said, 'I chose my work because of my Christian faith which makes me believe passionately in peace and justice for all people.' She said work had not always been easy 'as I have had a son and daughter to look after as they were growing up and also needed to care for my elderly parents before they died.' Later she was invited, thanks to her Brahma Kumaris' friends to be one of the very special 'Hundred Women of Spirit.'

Women of Spirit, including Mary, front row next to Dadi Janki.
Sister Jayanti is on Dadi's right and Sister Maureen is standing at the back

15. An International Interfaith Centre.

The main reason that Marcus and Mary moved to Oxford, as we have seen, was to help with establishing an International Interfaith Centre.

Many of those most active in the Year of Inter-religious Understanding and Co-operation felt it was important to maintain the links that had been built up and that a centre both of information and for research was needed. After careful consultation, it was agreed that Oxford would be a very suitable venue and Westminster College, which at that time, had a strong department for the study of religions, agreed to co-operate with the project. By the end of 1993, both the International Association for Religious Freedom and the World Congress of Faiths had relocated their offices to Oxford.

IIC Conferences

For its first ten years the Centre was based at the offices of IARF in the top floor of 2 Market Street, Oxford. Thanks to the efficiency and dedication of Sandy Martin (later Bharat) and Celia Storey, the co-ordinators, and other volunteers, the Centre established links with interfaith organisations around the world and was very active in arranging regular conferences and lectures.

The long term hope was to have a purpose-built centre at Westminster College. A fundraising campaign for the building and endowment fund was set up under the guidance of Mr Neville Sandelson, a former MP, whose family were known to Marcus. H R H Prince Charles wrote a message of support and Sir Richard Greenbury, Chairman of Marks and Spencer, agreed to be President of the Appeal. Neville was insistent that an outline plan of the building was essential before launching the appeal. Mary and Marcus, with help from David Goldhill, who was a retired architect and Marcus' brother-in-law, spent the best part of a year meeting with a few highly-reputed architects and going to see some of the buildings they had designed. Eventually the architects Evans and Shalev, who designed the Tate Gallery at St Ives and other well-known buildings, prepared an initial design for the centre. Sadly this ambitious project was frustrated, mainly because local residents objected to the proposal because it would increase the traffic on the access road. As a result planning permission was turned down by the White Horse District Council.

Marcus was in India at the time and came back to find that the Trustees had given up on the project, especially as Westminster College's new Principal showed no interest in it. Looking back, Marcus is sorry that there was no appeal, as very few ambitious projects get permission at the first attempt. The failure to build a centre continues to be a matter of regret and disappointment to Marcus and Mary. Similar centres, properly funded and with paid staff, now exist in different parts of the world. Perhaps as the Chairman of the Appeal said, the project was at that time 'a bridge too far' and, of course, Oxford is known as the 'home of lost causes.' Nevertheless, for some years IIC had a very busy programme, with several conferences, including one in Northern Ireland, looking at ways in which people of different faiths could help in situations of conflict. IIC also arranged regular meetings for staff members of the major international interfaith organisations, which now work more closely together. With changes to staff and lack of money there is now little activity.

Marcus' colleagues showed their appreciation of his work, by nominating him for the 1999 Templeton Prize for Progress in Religion. Their very generous letters supporting the nomination are still treasured by him. He was also 'lifted high,' at a ceremony in Oxford, by Sri Chinmoy, a tireless worker for peace, a poet, painter and inspirer of the World Harmony Run, who was physically strong and would literally raise up on a platform those he wished to honour.

Afternoon Tea with Mary and Marcus

Other Interfaith Links

To help make IIC known and build up its work of linking international interfaith organisations, Marcus, often with Mary, attended a number of international interfaith organisations. They, as we shall see, included the first five of the modern Parliaments of World Religions, at which both Mary and Marcus presented papers and arranged devotional gatherings; initial meetings to create the United Religions Initiative, gatherings at World Thanksgiving and meetings of the Peace Council.

The Faith and Belief Forum (Three Faiths Forum)

Sir Sigmund Sternberg and Sheikh Zaki Badawi

In the mid-nineties, Marcus was telephoned by Sir Sigmund Sternberg ('Sigi') whom he had worked with at CCJ. He always found Sigi rather difficult to hear on the phone and was busy with other work. Sigi said that he and a leading Muslim, Sheikh Zaki Badawi, who was also a good friend, wanted to start a dialogue group for Christians, Jews and Muslims – sometimes called the Three Abrahamic Faiths – as, under new direction, the Council of Christians and Jews made clear that dialogue with Muslims was not part of its agenda. Marcus said he thought it was a good idea and a few days later he was named as the Christian Co-Founder of the Three Faiths Forum (3ff), or as Michael Binyon put it in *The Times*, as one of 3ff's 'three pillars'.

Initially, the Three Faiths Forum (3ff) focussed on engaging religious, communal and civic leaders through seminars and events. However, in 2006 it launched its first schools programmes and now most of its activity is with young people. ParliaMentors leadership is a particularly successful venture. It brings together university students, who in small groups work together on a project under the guidance of a Member of Parliament. Recently, the name has been changed to the 'Faith and Belief Forum.' In 2008, 3ff started a cultural awareness programme in Israeli hospitals, which has gained government support. There are now also arts and cultural events which help to build bridges between communities through the arts. At first 3ff concentrated on relations within and between the Abrahamic faiths, but now works with people of all faiths as well as those who do not subscribe to a faith. The work has attracted considerable public attention and, in 2007, Marcus wrote a full page article for *The Church of England Newspaper* on 'Why the Three Faiths Forum is a vital task for the Church.' In the final paragraph, he said, 'As an alternative to terror and "the war against terror", religions should inspire us together to seek reconciliation rather than revenge, to provide for the poor and needy and to reverence all life with which we share this planet.' He would say the same today.

In recent years, as 3ff has become more established and as the only surviving founder, Marcus is treated as an elder statesman and was asked by the BBC to pay tribute to Sir Sigmund Sternberg after his death in 2016. Rachel Silveira, who was Deputy Director for many years, said, 'I am completely inspired by your grandparents.' Michael Sternberg, who has succeeded his father as Chairman of 3ff, says: 'I have known Marcus and Mary for at least 15 years. Marcus was instrumental in the setting up of the Three Faiths Forum (which he has supported consistently and vigorously since 1997) as well as being a hardworking Trustee of the Sternberg Foundation for over 20 years. His wise counsel has always aided us and we have always regarded his help as being vital in the success of both charities.'

In 3ff's early years, when Sidney Shipton was Director, Marcus went to a lot of meetings with interesting people. One of these was King Abdullah II of Jordan. An amusing aside is that as Marcus made his way from Victoria Station along Buckingham Palace Road, he came to a side entrance to the Palace and asked the policeman if that was the way in. He thought that for security reasons, as in many public buildings, admission would be by a side door. The policeman replied, 'If you are going to meet a King, you had better use the front door.'

There was another faux pas when Marcus was invited to join a small group of religious leaders for the Presentation of the Sir Sigmund Interfaith Gold Medallion to Her Majesty the Queen. Somebody came up to Marcus, who introduced himself and then asked the other person 'What is your name?' It was the Queen's Private Secretary, who was obviously taken aback that there was anyone who did not know who he was. (The same thing happened at some reception when Marcus asked Lord Falconer who he was).

Marcus has spoken at a number of meetings held in the Committee rooms in the House of Commons or the House of Lords. These rooms are often made available for charities to use. Marcus, however, never has felt quite at home in these surrounding or at London Clubs and did not take up a suggested nomination to join the Athenaeum. Maybe he still has that sense of only half-belonging to 'the establishment' that he had as a day boy at a boarding school. Also, although always respectful, he has never felt that grand titles make a person more important than anyone else.

Prince Charles with the Revd Tim Winter, Mary and Sidney Shipton, the first Director of the Three Faiths Forum

The Muslim College

Sheikh Zaki Badawi, amongst his many responsibilities, was Principal of the Muslim College in Ealing. His concern was that the Muslim community needed imams who were familiar with British culture. Many of the imams at the time had been hired from Pakistan and had poor English and little understanding of British life – and this contributed to the alienation of young Muslims. Marcus went with him and Sir Sigmund to meet the then Home Secretary David Blunkett and urge him to introduce language checks on imams coming into the country. Marcus was very impressed with David Blunkett and surprised that he knew about Marcus' visit to Sudan and that his suitcase had not arrived.

Zaki also wanted his students, some of whom came from abroad, to learn about other world religions. For several years, Marcus would travel once a week to Ealing to teach about Christianity. 'It was a challenge to help the students have a feeling for Christianity as well as information about it. I always arranged for them to visit a Christian church, often for a service at St Martin-in-the-Fields or Westminster Abbey. Marcus remembers one student from Nigeria who, after choral evensong at the Abbey, saying it was one of the most moving experiences of his life. Zeffirelli's film *Jesus of Nazareth* also helped students have a deeper empathy with Jesus – Isa, whom Muslims highly regard as a prophet.

Marcus says he learned a lot from this teaching. One student from Saudi Arabia was fully covered by a burkha – only her eyes showed: but Marcus soon discovered that she was a paediatric specialist and the most intelligent person in the room. Another student from Somalia was also outstanding and she 'showed how misleading stereotypes can be'. Rather hesitatingly, aware of the situation in Pakistan, Marcus asked if he could give the students a copy of the New Testament. 'Yes, of course,' was the reply and the College offered to pay for them. Marcus also wrote two distance-learning courses for the Hijaz College near Nuneaton. These had to be delivered to the camera with as little glancing down as possible. He was also asked to take part in some programmes for an online Muslim TV station.

The Peace Council

Another new initiative in which Mary and Marcus were involved was the Peace Council. Their friend Dr Daniel Gómez-Ibáñez, even before the end of Chicago Parliament of Religions—of which he was the chief organizer—was thinking of new ways to achieve 'effective interreligious co-operation', in places stained with blood and haunted by the memories of bitter conflict. He brought together a very small group of people, who became knowns as Peace Councillors, whose spirituality was expressed in practical commitment to a non-violent search for peace. The Dalai Lama – represented by a senior Tibetan monk – Desmond Tutu and Nobel Peace Prize winner Mairead Maguire, Fr Thomas Keating and The Cambodian Buddhist leader Mahā Ghosānanda were among the notable spiritual figures invited to be Councillors. Marcus was initially one of the Trustees, who included Peter Brinkman, Jim Kenney, Paul Knitter and their wives Patricia, Cetta and Cathy all of who became close friends. The Trustees were responsible for the running of the Council and Marcus attended at least one Trustees' meeting a year in the USA – usually at Maddison – as well as going to the full Peace Council meetings, which were more or less annual. Mary usually came as well. At first wives had to 'sit in the background and keep quiet' but gradually participated fully in the meetings.

Maha Ghosānanda, former senior Cambodian Buddist Monk, his assistant and Marcus

These meetings took Mary and Marcus to many unusual and sometimes dangerous places. The first meeting was at Windsor Castle (not too dangerous!) and included a moving interfaith prayer service in St George's chapel. The Dean at the time was Patrick Mitchell, who had been Dean of Wells when Mary and Marcus lived there.

Chiapas

The second meeting was held in November 1996 at San Cristóbal de las Casas in Chiapas, Mexico, at the invitation of Peace Councillor Bishop Samuel Ruiz Garcia, who for many years had campaigned to protect the Mayan indigenous people – or Indians as they are often called – from paramilitary groups working for multinational companies which wanted to seize their land. Because of other commitments, Mary and Marcus were a little late and to their disappointment when they arrived at San Cristóbal the Peace Councillors had disappeared – they had gone into the forest to a secret location to meet members of the rebel Zapatitsa National Liberation Army which had occupied the city of San Cristóbal de las Casas for a few days in 1994. There were meetings with many human rights groups. On the final night the cathedral in San Cristóbal was packed for the first interfaith service ever to be held in the Diocese, which Marcus helped to organise. It took place on Don Samuel's seventy-fourth birthday. Local indigenous people joined with a few local Buddhists, Jews and Muslims and with members of the Peace Council to offer prayers for peace and justice. The cathedral was decorated with banners, each of which showed the symbol of one of the world's religions. At the end, instead of processing out, the Peace Councillors mingled with the congregation, lighting candles until the whole cathedral was filled with light.

Following the meeting Mary and Marcus spent a few days relaxing at Cancun – although Marcus kept in touch with the parish on his travels, and had a fax there about the time of a funeral. They also visited the historic site of Chichén Itzá and the Basilica Santa Maria de Guadalupe in Mexico City.

Quite soon and quite unexpectedly Marcus was asked back to Chiapas. Just before Christmas 1997, a group of refugees, who had been expelled from their land, came to the remote village of Acteal to ask for help. The locals took them in and provided for them. But the refugees were pursued by the paramilitaries and forty-five of them were gunned down. The massacre lasted for four hours. Most of the victims were women and children, many of whom had taken refuge in the chapel.

Subsequently, Bishop Samuel Ruiz invited members of the Peace Council to come as witnesses and to accompany him on All Souls' Day 1998 – the Day of the Dead - to Acteal for the dedication of a memorial to those who had been massacred. The journey through the forests was difficult. Marcus travelled with the Bishop, who always had a bodyguard. The Bishop was afraid the army would stop them reaching the village. The soldiers, however, let them through the checkpoint and in pouring rain they reached the village and slithered down a muddy bank to the chapel. The service, with prayers offered by an Imam, a Rabbi and a Buddhist monk as well as by Christians of many traditions – all members of the Peace Council – was, Marcus says, 'intensely moving. One widow, who had lost several children, said afterwards, "My suffering is not over but the prayers have given me hope."'

Jerusalem

Other 'trouble spots' where the Peace Council met were in Israel/Palestine, Northern Ireland and Korea. The meeting in Jerusalem in May 2000 was soon after Pope John Paul II's historic visit. 'It was a fleeting moment of hope,' Marcus says, 'between the first and second intifadas, when it seemed that progress towards a peaceful two state solution was possible.'

Afternoon Tea with Mary and Marcus

The meeting took place at the quiet convent of the Sisters of Sion at Ein Karem, near the birthplace of John the Baptist. However, the Councillors were not shut off from the pain – both because of the visits to Arabs and Bedouins whose homes had been destroyed by the Israeli army – and because they listened to the testimonies of a large number of people with very varied views, who came to meet them. There were moments of hope as the Councillors met members of grass-roots organisations in Israel/Palestine who are working still to build bridges of understanding and trust.

Northern Ireland

Even when, as in Northern Ireland, there is a ceasefire or a negotiated political agreement, bitter memories of the past can jeopardise progress, as Peace Councillors soon recognised when they met in Belfast in June 2003. The Good Friday Agreement was signed on April 10, 1998 but in August of that year the deadliest incident in more than thirty years of 'The Troubles' occurred in Omagh, when a huge car bomb exploded at a market and killed twenty nine people. Mary and Marcus with another Peace Councillor, Sister Joan Chittester, went to Omagh, where Mary recalls, 'We listened to the harrowing stories of that tragic day and although we were told of the amazing efforts to heal and rebuild the community, it was clear that the wounds were still raw. There was little one could say, but our being there and listening seemed helpful. However, those who had taken an active part in the troubles avoided the question of repentance and forgiveness and just said,

Marcus, Mary, Sr Joan Chittester and Cathy Cornell

"Bad things happen in war."' Marcus still remembers, on a subsequent visit, the shock of sitting next to a member of Sinn Féin. 'I realised how much my opinion of them had been conditioned by repeated hostile reports of them in the media.'

Korea

In 2007 the Peace Council was invited to Korea by the Mayor of Hwacheon - Mary and Marcus had both visited the country before, for meetings arranged by the Won Buddhists or by UPF. Hwaechon is a small town situated close to the defensive lines, which separate the two Koreas, for the dedication of the Peace Bell Park. The Mayor wanted to make a bell that would be rung when Korea is reunited, and, Mary explains:

'We were asked to bring small bells or spent ammunition which would be melted down and used to make the bell. It proved almost as difficult to leave Heathrow with used bullets as it was to get through security with them on our arrival at Seoul. Our luggage was padlocked and we tried in vain to explain to ever more senior officers why we had bullets with us. It was only when I rang a small bell that we were we allowed to leave the airport. Did the officials understand or merely decide that the crazy English posed no security threat? Anyhow, when we got to the dedication ceremony, we were interviewed by Korean TV and showed them our bullets. That evening, turning on the television, there we were with our bullets on TV!'

During the time in Korea, members of The Peace Council visited the Korean Demilitarised Zone (DMZ) and looked across to North Korea. 'Talking to some bored South Korean soldiers,' Mary says, 'it was easy to see how one false move could quickly escalate into an exchange of arms. There were grim reminders of the enormous number of casualties during the Korean War. We passed a lake which was said to entomb the remains of thousands of Chinese soldiers. We heard also of the continuing sadness of family members who have been cut off from each other for over fifty years – although some occasional contact is now possible.'

Marcus has been back twice to other meetings in Korea organized by the Universal Peace Federation (UPF). The second time was in 2017. Unexpectedly when tensions between North Korea and the USA and the South were at their height, Marcus was asked to a big UPF conference of religious leaders. (He just missed meeting President Trump, who left the day before). The central event was a big peace rally held in the World Cup Stadium. Marcus was the last speaker. 'I had been very nervous at the thought of speaking to 80,000, but then I realised that they must have been as bored as I had been by some of the wordy presentations – so I spoke personally to the many young people about why I have worked for peace and challenged them to be true to their vision.' At the end he asked everyone to join with him in a prayer for peace of Korea. "Amen" echoed round the stadium. Three months later, there was the first contact for many years between the leaders of North and South Korea and later President Trump met Kim–Jong Un, the Supreme leader of North Korea.

Interfaith Networking

By the time Marcus and Mary moved to Clifton Hampden, it was clear that any hopes of an International Interfaith Centre being built had faded. They continued to be much involved in WCF and 3ff. The IIC also continued to encourage co-operation between international interfaith organisations at meetings, which were usually held at Harris Manchester College in Oxford, although one meeting was held in India. Such networking was the reason Mary and Marcus attended the Parliaments of World Religions, the meetings of the Peace Council, and numerous other international meetings. Yes – they are very aware of the environmental damage caused by flying, but they hope that real co-operation between religions will contribute to peace and more effective action to reduce global warming.

United Religions Initiative

We have already met Bill Swing, who inspired the creation and growth of the United Religions Initiative (URI). The idea came to him when in 1993 the United Nations asked him, as Bishop of California, to host a large interfaith service in San Francisco Cathedral to mark the 50th anniversary of the signing of the UN Charter. As he pondered the idea whilst he was trying to go to sleep, he asked himself, 'If the nations of the world are working together for peace through the UN, when are the world's religions going to do the same?'

To coincide with the interfaith service in the Cathedral, Bill, at Mary's suggestion, also arranged an exciting conference for young people in which some of the leaders, including Desmond Tutu, took part. Bill then travelled the world getting the blessing of many religious leaders, but ultimately they provided little active support. At the grassroots of the world's religions, on the other hand, he found a deep desire for co-operation and peace. From this inspiration, thanks also to the dedicated work of Charles Gibbs, there are now 800 Cooperation Circles spread across more than 100 countries. The signing of URI Charter by more than two-hundred people - including Mary and Marcus – took place at a ceremony in Pittsburgh, Pennsylvania, USA on June 26, 2000. They and Bill and Mary Swing have become great friends – as was evident at the meal in Salt Lake City – and Mary usually arrives with a gift of Stilton Cheese for these friends. Bill once described Mary as 'a benign missile' and Marcus as 'the Dean of Interfaith.' Quite different terms of endearment!

I wrote to Bill to ask him to share a few memories. He replied, 'Mary and Marcus have become dear, dear friends. And we seek them out for a dinner wherever in the world we find ourselves together . . . Barcelona, New York, London, San Francisco, Oxford, and on. Those dinners, as you have witnessed, dear Helen, have always been full of high humour, intense teasing, and occasional profundity.

Truth be told, Marcus speaks with such an accent and unique delivery, that I am not sure I have understood 5% of what he is talking about. But I am confident that his words carry weight, insight and, sometimes, hilarity. Actually he is such a hero for me, that I don't care much about the content. I just enjoy listening. Also, he has always seemed old to me. When I met him in 1993, I thought: "what a wonderful old man." Later I discovered that he is younger than I. Go figure!

As for Mary, she is a fun seeking missile. So many laughs along with so much profundity! And . . . she has been on a global mission to supply me with genuine Stilton cheese. She gets off of airplanes and presents me with Stilton.'

The Sikhs - Pattiala

The first international meeting that Marcus went to was in 1969 at the University of the Punjab in Pattiala. It was a scholarly gathering to mark the 400th anniversary of the birth of Guru Nanak, the founder of Sikhism, and to dedicate the new Gobind Singh Bhavan. Subsequently, he was invited back to Pattiala on a couple of occasions by Dr Dharam Singh. The second time, a group from WCF, after the meeting, went with some Sikhs on a pilgrimage to their holy places, including the Golden Temple at Amritsar. The pilgrims' hostel was very basic, but, Marcus says, 'getting up for the early morning devotions was very moving. The Golden Temple is surrounded by a blue shining lake. There is a small causeway leading to the shrine where the holy book, the Guru Granth Sahib, is placed. Everyone kneels before it and touches their head to the ground to show their respect for scripture.'

Amritsar

Marcus was also invited to a colloquium at Amritsar in 2004, to coincide with the 400th anniversary of the placing of the Guru Granth Sahib in the Golden Temple. The President of India, H.E. Abdul Kalam, was expected to attend the colloquium. Marcus like the other speakers had prepared a talk of about 30 minutes. 'Then,' he says, 'a message came that the President was delayed and would the speakers keep their remarks to about 20 minutes. Then another message, another delay and another cut to 10 minutes. When yet another message came, and another delay and another cut – the Muslim speaker said, "Why wait?" and left. But the President's charm and real interest, shown at the subsequent reception, made the wait worthwhile.'

On several of these visits, Marcus renewed his links with Mary Pat Fisher, and enjoyed the inspiration and hospitality of Gobind Sadan. Marcus has also been invited to the dedication of a multi-faith building in Kirpla Sagar and to events arranged by the Sri Ramanuja Mission Trust in Chennai – (Sri Ramanuja in the twelfth century founded an important Indian spiritual movement, called Visistadaita.) The Trust gave Marcus a Life-Time Achievement Award.

Ma with Mary and Marcus at Kashi Ashram.

Kashi Ashram

Marcus was also given a Life Time Achievement Award by the Kashi Ashram. We have already met its founder, Ma Jaya Sati Bhagavati at the Chicago Parliament of World Religions. They met again and spent time together at the Cape Town Parliament. The Ashram, a residential spiritual community, was founded in 1976 by Ma - a yoga master, author and artist. She is an unforgettable figure. Its eighty acres has a number of temples and shrines surrounding the sacred Ganga pond. Ma has given particular attention to those suffering with AIDS, both by combatting the prejudice which many of them have encountered, but also by caring for them at the Ashram. Mary and Marcus were particularly moved to visit the house for young children who had inherited the illness. The award ceremony clashed with an important event in the Baldons. Mary and Marcus went to the start of it, hurried to Heathrow and after an uncomfortable night at Kennedy Airport, got a very early flight to Miami and were there in time.

Marcus asked, if the following day, he might celebrate holy communion. He thought perhaps half a dozen people would come – but there must have been well over a hundred for what became an amazing interfaith communion service. One Jewish person who participated said afterwards that he never in his life thought that he would be handing a bottle of wine to a priest at a communion service. Whilst they were there, they also went on a boat ride on the sea - but a hurricane suddenly threatened and they only just reached the shore in time.

A Lambeth Doctorate

In 2004, shortly before Mary and Marcus left the Baldons, Marcus was awarded a Lambeth Doctorate. This is a proper degree – not an honorary one. Before the Reformation, the Pope had power to award a degree to someone whose work was of sufficient worth, but, perhaps because of plague or war, had been unable to meet the necessary residential qualification. At the Reformation, Henry VIII transferred the power to do this to the Archbishop of Canterbury, although any award needed royal approval.

Afternoon Tea with Mary and Marcus

The Archbishop of Canterbury

Lambeth Degrees 2004
COMMENDATION
Marcus Braybrooke
Doctor of Divinity

A Hindu has said, "Marcus Braybrooke has probably contributed more than anyone else to the development of inter-religious co-operation and understanding throughout the world." A Christian bishop testifies that Marcus "more than anyone in the Church of England at the moment, has been associated with constructive interfaith dialogue". I could carry on, for many Jews, Christians, Muslims and Hindus alike have used similar words to describe their great respect for Marcus' work in inter-faith matters and he has been doing it for so long! Once, when he was lecturing on the history of the Inter-Faith Movement and brought in the 1893 Parliament of Religions, a student at question time asked Marcus whether he had been present at it.... Nevertheless he has been active in inter-faith work for the whole 40 years since his ordination. There are probably two aspects in particular which account for his success in this very difficult field; his scholarship and his spirituality. Marcus has a wealth of knowledge of different faiths which he shares with compassion, enthusiasm and deep humility with whomever he meets. He truly understands and respects other faiths, celebrating the differences, while acknowledging and worshipping the one creative force that guides us.

Over the years his published work ranges across a breadth of concerns and interests, including the doctrinal and theological issues of the Christian encounter with other traditions. If I have to single out one book it is probably his *Pilgrimage of Hope: One hundred years of global interfaith dialogue*, published in 1992. It is the kind of meticulously researched historical study which not only chronicles all the major events and people who contributed to the development and steady growth of interfaith dialogue over the last hundred years, but it also provides a mature assessment of the significance and implications of such dialogue for the Christian churches and the world at large. Quite rightly it has been called a global "history of the inter-faith movement". His spirituality is manifested in the way he has been able to put his scholarship into practice, a quality which has broken down the often vociferous opposition to his stand in some parts of our church; but he is invariably courteous with such people and continually wins their trust and understanding. A clergy colleague of Marcus' told me that he had difficulty persuading some of his more evangelical parishioners that the parish should welcome Marcus and in fact it proved necessary for my predecessor, Archbishop Carey, to write in the parish magazine on the incumbent's behalf. A year after Marcus' arrival the colleague was visited by one of those who had needed persuading; he said he had come to apologise and to say how much he was learning from Marcus – that is how to hold true to the Christian Gospel while also remaining open to those of other World Faiths.

Marcus' practical involvement in inter-religious dialogue has included his work for the Council of Christians and Jews, co-founding the Manor House Group in the 1980s and playing an integral part in the founding and development of the International Peace Council in 1994. While executive director of the Council of Christians and Jews Marcus realised that the work of CCJ needed to move on from social pleasantries to a theological agenda. He did this by gathering together a group of people who were personally interested in understanding the relationship between Christianity and Judaism, who were open to change and growth and who were prepared to meet and talk on a regular basis, not for political reasons, but in the knowledge that in building trust and friendship they would be changed by the experience and would influence others because of it. In Bishop Richard Harries' new book, *After the Evil*, the Bishop says he was a member of the group and acknowledges its significance in influencing his understanding of Christian/Jewish relations. Marcus subsequently used this model to form the Manor House group, a group of Jewish, Christian and Muslim individuals who meet to discuss problems that they share. A Jewish rabbi who was part of these groups says that such is the respect he has for Marcus that he would trust him with his life, a testimony indeed to Marcus' insight, integrity and love.

I particularly welcome his wife Mary here today. I know how much she has contributed to Marcus' work in the giving of her time while pursuing her own career; she has shared in his conferences, she has entertained in their home many visitors of other faiths and on several occasions has actually helped to finance her husband's work out of her medical salary. I have the greatest pleasure in awarding Marcus Braybrooke the degree of Doctor of Divinity in recognition of his contribution to the development of inter-religious co-operation and understanding throughout the world.

Global Co-operation for the Common Good

Marcus and Mary have also attended several conferences arranged by 'Global Co-operation for the Common Good' (GCCG), to which their good friend Kamran Mofid has dedicated his life. Kamran, a lecturer in economics, became increasingly dissatisfied with teaching about 'wealth creation' without any thought about how wealth should be used. He and Marcus wrote a book together called *Promoting the Common Good: Bringing Economics and Theology Together Again.* The book was launched at the Second GCCG conference in Kenya by the country's Vice-President. Marcus, in an article in *The Church of England Newspaper*, began with the quotation, 'A New Economy Needs a New Morality – there's a moral vacuum at the heart of the New Economy that needs to be filled.' He then pointed out that this was not something said by an Archbishop, but by Michael Mandel, the then chief economist of *Business Week*. Marcus pursued this concern in his book, *A Heart for the World; the Interfaith Alternative.*

Universal Peace Federation

Over the years Marcus and Mary have attended a number of meetings arranged by bodies linked to the Unification Church, which was founded by Rev Sun Yung Moon in Korea in the 1960s. There has been a lot of controversy about the church partly because of the recruitment tactics used in early days in USA, which was said to include deprivation of freedom and brainwashing. There have also been claims of financial dishonesty. The most serious concern for Christians is Rev Moon's alleged claim to be a New Messiah who will put right the failure of Jesus.

The first approach was from Dr Warren Lewis. He has vividly recalled the initial meeting. 'I walked up to their front door, and Mary smilingly opened to this complete stranger and welcomed me in. A lovely and sumptuous tea was already spread, and the tea was hot in the pot. She had baked a tea cake with chocolate frosting. Among topics of conversation, besides the Global Congress, was the difference between "vegetable marrow", "zucchini" and "squash."'

Mary and Marcus attended some of the early Congresses and have visited Warren and Judee in their various homes. 'Once' Warren recalls, 'on a very hot day in Vancouver, passing a nudist beach, Marcus and I went swimming in the buff' – much to the embarrassment of Mary and Judee.'

Very few of the international interfaith organisations wished to have any contact with the Unification Church and some members of WCF were critical of Marcus' and Mary's participation in events sponsored by them. They have never felt under any pressure and several members of the Unification Church have said that their friendship has changed their rather unfavourable view of the main-stream churches. 'More important', Marcus says, 'UPF and other related organisations are doing good work and the conferences have given us the opportunity to meet an amazing range of people from all walks of life and from many religions who all recognize the good work being done'.

Because of its aim to unite all people as one family of God, it was natural that the Unification Church would support efforts to bring the religions closer together. The World Congress of Faiths is a fellowship of individual members and unlike many other interfaith organisations participants are not seen as representing a religion. The founder Sir Francis Younghusband even said that 'spiritual atheists' could join WCF. The WCF Executive therefore agreed that Unificationists and Scientologists could join – provided like all members they avoided canvassing for members or promoting a political agenda at meetings of the WCF.

Afternoon Tea with Mary and Marcus

After Dr Warren Lewis left his position, contact was mainly with Dr Francis Clarke, a devout Roman Catholic, who arranged a series of carefully organised meetings for dialogue. Participants had to submit a paper well in advance, which was then circulated to other participants. The time together was therefore spent in discussion rather than in listening to papers. 'The meetings gave us a chance to converse with many stimulating people from a great variety of countries and creeds as well as seeing new parts of the world'.

More recently the contact has been with the Universal Peace Federation, which has a more practical agenda, often on human rights or peace initiatives. Marcus has spoken at a number of meetings in Britain arranged by Margaret Ali and Robin Marsh. These are often held in the Houses of Parliament with some MPs or Peers present as well as representatives of a wide range of charitable and campaigning organisations.

Marcus has also taken part in some international meetings and was asked to say an opening prayer at a meeting in South Korea where a dozen or more heads of state were present. By the end of the protracted proceedings Marcus was feeling ill – some strange food the night before – and dashed from the dais, leaving his papers behind. By the time he went back, the stage had been cleared and his file was no longer there. In it was the text of the talk he was to give later in the day – so instead of sleeping off the sickness he had to try to remember what he was going to say. 'In fact, it was a good thing as I realised I would have to come straight to the point about human rights abuses and their responsibilities if I were to have any impact . . . Afterwards, a Canadian ambassador said it was just what needed saying.' After another talk about the need for changes to the UN if it is to act decisively to prevent genocide, an MP asked Marcus for a copy of the talk.

Marcus says, 'I always try to be polite, but it is good for those in power to hear what their officials are not telling them. I know also that some of my colleagues disapprove of the company I keep. Certainly there can be a risk of being used, but there is always the hope that the other person may be influenced. Also, one may disagree with a person's beliefs, but find a shared commitment to peace and justice.'

International Women's Day - Several Years Ago

Mary has also often been asked to speak at meetings. At a large gathering in Birmingham, organised by leading members of UPF there, on International Women's Day, she began with this amusing story of a conversation that God had with Adam:

'One day in the Garden of Eden, Eve calls out to God. 'Lord, I have a problem!'
'What's the problem, Eve?'
'Lord, I know you created me and all of these amazing animals and that hilarious snake,
but, I'm just not happy'
'Why is that Eve?' came the reply from above.
'Lord, I am lonely and I'm sick to death of apples.'
'Well, Eve, in that case, I have a solution. I shall create a man for you. But he may give you a hard time. He'll be bigger, stronger, and will like to hunt and kill things. He'll look silly when he's aroused, but since you have been complaining, I'll make him in such a way that he satisfies your physical need. He will be witless and will revel in childish things like fighting and kicking a ball about. He won't be too smart, so he'll also need your advice to think properly.'
'Sounds wonderful,' said Eve, 'but's what the catch, Lord?' 'Well . . . you can have him on one condition.'
'What's that, Lord?'
'As I said he'll be proud, arrogant, and self-admiring . . . So you'll have to let him believe that I made him first. Just remember, it's our little secret . . . You know, woman to woman.'
(https://www.funny-jokes.com - attributed to Beverley Glock)

16. Farewell to the Baldons.

Once again, Diocesan re-organisation was to change Mary and Marcus' lives. The plan was to reduce the number of clergy in the Dorchester Team. As a result, the Diocese did not wish to continue the cost of providing a clergy house in the Baldons and planned to sell Marsh Baldon Rectory. As Marcus' appointment was 'at the bishop's pleasure,' Marcus and Mary had no choice. The bishop did however, allow them to stay on until the end of 2004 so that Marcus could complete 40 years of active ministry.

At the Farewell service their good friend Graham Hobbins spoke warmly of their time in the villages:
'I am certain Marcus and Mary would now like to slip quietly away with no fuss and next be seen on the Green, walking Toffee, without any of the responsibilities of being our vicar and vicar's wife. But we cannot let you go like that! Several weeks after Marcus and Mary arrived in our Parish, in September 1993, I got talking to Mary (something that is very easy to do!) outside St. Lawrence's and said to her what a wonderful preacher her husband was. She replied, "Do you know that in all the years I have known him, I have never heard him give a bad sermon". Some 12 years on, Mary, we would certainly all agree with you! God uses Marcus to preach, teach and live His loving word and, in a world that seems to lack clear moral leadership and direction, Marcus stands out like a shining beacon.

It is impossible to think of either Marcus or Mary without the other coming into the equation somehow. They make a unique team. Some words by Gibran come to mind when thinking of this formidable pair, "Sing and dance together and be joyous, but let each one of you be alone, even as the strings of a lute are alone though they quiver with the same music."

A number of us have had the good fortune of going on some of Marcus and Mary's trips abroad. These trips have without exception been highly informative, exhausting, fun and never without incident. Some moments come to mind readily: Marcus leading a communion service on the shores of Lake Galilee; climbing Mount Sinai with Marcus at 3 am and watching the sun rise; in India, during that horrendous earthquake, the image of Marcus standing on the dusty grounds at the rear of our hotel watching bits fall off the building, the earth moving beneath our feet, and Marcus holding a jar of instant coffee in one hand and a jar of marmite in the other; and Marcus and Mary leading groups around parts of Europe, following the footsteps of St Paul. Marcus has an extraordinary store of relevant information, which he seems able to produce at the drop of a hat, on any topic you like to raise!

We are also aware of the work Marcus undertakes within the international peace and interfaith movements, though I suspect none of us fully appreciate the huge contribution he makes towards peace and understanding in our world. This, together with all his books and academic work was recently acknowledged by the Archbishop of Canterbury when he granted Marcus a Doctor of Divinity Degree. The Archbishop also specifically recognised all Mary does as well. Having Marcus and Mary living within our communities these past years has been a great privilege. To all of us, you are very special and we thank you both for your friendship, leadership, wisdom, humour, patience and ability to listen and understand. These qualities have been visible within every area and activity of our village lives and have touched everyone.

Marcus has the exceptional gifts of being highly intelligent, an original thinker, incredibly well organised and efficient, he will always recognize and acknowledge the work of others, and he is a wonderful communicator. All he does is undertaken with great humility—he regularly mixes with world leaders in many fields, yet still has time for each one of us.

Afternoon Tea with Mary and Marcus

Throughout her time here, Mary has kept all her social work going, dispensed justice within the County, attended numerous international events with Marcus and kept a welcome at the vicarage for any of us 24 hours a day. With her finely tuned antennae, Mary has always been well informed about what's going on in the village and the world and she has strong, independently formed opinions, to go alongside. Mary thrives on being a wife, mother and grandmother and loves having all her family around.'

Graham and Sonia Hobbins have been very special people in all our lives—one very vivid childhood memory for my sisters and I involves being pushed about by Graham in a wheelbarrow— he always seemed, and does to this day, a towering strong giant, with a kind, deep voice. Later, when Sarah, Anna, Dad and I joined our grandparents on one of their wonderful tours through Israel, we taught them both how to play the card-game 'cheat', in which the objective is to reduce your hand to zero. Graham was a complete natural, and by his second round I was only barely catching him as he passed off five cards while nonchalantly announcing 'two Jacks'.

Parish fellowship in the Baldons

The Team Rector, Canon John Crowe, retired at the same time. He could not be at the service but wrote of Mary and Marcus, 'They are a wonderful example of true friendship and collaborative ministry. I can see now in my mind's eye - Marcus at a Tuesday morning staff meeting, listening as a difficult pastoral matter is being discussed with alertness, a slight smile and readiness to offer wise advice - Mary providing a generous breakfast and shrewd and forthright advice on any subject that is being aired - Marcus sitting quietly and prayerfully in Marsh Baldon Church waiting for colleagues to arrive for the early morning Eucharist – Mary acting in a village pantomime - Marcus brilliantly adapting his sermon on the spur of the moment at a Team Eucharist on the day Princess Diana died – Marcus and Mary with their video camera on the Team Pilgrimage to the Holy Land in the mid 1990s - there are so many other memories that could be mentioned!

'Marcus's skill with liturgy has benefited special services. His ability as an adult education specialist has been on offer to the Team as Lent courses and other similar initiatives have been planned. Marsh Baldon Rectory over these last 12 years has been the venue for countless meetings, meals and parties - the hospitality given by Marcus and Mary has been outstanding.'

Ron Hewitt, one of the church wardens, also paid tribute to Marcus' ministry and on a lighter note, mentioned that they hosted well attended fetes at the Rectory and even wrote their own sketches to perform at the Harvest Festival suppers and that- both are more than capable of' letting their hair down when circumstances permit and both have a great sense of humour. He noted too that Mary had given several performances for the Baldon Players, notably as a "'not to be trifled with' Good Fairy supported by fairy grandchildren and a formidable opponent to my Demon. We were both more conventionally dressed in a recent production of 'The Boyfriend' in which she was a bit of a battle-axe in contrast to her gentle portrayal of the house keeper in 'Oliver'". (He did not mention how often on stage they were husband and wife!)

A window 'to the Glory of God.'

Upon their retirement from official parish work, my grand-parents received an extraordinary gift. The parish, in an amazing tribute, had commissioned a stained glass window to recall their ministry – a beautiful design with an array of natural colours depicting trees, rivers and light (my cover design is based on it). However, when the Bishop of Dorchester unveiled the window and pointed this out to the grandchildren, Mary promptly interrupted him. Their friend David Winter wrote about what happened in the *Church Times*. (She is still not sure if 'redoubtable woman' was a compliment!): "I guess it's quite rare for an incumbent's ministry to be commemorated in a stained-glass window while he is still very much alive. But our neighbour and friend Marcus Braybrooke, as well as being a world expert on interfaith matters, was for 12 years the much-loved non-stipendiary parish priest of a delightful trio of Oxfordshire villages: Marsh Baldon, Toot Baldon and Nuneham Courtney.

To mark the end of his ministry there, the parishioners raised money, and commissioned the artist Nicola Kantorowicz to create a new window for the south aisle of the church at Marsh Baldon. Using symbols drawn from creation, Church, and faiths expressed in a heavenwards movement of light and colour, it is truly amazing and beautiful. The occasion of its dedication by the Bishop of Dorchester filled the church with friends and well-wishers. Marcus and his wife Mary, a redoubtable woman of strong principles, greatly loved in the parish, stood by as the Bishop introduced the short ceremony. "Today we are dedicating this beautiful window as an expression of gratitude for the ministry of Marcus and Mary", he began. "And to the glory of God," interjected Mary firmly. Bishop Colin continued with unswerving concentration. "And to the glory of Almighty God she said. Quite so."

The stained glass window in Marsh Baldon Church.

17. Clifton Hampden

For this new chapter in their lives, Mary and Marcus spent some time wondering where to move to, and at first planned to buy a bungalow – because of Mary's arthritis: but then decided a stair-lift would be better value.

Independently they both noticed a house for sale in Courtiers Green in Clifton Hampden. The difficulty was that Clifton Hampden was the next village to the Baldons and the Bishops had just sent a circular to clergy saying, in effect, that when they retired they should move at least twenty miles away from their last parish and not be seen there for ten years. The letter arrived just as they were about to put down a deposit on 17, Courtiers Green. They went ahead and did so! Many good friends from parishes where they had been came to visit them in their new home.

As always, Mary and Marcus had more stuff than most people would have in an eight bedroom house. Nancy Traer recalls, 'Your grandparents are indeed extraordinary and they have made strenuous efforts to increase peace and understanding in all parts of the world. I also remember their ever-warm and wonderful hospitality, good food and energy. I was helping Mary move house when she looked around at the stuff to pack and sighed, "I have lived too long..." I remember saying that I hoped she would live MUCH longer, and I am glad she has.'

Friends from Bath: Margaret Heath and Audrey Sheppard

Years ago I was commissioned to help my grandmother sort through her papers, and after hours of her saying 'Oh I can't throw that away, we might need it', as we essentially moved a large pile of documents from one side of the room to the other, I unashamedly gave up. Bishop John Pritchard also comments on the house: 'We hugely enjoyed going to have meals with Marcus and Mary when we were in Oxford. We would be taken into this house, full of cluttered memories, and shown their various enthusiasms, from the garden which they had rescued and loved, to the attic prayer space into which you climbed at your peril.'

Wherever he lives my grandfather's gardens are beautifully cared for, and always full of grateful little birds, from blue tits and wrens to robins and goldfinches, making use of the seeds and bread faithfully put out for them. One bird table is even in the shape of a church, although the congregation attend and depart rather haphazardly! And my grandmother lovingly feeds the goldfish whenever her pond is occupied. Marcus says that his most satisfying garden has been the one in Clifton Hampden. He always makes an effort to grow vegetables and plant fruit bushes, among the bulbs and roses.

Despite having a smaller house, there were still many visitors, children or grandchildren. Lizzie, who was born in the Baldons says, 'One of my favourite memories is definitely playing with Mama's dolls and learning all about where they came from. I also remember all our bike rides by the river with Toffee which were always fun'.

On one occasion, during a walk with Marcus, Toffee mistook the thick green layer of weed or algae at the edge of the still water for solid ground, and fell into the deep part of the river. He never was keen on swimming or getting wet, and panicked. Without hesitation my grandfather plunged in after him, and was later seen trudging back home, soaked through and holding a shivering, rather sheepish looking poodle.

Christina also added, 'Visiting Mama and Grandpa was always an exciting event. As soon as Lizzie and I went through the door we would eagerly race upstairs to see what treats had been thoughtfully laid out for us on the beds. They have always encouraged and respected our independence. Grandpa would provide a range of bikes in various sizes and states of repair, before handing us some change so that we could go on an adventure to the village shop. We would carefully calculate the optimum combination of sweets and magazines that our precious pounds could buy before returning home full of glee and fulfilment. Despite being young, we had been gifted a trust and independence that has stayed with us both.'

Lizzie and her 'Mama', or Grandma.

My sister Sarah wrote,

'How my Grandpa has the time and energy for gardening whilst doing so much for others I have no idea – that is something I have always admired about him. Grandpa has the kind of gentle leadership that draws you to him without him having to say anything. When he speaks it makes you want to listen and absorb every word, regardless of whether it is in the context of showing us how to be quiet and kind when we met their new puppy Toffee, or whether it was teaching us more about our faith as he took my sisters and I through our confirmation. I hope that just by sitting beside him I am absorbing some of his perception of the world. My husband and I are so blessed to have had Grandpa take us through marriage preparation and marry us on our special day – we will never forget that or take that for granted. My Grandma reading Corinthians during the wedding service made it all the more special'.

While looking through old photo albums and documents, I came across a poem, entitled 'Grandpa', written by my sisters and I, when we were children. Sarah had the first stanza, then Anna, Kathryn and myself. It reads:

Afternoon Tea with Mary and Marcus

"*Down in the garden, Grandpa is there,
Picking his tomatoes with patience and care,
Digging up the vegetable patch and watering it all,
Our Grandpa cares for everything big and small.*

*Down in the Woods where grandpa is walking,
Grandpa is thinking and grandpa is talking,
Toffee's barking and having fun,
And everyone is walking along.*

*Down in the study, Grandpa is writing,
His books encompassing all faiths and uniting,
Moral and true – an example to us all,
Grandpa: a member of the community, standing tall.*

*Down in the churchyard, Grandpa is teaching,
Holding young hands, his peace always reaching,
wisdom and kindness, loved through the earth,
Grandpa, Dad, Marcus; special since birth!*"

Sarah with her cousin Ella Walker

Church Life

Mary and Marcus both miss parish life and sometimes wish, like Victorian clergy, that they had been allowed to stay on until they dropped, but Marcus' health was uncertain and his growing deafness meant it was difficult to hear what people – and especially children - said.

After they moved, although they both go to Clifton Hampden Church when they can, Mary got very involved in the life of Dorchester Abbey, which with the able and imaginative leadership of Canon Sue Booys, talented organist, Jeremy Boughton, and a large choir, has beautiful worship and many interesting events. For many years she was a member of the Church Council and of the Deanery and Diocesan Synods. She also helps with the chalice and often leads the intercessions.

Mary, as well, was the Diocesan officer with responsibility for caring for widows (and now some widowers). This involved sending each of them a Christmas card and offering support, especially after a bereavement. She also helped Wendy Pritchard, the bishop's wife, at social occasions for Oxford's clergy wives. In addition she was for a time Deanery Vocations Officer, for which Bishop Colin Fletcher wrote to express his grateful thanks. Marcus, 'like a dentist filling in holes' has taken services in a lot of neighbouring churches, where there is a vacancy or the vicar is ill or on holiday. He is grateful that he has been invited to take services in various churches in the Team area and to go back to the Baldons for some weddings and baptisms. Mary and Marcus have also taken one or two services for several years at Harris Manchester College. The Chapel Society keeps up the College's historic links with Unitarians, although ministers of other traditions are very welcome. Mary and Marcus enjoy the chance to plan a service without the constraints of a set liturgy.

Afternoon Tea with Mary and Marcus

Social Work

Even after she retired, Mary was asked to supervise some colleagues. Stephanie Stott, who worked at Sobell House and then Katherine House, wrote to Mary saying, 'Thank you for the supervision you have given, which I value highly, and I want to say that you really do enable me to reflect on what I am usually "rabbiting on about" at length.'

Mary was additionally chairperson for several years of the Oxfordshire branch of BASW (The British Association of Social Workers). She was well supported by the Secretary Tony Garrard, who also on occasion played the organ at Clifton Hampden church. She also 'in her retirement' is an active member of various consultative bodies about the future of the NHS, and chairs the local Patients' Participation Group of Clifton Hampden Surgery, whose doctors and nurses have given them so much help for a quarter of a century.

In 2015, Mary said, 'Following final retirement in 2009 (having 'retired' hundreds of times) I found it quite difficult to come to terms with not having a regular routine and I kept needing to consult my diary. It was also difficult for Marcus, as he was used to having time on his own at home, and now I was around even for lunch.

However, we settled into a fairly comfortable routine, and I was out most of the time anyway, helping to run coffee mornings at Dorchester Abbey, visiting friends and also older people in need from the pastoral committee at Dorchester Abbey. I also continued supervising a social worker working in a hospice at her request. Marcus and I had more time to go out for walks with Toffee, who spent a great deal of time sitting on my lap—although he would hardly ever come up without asking me.

Toffee and Mary on holiday in Devon. He loved chasing around on the sand, but would never swim.

My sister Sarah has said, 'I'd like to think I have inherited some of my Grandma's feistiness. I have certainly inherited my Grandma's passion for helping others and working in healthcare – passed down from my Grandma to my mother and now to me. Grandma and I have spent many happy hours exchanging stories of supporting others and laughing with exasperation at how little common sense seems to prevail. Grandma also taught me to like black coffee which, especially working in healthcare, I appreciate on a very necessary level! One of my favourite memories is when Grandma and I once went to France together when I was about eleven. At the airport she was being interrogated by a fairly unpleasant woman for setting off the metal detectors due to the metal in her knee replacements. Having none of it, I emanated my Grandma's sassiness, declaring to the woman involved that my grandmother was clearly not a terrorist and so to leave her be! We could not stop laughing.'

Mary's brother Paul wrote to me, 'Whenever I think of Mary I have a picture of someone I would like as a colleague and advocate when attending a difficult meeting – especially a meeting where I expected resistance. Integrity and fearless honesty come naturally to Mary. In the nicest way she has no fear of entering ground that angels fear to tread! So often we (I) hold back and the moment is lost. Maybe Mary has something of our mother's fearlessness.'

A Royal Wedding

In 2011, the newspapers for weeks were full of stories about the forthcoming marriage of Prince William to Kate. The event itself had worldwide coverage. In Britain there were over 5,000 street parties, Mary and Marcus managed to go to three of them. As Jeremy and Amanda were away at the time, Mary and Marcus stayed at East Horrington to accompany Lizzie and Christina to the local celebration. Sadly there was a downpour, but even so everyone did their best to enjoy themselves. Marcus the following day went back to the party in the Baldons and looked in on the one in Clifton Hampden. And over in Harwell, our celebrations included a huge barbeque and an amazing cake made by my mother, with fresh cream, strawberries, raspberries and blueberries depicting a union jack. The patriotic national events reminded me of my grandmother's 'celebration society' back in her garden shed.

The London Olympics

In 2012, the gloom of the 2009 Financial Crash was, in part, relieved by the preparations for and the excitement of the Olympic Games. When the family went to see various events, Mary and Marcus were delighted by the friendliness and happiness of everyone they met.

There was some hope that the Olympic Committee would sponsor a religious event to mark the beginning of the Games, but the Committee showed no interest. The World Congress of Faiths, therefore, arranged an interfaith service at St Martin's-in-the-Fields, a week before the start.

It was a moving occasion and Jeremy had managed to obtain one of the Olympic torches that had been used when the Olympic flame was brought to Bristol. Lizzie and Christina held the torch in the Opening Procession and read a story from the Seattle Special Olympics; in the 100-yard-dash, when one of the children fell over, all the children came to help and then, holding hands, walked happily together to the finishing line.

The title given to the service by Marcus and the Revd Richard Carter, who together mostly arranged the event, was 'Go for the Golden Rule.' It highlighted the fact that, even if in rather different forms, the Golden Rule – 'Do unto others what you would wish them to do to you' - can be found in the teaching of all religions.

My Grandparents' Golden Wedding

Mary and Marcus' Golden Wedding celebration in June 2014 was a wonderful occasion. It was beautifully organised by Rachel and Peter with help from Jeremy and Amanda and held in the garden at Harwell on a sunny day. There was an amazing array of food and an excellent celebration cake made by Anna, presented amid confetti and champagne. Rachel's close friend Jenny made beautiful bunting to decoration. Jeremy gave a generous and amusing speech to which both Mary and Marcus replied—despite being notoriously good listeners, neither of my grandparents seem to be able to make it through a speech about themselves without adding their own two pennies' worth! Sarah and Chris gave a brilliant musical recital and the granddaughters helped look after the eighty or more guests, including Bryony, Paddy and Paul and Pepita and their families, other relations and many friends. Even Toffee seemed to enjoy the event, but having said 'hello' to most of the guests, he found somewhere quiet to have a snooze. Maybe by the end my grandparents would have liked to do the same!

Anna's incredible cake for the Golden Wedding Celebration

Several people sent messages. Marcus' cousin David recalled many happy family events, especially the wedding, which Marcus took, of their son Richard to Sophie; 'Marcus produced a bottle of wine from Cana for the bride and bridegroom. A wonderful moment and much appreciated.' David also recalled family funerals at which Marcus officiated and his and Anne's delight when Mary travelled with Marcus' mother to stay with them in Jersey. 'It was so nice to have a few days of family time together and to enjoy each other's company.' Mary too remembers it as a special time and especially Marcia's happiness on what was to be one of her last holidays.

Mary and Marcus also had a London celebration for their interfaith friends at Golders Green Unitarian Church, thanks to Feargus O'Connor, who has asked Mary and Marcus to take part in several services at his church. Once again Anna made a special cake—she has taken after our mother as a talented and enthusiastic baker, with endlessly creative ideas for important events. My grandparents also celebrated the year with a trip to Australia – including a stop-over in Hong Kong – accompanied by Jeremy, Amanda, Lizzie and Christina. It has been such a pleasure for all six of us granddaughters to get to know the large Australian branch of our family. When I first went to the east coast of Australia in 2007, with my family and grandma to meet some of our two-to- three-hundred-strong family, we had an incredible welcome barbeque hosted by Barry and Gwenda.

I was later taken in by countless kind members of the family when I returned to travel solo in 2012, and had wonderful adventures, from exploring local sights and lighthouses with Sue Walker to spending several weeks 'helping' Linda on her incredible farm in Megalong Valley. Sarah and Chris made the same journey a couple of years later, also heading west to Perth, where Chris grew up. It is comforting to know that, even on the other side of the world, the connections and friendships lovingly maintained by Mary and Marcus mean that we all have so many doors open to us.

Sad Times

There have also been sad times as friends and loved ones have become house-bound or set out on their final journey. My Grandad, Terry—my father's father—passed away quite suddenly on 17th November 2012, and I received the news with my mother Rachel, who was visiting me at The University of York. Grandad had always had a wonderful sense of humour, akin to that of Marcus, and in my childhood used to make me giggle by calling me a 'silly sausage'. One of my favourite photos of him shows him patiently holding the lead-rope while I, at three years old, ride my hobby-horse along (although there was little danger of this particular steed bolting!). It's always been a pleasure that I take for granted, how well both sets of my grandparents get on—though for so many families that would not be a given.

My granny Hilda is a talented crafts-women, and over the years has cross-stitched many treasured gifts, from the Christmas stockings that my sisters and I received at birth and still use now, to special designs that mark events, such as Sarah and Chris' wedding. During one Boxing Day at Springend Cottage, my family's home now in Devon, Mary and Hilda both became utterly engrossed in a film they'd first seen when it was released in the cinema during their teenage years. Enjoying the nostalgia, they proceeded to ignore the rest of us and ate their dinner on lap trays, even going so far as to pull the dividing curtain closed!

Afternoon Tea with Mary and Marcus

With Kathryn's birth, four new grandparents were also created! Hilda and Terry Hobin, and Mary and Marcus Braybrooke.

As mentioned, both Susan and David Goldhill have now passed away, but in addition to being the person who first introduced Mary and Marcus, Susan has left beautiful artwork. Her watercolours, often of woodland creatures, birds and wild flowers, brighten up many of our homes, and whenever I see my grandfather beginning a painting of the seaside whilst in Devon, in reminds me of the artistic inheritance we share, from Marcia's depictions of local flora to the current sketches undertaken by myself, my sisters and my mother.

One of the few downsides of having so many dear friends throughout the world, is that there are so many more people to miss when these times do come. Among them is Hew, a dear gentleman of Marsh Baldon. He was always soft-spoken and kind despite having to endure the frustrations of Parkinson's disease, and my mother—as an Occupational Therapist—helped to care for him for several years. His wife, Oni Sandilands, has been an endlessly patient piano teacher to Sarah, Anna and myself; although the former has always been extremely musically gifted, and now still regularly makes use of all she has learned from Oni. And although he is physically gone, Jack Greenaway lives on at the Baldons in the form of the daffodils in the fields, the wind in the huge, old trees and in the birdsong—he always was so much a part of the grounds he tended.

I was perhaps better at leaping through the long grass in the fields of Marsh Baldon House, pretending to be a lion to entertain Alexander and Angus, her grandchildren, than at actually progressing with my piano skills. My grandmother has also been an impressive musical figure, playing the piano and singing beautifully in choirs. As her mother was a soloist contralto, musical ability has always meant a lot to Mary.

Amanda's mother Bobbie passed away in 2016, and is greatly missed by Amanda, her father David, and siblings Jo and Tim, as well as the rest of the family. Mary and Marcus got on very well with her, and Marcus took Bobbie's funeral.

It would be impossible to list all of the wonderful people who have had an impact on the lives of my grandparents, but as we go through life we shape each other, and I know that Mary and Marcus are grateful for every soul they've gotten to know, and for the richness and variety that each person has brought to their lives.

Getting Older

My grandmother has mentioned once or twice that it is not always easy to live with somebody who is as good as Grandpa. In 2016, I asked her how she has found the experience of getting older. She answered honestly;

'I miss my social work even more than I had expected and still, several years later, dream about working from an office and visiting people. I didn't dream about being a magistrate at all. Fifty years is a long time to give up something.

Getting older is extremely challenging. Everything takes longer, and one's memory for names, having met so many people, gets occasionally jumbled, so you give people different surnames. Having had the last five weeks with a chest infection, I'm learning now to say 'No' to a few more things. Marcus will always include me, if I want to be involved - lots of husbands wouldn't. But I do or have done some things which don't really involve him – like my work with kidney patients. Unlike me, he's quite happy with his own company. I do need people.

As we have got older, and because Marcus is very deaf, especially during a break from his hearing aids, it has been difficult not to be irritated at having to repeat sentences several times. I also find that when I mention something that needs to be done in the house, that Marcus feels he is being asked to respond immediately, and gets fretful, but does it anyway - that's what's so tiresome, because then I feel guilty.

He's actually the stronger of the two of us, has better ideas and makes most of the decisions in the end - even if it doesn't appear that way. Because of his heart problems, it is almost impossible to have an argument - in my family we had plenty of arguments and it was healthy, but due to his background, he was more sensitive to them. I don't feel I can always say what I want to— so it's very unlike me, but I do hold back. Regardless, I love him more and more as the years go by.

But I see that he is becoming an old man and I am becoming an old woman, and I find that *really* hard. I remember his mother saying to me "You are a very argumentative person" when she first met me, but later she loved me. She used to bet on horses, and told Grandpa that he'd picked a winner!

Being a grandmother is one of the greatest joys in life. And we saw all our grand-daughters within 24-48 hours of their birth – we tore up to Farndon when we thought Rachel was going to give birth. We particularly enjoyed having Kathryn, Helen and Sarah to stay when Anna was being born, and also for 3 months during their house extension. I began to feel almost that they were my own children. Whilst losing Helen in the arboretum was frightening, even more terrifying was when, at the age of six or seven we lost Lizzie. We were at the Eden project, and Grandpa had gone to buy something – she went off to look for him, and for twenty minutes we couldn't find her. Jeremy and I put an announcement on the loudspeaker, and eventually found her hiding by the car, afraid that someone would take her away. Christina was a little imp—very courageous and outspoken, with an inquiring mind. When she was ten she sent off for a touch typing course without telling her parents, and they were left to foot the bill when it arrived!'

'We're so proud of both Jeremy and Rachel', my Grandmother continued, 'They were model children growing up. They never went through a rebellious teenage phase and we always felt that children were to be respected, as people in their own right. Jeremy always loved football and had good friends but was quite happy in his own company too. We're very proud of him becoming a doctor and also that he did a doctorate and a degree in psychology (and did it in a year!), and that he has now become an eminent oncologist.

We were also very proud of Rachel when she became an OT and a riding instructor. She's a wonderful daughter, totally caring (almost over caring – there aren't many daughters who offer their parents a home for the rest of their lives). We used to meet for lunch once a week, and I feel I can really talk to her about anything - nothing is barred. It's a lovely relationship - she is my best friend. I would talk more to her than anyone else about anything.'

'We are also very grateful to have such a delightful and helpful son-in-law, Peter and Amanda who is a beautiful and charming daughter-in law,

A recent family celebration for Lizzie's 18th birthday.

18. Books, Gardening and Much More

My grandparents have many other interests besides their more public activities, on which I have so far concentrated.

They are, for example, surrounded by books. The study is full of them; there are over-flowing book cases in every room, there are books on the window sills and in the attic. It is surprising how many of them they have read (and perhaps more surprising still that they can recall the contents!). In the porch, as well – boxes of Marcus' unsold books. He is a wonderful writer, but has never had a businessman's approach to selling his work.

Mary has always loved reading – and as mentioned belongs to three book clubs, despite problems with her eyes. One of the good friends she has made is Trish Morgan, who has written to me, 'I first met Mary when I retired and joined the same book club. I have truly appreciated the friendship that has developed. I have always been impressed by her intellect, stoicism, supportiveness and kindness and how she truly lives out her Christian faith and values. Although I know Marcus less well, on the occasions we have met I have found him always to be thoughtful and kind, with an aura of calm about him. Clearly they have a very blessed and successful marriage made richer by their wonderful family. One thing that shines out from both of them as they get older is that they retain a youthfulness of spirit which is so appealing. I loved it that they chose a disco for Mary's 80th birthday, possibly for the grandchildren (!) but that didn't stop them getting up and dancing enthusiastically to the beat. The energy they have for constant travelling also amazes me – they are truly inspirational in so many ways.'

Marcus also taught himself how to self-publish his work. People sometimes come up to my grandfather and announce, "I have read your book!" He rather hesitantly asks, 'Which one?' An understandable reaction, given that he has written or contributed to more than fifty books. His first book, as we have seen, *Together to the Truth*, was published in India in 1971.

It was only after he retired from the Council of Christians and Jews that Marcus really started writing. Up till that time, he says, 'I had to write balanced reports, which reflected the views of the Council. Now I could speak for myself.' He acknowledges the great help he received from the stimulus of working with his friends Rabbi Tony Bayfield and John Bowden, who was editor of SCM Press.

Time to Meet – his first post-retirement book - was an attempt to convey to the Christian public the dramatic changes in how scholars and the Churches now see the relation of Christians to Jews and Judaism. Among these changes in perception he discusses the following; Jesus is acknowledged to have been a faithful Jew, who was popular with the Jewish people; he was put to death by the Roman ruler; and God's covenant with the Jewish people has never been revoked - which calls in question attempts to convert Jews to Christianity. There were also chapters on the challenge the Holocaust makes to all faith in a loving God, as well as how Christians should relate to Israel.

The shed in Box where Marcus started his writing

Marcus has also written books which introduce Christian readers to the riches of other faith traditions - *Meeting Jews*, of which a reviewer in the *Journal of Ecumenical Studies* wrote 'the value of this book is above rubies'; *What We Can Learn from Islam* and *What We Can Learn from Hinduism*, and in February 2019 he published *Sikhism: A Christian Approach*.

Other books are about the history of interfaith movement, including *Children of One God - Widening Vision,* a history of WCF and what he considers to be perhaps his most important book—and *Pilgrimage of Hope*, which recounts the growth of the worldwide interfaith movement from the 1893 to 1992 – and which he has updated as *Faiths Together for the Future*.

Drawing on his knowledge of world religions Marcus has edited a number of anthologies of prayers and inspiring quotations and stories. One of these, *The Bridge of Stars,* was published shortly before 9/11. Marcus treasures the message he received from someone who lived in Washington, and who, after making sure all his family were safe, unpacked the book and opened it at this Jain prayer:

I give amity to all, enmity to no one.
Know that violence is the root cause of all miseries in the world.
Violence, in fact, is the knot of bondage. "Do not injure any living being."
This is the eternal, perennial, and unalterable way of spiritual life.
A weapon, however powerful it may be,
Can always be superseded by a superior weapon;
However no weapon can
Be superior to non-violence and love.

Learn to Pray, for people who had never prayed, was part of a self-help series, but Marcus felt is should also be about God's help. This raised the question – in lots of emails to the editor – as where first to mention God? If God was on the first page, the enquirer would read no further – it you waited to the last page the reader might feel conned. So God was introduced on page 16, but with the suggestion it is better to think of a 'Light Within' rather than an 'old man in the sky.' This book sold well in America, as its publishing happened to coincide with the tragedy of the Twin Towers.

Marcus' *365 Meditations for a Peaceful Heart and a Peaceful World* (reprinted as *Peace in Our Hearts: Peace in Our World*) also uses material from many countries and traditions. Each page is in three parts: a quotation, a story and reflection and a practical suggestion.

Beacons of Light: 100 Holy People who have shaped the History of Humanity is Marcus' longest book, with nearly a quarter of a million words. The publisher's challenge was to choose the 100 people who have had most influence in shaping the spiritual life. He realized, however, that the book would have to be chronological, but in appendix he accepted the publisher's challenge. Not surprisingly, he put Jesus first, but it was more difficult to decide whether to put the Buddha or the Prophet Muhammad second. He decided on the Buddha, because, he wrote, 'I believe that his message of non-violence will grow in influence and now has a world-wide appeal.' Christopher Morgan, on Amazon, said of the book, 'It is a brilliant and timeless work written with great authority – light and inspiring as a beacon should be.' Swami Dayatmananda, head of the U.K. Ramakrishna Centre, who recommended 'this wonderful book to one and all' quoted Swami Sivananda's definition of a saint as 'a spiritual washerman. He applies the soap of devotion and knowledge and removes the spots of sin in worldy people. In his presence, people become holy.'

One paragraph from the Introduction to his *Beacons of the Light* gives a clear summary of Marcus' understanding of the interaction of spiritual paths and that we can learn from the experience of many people of different traditions. He speaks of himself as a follower of Jesus, whom he seeks to serve and to whom he gives witness, but sees no reason to pass judgment on other people's spiritual experiences. As Jesus said to Peter when he asked what would happen to John, 'What is that to you?'

'The book is intended to be read as a whole and not just used as a reference book or dictionary to look up particular people - although of course it can be used in this way. What I have found fascinating is the interaction between spiritual movements through the ages. Interfaith dialogue in the way we think of it today may only date from the end of the nineteenth century, but different religions over the centuries, have in many places interacted sometimes by disputation, sometimes by borrowing and learning from each other. I have found it helpful to picture the spiritual history of humankind as a great river with various springs, sources and tributaries, always changing, sometimes dividing, maybe with backwaters, but moving forwards and enriching the present with what is carried forward from the past and opening up new vistas for the future. Diana Eck, a renowned scholar of religions, I have discovered since writing this, uses the same image. 'Religious traditions are far more like rivers than stones' in that 'they flow and change, sometimes drying up in arid land, sometimes dramatically changing course in new territories. All of us contribute to the rivers of our traditions. We do not know how we will change the river or be changed as we experience its currents.'

And, yes - Marcus has written some Christian books! Indeed *The Explorer's Guide to Christianity* is an overview of the history, faith and practice of the religion. *The Wisdom of Jesus* and *The Miracles of Jesus* were commissioned by the American Readers Digest. Some of his sermons have also been printed, many of them typed by Sally Richmond, who with her husband Alan were very loyal members of Christ Church in Bath. For one of the collections, Sally wanted a preface from George Carey, the then Bishop of Bath and Wells and hunted him out at the Palace in Wells. It was the day that it had been announced that he was to be the new Archbishop. Sally was told that he was far too busy to see her: she replied, "This is the Lord's business, which is more than most of what he is doing. I am sitting here till I see him." He wrote a very generous preface. Bishop George Carey also invited Marcus to be a Prebendary (like a Canon) at Wells Cathedral, whilst he was serving in Christ Church.

Several of the books are out of print, so recently Marcus has learned how to self-publish them, first as e-books and then as paperbacks. Marcus describes the process as 'fascinating and frustrating.' One hard-earned achievement is to learn to do an index. Self-publishing, of course, means self-publicity, which Marcus finds difficult. Mary is much better at selling his books as well as at spelling and carefully checks the texts.

If it is true that "the pen is mightier that the sword," Marcus hopes his books have made 'a miniscule contribution to a more caring world.' Mary too is a writer and speaker, but she has confined herself to articles in journals. Over the years Mary has written social work articles, given numerous talks on her work to audiences from general practitioners to women's groups, also discussing being a magistrate and a clergy wife. She has researched attitudes towards transplantation in different faiths and her articles have been published in various magazines and journals, with several interviews on local radio.

Afternoon Tea with Mary and Marcus

Other Interests

Mary particularly loves going to the theatre. Marcus used to enjoy it, but for some years he has been too deaf to hear what is being said and has to rely on sub-titles when he watches TV

My father Peter recalls, 'Marcus's connections have led to many prestigious invitations and sometimes he could also invite guests to join him. On one occasion Rachel and I joined Mary and Marcus for a Royal reception in London. A little bit more bizarrely, Marcus regularly got invitations to the London premiers of Tom Cruise's films. On one such occasion, we found ourselves walking down the red carpet entrance at Leceister Square with hundreds of Tom's fans surrounding us looking for autographs (Tom's not ours!).'

I have had several special theatre trips with my grandparents which, as a student and later a graduate of literature, were immensely enjoyed—from *Othello* and *The Duchess of Malfi* to a family trip to see *The Lion King* on Broadway—at the time I felt as if I knew almost all the words for all three.

Marcus has gradually become more skilled at D.I.Y., especially as he has slowly collected the appropriate tools for each job over the years. As a child they had a hammer and a bent screw-driver and not much else. Partly D.I.Y. has been a financial necessity—the Diocese rightly want to spend as little as possible—but as he has become more competent he has begun to quite enjoy it, although he never expects anything to work. His sense of humour is perhaps his most valuable tool in these situations! He and Jeremy once did a car-maintenance course, which has helped them to recognise what has gone wrong, but has not often equipped them to be able to put it right.

Pets

Animals have always been part of my grandparents' lives, both as children and in their own married home. At Frindsbury, when the children were little, there were hamsters, guinea pigs and rabbits and then in Swainswick a puppy, Rex, and a kitten, Harvey, joined the family. Poor Harvey, who loved climbing up the curtains, was sadly run over when he was quite young—cars came very quickly along the nearby road and it was known for being dangerous. Later a beautiful long-haired cat, Felix, adopted the family. Rex, who was very loving, liked to roam when he got the chance. He also was a terrific barker when he was travelling in a car. He didn't seem to mind other cars, but would bark very loudly as soon as he saw pedestrians, other dogs, cyclists, motorbikes and more. As the family were already quite squashed amongst the luggage when they went off on family holidays, the addition of never being able to hear themselves or each other made long journeys rather tiring.

Once, when Rachel was a child, Rex (pictured on the right) dug up a wasp's nest. He began to yelp as they stung him, and so my mother flung herself over him and they both came home covered in stings. The family also adopted some ex-battery-shed hens, who gradually grew their feathers again and laid quite a lot of eggs. Sam Walker, one of Mary's great nephews, remembers a rather humorous story passed down through the family about these hens.

'Once upon a time, when my father was much younger and had more hair on his head, he was sent to stay at the house of his Auntie Mary and Uncle Marcus, who were away. At this time, his Auntie Mary and Uncle Marcus kept chickens, and my father was put in charge of feeding said chickens until the return of his aunt and uncle. My father, in a moment of rascally genius, decided that he would improve the manners of these chickens by instructing them that the appropriate place for them to take their meals was in the house's kitchen. He spent the next few weeks educating these chickens, who made themselves most at home. The response of his Auntie Mary and Uncle Marcus, when they returned to find the fowls roosting in the frying pans is not recorded, but my father ranks this as one of his finest achievements. There was never going to be much hope for me.'

When this biography was first begun, my grandmother made it clear that all stories about herself and Marcus were to be told 'warts and all', and she was not keen on having a 'book full of compliments'. Unfortunately, they are both very well loved, and it is difficult to find someone willing to insult them. The closest I have come to this is Sam's other comments, which describe Mary and Marcus as being 'the chief-high inquisitors of God'. Sam claims that 'even Saint Peter would find their excruciating moral clarity a tad too close for comfort', and goes so far as to imply that they are frightening. He continues: 'Now, you may be wondering what it is that's so scary about my great aunt Mary and the Rev. Marcus, wonderful, kind and good people as they are. The answer is that it's their immense and expansionary goodness in itself that strikes terror into the hearts of all dissolute and wayward Walkers, such as myself'.

He describes a family gathering, in which his turn came to be investigated by my grandparents. 'Interestingly, throughout the interrogation, Great Aunt Mary and the Rev. Marcus Braybrooke, would play very different roles. Great aunt Mary was the asker of questions, the renderer of advice and the giver of counsel, while Rev. Marcus was the keeper of silence. This silence, however, was integral to the overall effect:

his silence was saintly, even divine. His quiet smile and gentle lightness always gave me the vague impression that he was just on the verge of floating away, and that he tarried on this earth only to sanctify and solemnise great Aunty Mary's practical pedagogical mission.' This, I hope, is close enough for you Grandma!

Sam's grandfather, Paul, had much shorter additional comments. Mentioning Marcus' humour, kindness, faith and courage, he added. 'I am grateful for the guidance he has provided – usually when I needed it most. Whether it was a career decision – or theological struggle – Marcus was always gentle while being positive. He never has enough time, but always has time.'

To turn back to the animals, as mentioned earlier, there was also great excitement when Taffy moved into the churchyard. Rex and the hens went with the family when they moved to Wells and soon Rachel was the proud owner of Shaman.

When Mary and Marcus moved to Box, Rex came too and enjoyed walks along the valley or up to the woods beyond the field which was opposite their home. Eventually, when he was very old, he would sit down in the middle of the field and watch Marcus or Mary go for a walk.

Mary with Rachel and Shaman.

After a time, when they had settled in Marsh Baldon, they decided, with advice from Denise Daly to get a poodle puppy. This was partly for the grandchildren, as 'Daddy wouldn't buy them a bow wow.' It was also soon after one of Mary's retirements, but as she was soon once again employed, parishioners got used to seeing Toffee and Marcus walking across Marsh Baldon Green. Toffee, as has been said, was a very loving dog and went with them to Clifton Hampden. It was a sad day when, like Rex, cuddled in Marcus' arms, he had to be put to sleep. There was no longer any joy in his life. At the Baldons, also, as we have seen, part of the Rectory garden was fenced off for Rachel's horses, which have always had wonderful loving care.

Mary for some time had tropical fish as well as gold fish, which like the birds are waiting in the morning for Marcus to feed them. They thought they were too old to have another dog after Toffee died, as they were afraid a young dog would out live them. 'He was very sensitive,' Mary said, 'I miss him terribly. He had looked at me and asked to be put down - he was losing his sight, was very deaf and had some bowel problems. He no longer had any joy in him. The vet was very understanding and we took him home, and Marcus built a beautiful grave with flowers in the garden. It is amazing how much one misses a family companion like Toffee, who seemed like our own child, as all the others had grown up.'

The hardest part of having animals in one's life is often outliving them. But growing up alongside so many animals has been a wonderful aspect of our childhoods, as well as a huge source of pleasure in my grandparent's lives, and Toffee could not have asked for more doting parents during his long and happy life.

Holidays

Mary and Marcus have always regarded holidays as important to ensure that, in busy lives, they had time for each other and for Rachel and Jeremy. The first family holiday, as already mentioned, was to the Isle of Man - perhaps rather ambitious with Rachel not quite six months old. When the children were young there were happy holidays at Broadstairs and Dymchurch as well as with parents at Kersell or Box Cottage. All the grandparents really loved their grandchildren. Twice Mary and Marcus exchanged their homes with families in Holland.

After Mary's father died, they went to a Time-Share presentation and to their and everyone else's surprise bought one near Fungiorola in Spain. Having heard time-share horror stories, they were relieved when they arrived at Match Room to find their apartment actually existed. Some years later, they exchanged this for Club Playa Real, which was right by the sea near Marbella.

Mary and Marcus have always enjoyed swimming. Here they are teaching the grandchildren to swim.

Children and grand-children have happy memories of holidays there. When the grand children had grown up, after they exchanged it for Passage House, near Teignmouth, this saved travelling abroad and—far more important—it was one of the few time-shares which welcomed dogs. Toffee loved playing on the beach, but never ventured into the sea 'Like many other people,' Marcus says, 'we have lost money to one time-share shark, but this has been outweighed by so many wonderful family holidays and exchanges to other beautiful and historic places'.

There have also been very special holidays to Australia, an unforgettable safari in Zimbabwe and afternoon tea at the Victoria Falls Hotel – 'the Falls themselves were even more special'.

Afternoon Tea with Mary and Marcus

Mary with a small selection of our many dear Australian relations, at the home of Gwenda (to Mary's left) and Barry Wellham.

They have also had many holidays in Devon. My mother Rachel says 'I loved these holidays, which built on my mother's love of the county, which had developed during her own childhood. In the last five years Peter and I have achieved my dream of moving there permanently. Among many other benefits I have been able to get to know another branch of our family—the Leach's.' Marcia Leach, Marcus' mother, was a cousin of the famous potter Bernard Leach. His pottery in St. Ives was a favourite haunt for Susan and David, and for Jeremy and Amanda—who have a fine collection of Leach pottery in their study.

Several years ago, Jeremy Leach — Bernard's grandson and fellow potter — told me that he remembers two unknown people coming into his showroom in Bovey Tracey. They introduced themselves as Mary and Marcus and "suddenly we were discussing the family tree. I always knew of the Braybrookes from the Leach family tree, but I never thought I would meet one."

Jeremy is now kindly teaching my mother basic pottery skills, which she is thoroughly enjoying.

Mary with Jeremy Leach.

When my sisters and I got to spend one-on-one time with our grandparents, both at the time-share holidays, and when staying over in their homes in Marsh Baldon and Clifton Hampden, it was always a lovely opportunity for some quite deep discussions.

My sister Kathryn said, 'Grandma and Grandpa are a huge part of my life and I'll always feel lucky that we've been such a close family. They've looked after us all through our childhood, including for three weeks when my youngest sister was being born and we all had flu (fun times!) - and we've had some of the most fantastic holidays together, too. They're the kind of people you can talk to about anything without worrying what they might think – and despite having very firm morals and beliefs, they're some of the most open minded people I've ever known. I remember late-night conversations in Spain or Torquay when I'd share a room with Grandma and we'd question the meaning of life together, and it still somehow surprises me that Grandpa has read every one of the somewhat explicit romance novels I've started writing without batting an eye! It's not surprising I've never understood what people mean who say 'Your grandfather is a vicar!'

Pilgrims to the Holy Land in 2019 - Christina at the Passover Seder and Kathryn on the Mount of Olives

Kathryn continued, 'They've been at the centre of some of my favourite places as a child – the Baldons in Oxfordshire with their beautiful Rectory house and the lovely village there, and the Osborne Club in Torquay where we would go on holiday every other Easter. I've got endless memories of Grandpa teaching me to swim at the Osborne, playing in the Rectory house (finding endless amusement with Grandma's power-assisted armchair), running through the large gardens, the slightly dodgy swing under an old tree – and seeing it transformed into a country fete full of games and people and activity. Being at the centre of the community has always been part of Grandma and Grandpa's lives, wherever they've been, and throughout my life they've always been the people bringing everyone around them together. Whether it's Grandma's penchant for starting conversations with random people in waiting rooms and on planes, or Grandpa's constant willingness to be there and listen to whoever needs him. Although it happened before I was around, Grandma's outrage at Margaret Thatcher's claim that "there's no such thing as society" has always stuck with me, and while I might not have understood it much when I first heard it, I can see how everything about my grandparents' lives has always proven the exact opposite. It isn't until recently that I've realized how much their value for community and society has affected me, until I've found myself seeking smaller places where you can have that sense of *'knowing your neighbour'* and the genuine feeling that everyone is looking out for each other that I felt whenever I visited their home in the Baldons'.

Anna has also been influenced by their globe-trotting and worldwide friendship. She writes, 'You know your grandparents are great people when they have more social life than you, a 21 year old. I have memories from my childhood of inviting Grandma and Grandpa to a party or event of mine, to be told of course they'd be delighted to attend, but might have to leave a little early to arrive at their second party. I can see traits in my personality that I was lucky to get from both Grandma and Grandpa. Grandma and I both have a passion for Sociology, we love observing the world around us, people watching, and questioning everything. This always makes going for coffee with Grandma wonderful - as we can people watch together! Additionally, grandma is fantastic at languages, and whilst it's taken me a bit longer, I'm really keen to learn Spanish, and practising with Grandma is great!

Now not to sound too boastful, but I think Grandpa is one of the wittiest people I know, and I like to think that I have inherited that wit! We both hold the ability to find our own jokes so funny that we make ourselves laugh. As well as Grandma, Grandpa has a passion for travelling, and has been to more countries than I can remember. I went travelling in my gap year, and it ignited a passion for it that I didn't realise I had. There's nothing better than getting advice about a country I'm going to, than getting it from someone who has quite literally been, and probably got a T-shirt! My grandparents are incredible people. They never stop, they are always having new adventures, and they are just so kind and loving. I have such fond memories of strawberry picking in the summer, and taking their dear beloved dog, Toffee, for walks with them. As a couple, they are so happy, and are such a good team. If I have done half as much with my life as they have, by the time I'm their age, I believe that I would have done a good job at this life thing.'

Anna, spent part of her gap-year in Costa Rica saving baby turtles. She also accompanied Grandma on a cruise along the Seine to Normandy. She was brilliant at looking after Mary when she had a fall in Paris. Anna is now at Sheffield University.

Afternoon Tea with Mary and Marcus

Tours and Pilgrimages

Besides the many conferences, Mary and Marcus have led a number of pilgrimages and tours. Neither were exactly holidays, although parishioners tended to think they were.

To India

We have heard already about one tour to India. Others also have not been without problems. The first tour to India had to be rearranged at about two weeks' notice, because of extensive flooding in parts of Northern India. On another, the party was stranded in Gujarat, because a devastating earthquake in Ahmedabad meant all flights had been cancelled. News of the earthquake was on the early BBC news and naturally Mary was very alarmed. It was not until the evening that Marcus and Mary could get through to each other on the telephone. When the group were able to get to Poorbandor, Jeremy sent a reassuring email to Mary:

'We are having a really good trip. The earthquake has made things complicated. It is a real tragedy for India and the people involved. We were having breakfast at the time at our hotel in Junagadh. I was upstairs picking up the marmite when I felt the hotel shake. I realised straight away that it was an earthquake and ran outside. Bits of plaster and a few lumps of concrete fell off the hotel! The quake lasted about 45 seconds and was about 5.5 in our area. At first we did not realise how severe the quake was and carried on our schedule. No major damage in the area that we were at. Apart from the earthquake, we are having a really good time. We stayed in Bombay and then flew to Bhavnagar. From there we went Palitana and climbed the holy Jain mountain of Shatranjayha - a really enjoyable climb and fabulous temples.

We are now at Gandhi's birthplace and will stay here for two or three days. The plan is to fly to Bombay on Tuesday and then from there onto Udaipur. We will stay there for one day and then continue with the planned trip to Mt. Abu etc. I'm sorry this message is a bit rambling but you can imagine an Indian internet cafe with lots of people all talking and all trying to do things at the same time, plus pictures of Indian film stars all over the walls.

Dad is really well and coping brilliantly. He seems relaxed about everything and is enjoying himself. He was the first up the holy mountain. Marcus says that Shatranjayha is the most beautiful and peaceful place he has ever visited. People are only allowed to be there during the hours of daylight.'

To Egypt

The tour to Egypt had to be abandoned because of riots at the start of the Arab Spring. Later, however, with their good friends, Graham and Sonia Hobbins and George and Joanna Cacanas, they went on a wonderful cruise — but had to start at Lucknow, as Cairo was still unsafe. There were problems too before a pilgrimage to the Holy Land, because of fighting on the Lebanese border. There was a cease-fire just in time for a small group of fearless pilgrims to travel. There was only one other pilgrim party in Jerusalem – a beautiful choir from South Korea.

Oberammergau

They also led quite a large party to Oberammergau to see the Passion Play in 2010. They arrived just as all the locals were celebrating Germany's football team's victory in the World Cup. The delightful family my grandparents stayed with spoke hardly any English and Marcus tried to unearth his long forgotten German.

The play was very impressive – some of it, for the first time, acted as it was growing dark. Marcus was pleased to see that the revised text had removed the anti-Jewishness of previous versions.

The Holy Land

*Jeremy, Mary, Marcus, Lizzie, Kathryn and (front) Christina
in the 2019 pilgrimage for Easter and Passover
Picture taken by Christopher Wolff*

Several pilgrimages have been to the Holy Land. Although visiting Christian holy sites has always been a priority, most pilgrimages have given people the opportunity to meet Jews, Muslims, Baha'is and members of the Druze religion and to visit their holy places, as well as visiting refugee camps, hospitals schools and orphanages. On one tour – the coach broke down in the Sinai desert. Soon people produced the food that they had squirreled away at breakfast. Eventually two policemen escorted the coach which could only engage second gear all the way back into Israel. They have also led three pilgrimages 'In the steps of St Paul' to Greece, the churches of Asia Minor and to Malta and Rome, where they attended a Papal general audience. Two members of the group were in wheel chairs and were taken to sit close to the Holy Father.

Other tours to India, Tibet and Jordan were a way of introducing people to members of other faiths and to seeing their holy places. They were also enjoyable and a way of making lasting friendships, as Mary said in the parish magazine, in the following article: 'Can a Pilgrimage be Fun?

'We have just returned from a wonderful trip to the Holy Land. There were 16 of us, all warm and friendly and so enthusiastic that the coach was never kept waiting. No one complained about anything, even the incredibly hot weather (43C). Nine of us were from the Dorchester team.

Besides inspiring visits to holy sites, we travelled from the Golan Heights in the North to Eilat, on the Red Sea, and back through the Negev desert and wondered at the varied and beautiful landscape. The Bible came alive as we visited the Sea of Galilee and saw how the fishermen used to put their nets out to sea. The boatmen even played 'God Save the Queen' to greet us and listened as we sang 'Dear Lord and Father of Mankind'. We bought wine at Cana in Galilee and saw the springs of the river Jordan. We climbed down from the Mount of Olives to Gethsemane. Bethlehem was a highlight, especially the visit to a refugee camp where we watched a group of dancers. The Wall upset us.

We had a highly knowledgeable Palestinian Catholic guide from the Village of the Shepherds, a Muslim driver and later a guide who was a Messianic Jew. We listened and we learnt and we wept over Jerusalem and visited the Yad Vashem, the memorial to the Holocaust. We swam in the Red, the Mediterranean and the Dead Seas. Some rode camels, and two teenagers (our granddaughters) swam with dolphins.

We laughed, we sang, we shared communion, we discussed our sadness at the divisions in the Holy Land but saw signs of hope at Neve Shalom, a village where we stayed and where Jews, Christians and Muslims live together and their children are educated together.

We all have very special memories, and I have only mentioned a few of the places we visited. We are happy to share more with anyone interested. Pilgrimages bring us closer not only to Our Lord but also to fellow believers. Yes: they are fun as well as inspiring.'

India

Because the study year in India was so significant, Marcus has been glad to keep contact with India and has been back for several meetings.

His friendship with Fr Albert Nambiriambii, a Roman Catholic priest who has been a pioneer of interfaith sharing in India, goes back a long way. Fr Albert established a World Fellowship of Interreligious Councils and Marcus has taken part in several meetings - many of which have been held in Cochin.

Mary Pat Fisher (Kaur) has also been a friend for many years. She has written beautiful books about world religions and some years ago found her spiritual home at Gobind Sadan, which is an ashram founded by Baba Virsa Singh - a Sikh with a universalist outlook and deep compassion for the poor. The ashram is in the outskirts of Delhi near the airport and Marcus has often enjoyed their hospitality and spiritual refreshment after a night on a plane. At the ashram, there is a beautiful place which marks the spot where the Guru had a vision of Jesus. There is a carved wooden figure of Christ - in the cold winter one of the Sikhs puts a woolly hat on 'Jesus'' head to keep him warm. Prayers and offerings are made to Jesus every evening. The Guru believed that people can find inspiration from the holy people of each tradition.

Marcus, because he has worked closely with the Brahma Kumaris in Britain, has usually tried to maintain links with BKs in India either by speaking at their centre in Delhi or by a visit to Mount Abu, which he first went to with Mary and Rachel in 1989. A memorable few days was for a retreat called 'The Inner Voice of Silence.'

My sister Sarah and I followed in our grandparent's and our mother's footsteps when we travelled together to India for the 'Peace of Mind' Retreat in 2016 at Mount Abu. It was an incredible week of mingling with people from all over the world, and we have so many memories; attending 4.am meditation, walking through the landscape in a silent single file, with Brother David leading and playing musical instruments, visiting the Global Hospital to see the amazing work undertaken, and sharing in the lovingly prepared all-vegetarian food.

When my mother was sixteen years old she saw a documentary about factory-farming and proceeded to become a vegetarian—at the ages of thirteen and twelve, myself and Sarah followed suit, followed a couple of years later by Anna, and so the diet on the mountain has suited us for generations. A couple of very special moments on the trip include trekking to Baba's Rock to watch the sunset, and meeting Dadi Janki, who is over one hundred years old, but still remains the spiritual head of the Brahma Kumaris. It was a pleasure to get to know our grandparents' BK friends even better. Among them was Rachel Priestman, who looked out for us throughout, and Maureen Goodman.

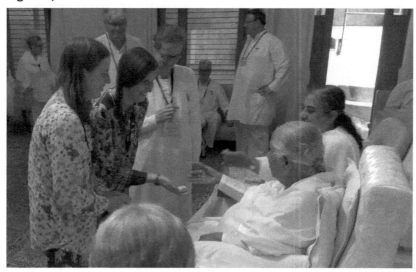

Sarah and I receiving 'toli' – a special sweet - from Dadi Janki, alongside Rachel Priestman.

Maureen has mused on my grandparents that 'neither of them ever complain—they get on with life, and know what's really important,' as people who focus on 'giving, not taking'. It helped, she said, that of each other they were 'never jealous,' but had 'so much respect and support between them,' with 'no façade' and a 'genuine insight into people.' Maureen has continued to be a treasured friend to all the family. Even though we did not travel with them, throughout our trip to India, Sarah and I could feel the presence of our grandparents.

19. A Rather Large Afternoon Tea

Much has happened in the last few years, whilst I have been, admittedly very slowly, writing this biography. My grandparents have now bought a lovely little flat in Teignmouth; it has a view of the sea and is very close to where my parents live. They are beginning to move across some of their many books, paintings and treasured items. It is within walking distance of the local theatre, the doctor's surgery and, perhaps most importantly, the ice-cream and fish and chip shops. From their childhood holidays to my own, I have always found Devon to be rich in association with my grandparents— from building sandcastles with Grandpa, to watching the waves as my grandmother quotes John Masefield, 'I must go down to the seas again'—those waves have been the backdrop for our 'Toffee to the Rescue' films, and the distant soundscape to many deep and honest conversations between us all.

Gathering at Springend Cottage, Devon, in November 2018, we celebrated Marcus' 80th birthday. It was a truly special day for many reasons. We were surrounded by loving family and friends. The house itself seemed full of light, amid the decorations and the marvellous spread of food. Rachel had created an incredible cake in the shape of a church, and Jeremy handed out flutes of champagne and gave a wonderful speech. But, most special of all, as well as all talking together, we took the time to listen. At my mother's suggestion, each of us present took it in turns, from the youngest child to the eldest friend, to ask my grandfather a question about his life and his work.

My grandparents held hands, and often Marcus would turn to Mary to complete the story or the answer they both knew so well. As ever, they were a perfect team. They have done and achieved so much, but being modest do not often get to speak at length of their many amazing experiences. Everyone present listened with rapt attention, and among the laughter and the more serious pauses, I had the wonderful feeling of familiarity. Each of the stories they told felt like an often-handled piece of fabric. I could remember the stitching of the narrative from having written it out in this book. And as we draw to a close it seems that the patches of memories, stories and experiences that they have shared have become like a patchwork quilt— colourful, varied—perhaps a little haphazard on occasion—but all part of one shared whole.

And on that day, amid a particularly large afternoon tea, most wonderful of all was seeing the genuine love and respect with which Mary and Marcus still look at each other, as they answered our questions together, and we listened.